TRAINING TECHNOLOGY PROGRAMME
Produced by the North West Consortium

Volume 2

METHODS OF TRAINING: GROUPWORK

Bob Wilson

Supported by OPEN TECH **MSC**

Parthenon Publishing
THE PARTHENON PUBLISHING GROUP LIMITED

To Saffron

The Training Technology Programme is published on behalf of the North West Consortium by:

In the U.K. and Europe

    The Parthenon Publishing Group Ltd
    Casterton Hall
    Carnforth
    Lancashire LA6 2LA
    England

ISBN 1-85070-159-8

In the U.S.A. at

    The Parthenon Publishing Group Inc
    120 Mill Road
    Park Ridge
    NJ 07656
    U.S.A.

ISBN 0-940813-31-9

Editorial Note

The male pronoun has been used throughout the Training Technology Programme for stylistic reasons only. It covers both masculine and feminine genders.

This work was produced under an Open Tech contract with the Manpower Services Commission. The views expressed are those of the authors and do not necessarily reflect those of the MSC or any other Government Department.

Printed in Great Britain

THE TRAINING TECHNOLOGY PROGRAMME

The Training Technology Programme (TTP) aims to provide materials which will help improve training and learning.
The Programme is presented by the North West Consortium, consisting of Lancashire Polytechnic, S. Martin's College and Lancashire College.
TTP is a set of distance learning materials in two versions. There is a choice between a hard-back Volume edition and a soft-back Package edition.

PROGRAMME PRODUCTION

Project Manager .... *Bob Wilson*
Co-ordinator .... *John Stock*
Programme Co-ordinator .... *Kath Litherland*
Video Advisor .... *Fred Fawbert*
Audio Advisor .... *Peter Darnton*
Main Illustrators .... *Angela Pour-Rahnema*
David Hill & Lesley Sumner
Editors .... *Andy Davies & Derek Oliver*
Production Team Members .... *Lynne Hamer, Judith Hindle*
Caroline Nesfield (Programme Secretary)
Susan Western, Bobby Whittaker

ACKNOWLEDGEMENTS

With gratitude and appreciation to the many who have supported the Programme including the Directorate, Principals and mangement of Lancashire Polytechnic, S. Martin's College and Lancashire College; David Bloomer, Norma Brennan, Cyril Cavies, Ryland Clendon, Noel Goulsbra, Stanley Henig, Tony James, Peter Knight, Joe Lee, Ken Phillips, Alan Sharples, Ross Simpson; The Director and members of MSC Open Tech, especially Steve Emms, Les Goodman, Fiona Jordan; last, but certainly not least, The Authors' Families.

FOR FURTHER INFORMATION

Write to Bob Wilson, Programme Director,
Training Technology Programme, Lancashire Polytechnic,
PRESTON, PR1 2TQ.   Tel. (0772) 22141

Foreword
to the Training Technology Programme

Today we see technology being applied to every department of civilised living. It comes in many forms and its applications are virtually limitless. What we see today, although it is transforming society, is but the beginning, and the extent and pace of change is likely to increase many times.

It is most fitting and timely therefore that a systematic effort is being made to apply technology to training. The techniques available are very varied ranging from computers to audio visual equipment. It will enable training to be undertaken privately at home or at the work place in a group, in the remote croft or in the city.

Technology is revolutionising training; I welcome therefore this Training Technology Programme developed by the North West Consortium and Parthenon Publishing, supported by the Manpower Services Commission. It brings training in technology, through the medium of technology, to more people than ever before.

I commend it and I am delighted to have been invited to contribute this foreword.

John Banham
Director General CBI

Contents

> **Editorial Note**
>
> *Study Units and Figures throughout Volumes 2, 3 and 4 are numbered consecutively, as they form a series which is best read in sequence.*

Study Unit 1

Methods of Training: Groupwork

Component 1:

Communication in the Processes of Training and Learning (1)

Key Words

 Training methods and the design system; defining communication; aims and success of communication; one-way, two-way models of communication; sender, receiver, medium, message, receiver's response, channel; feedback; Shannon and Weaver model; "gatekeeper"; SMCR model; receiver's perceptions of messages; barriers.

This Study Unit examines communication, models and strategies of training and learning.

Introduction

In Package One of this Training Technology Programme we examined the systematic approach to designing a course. We followed through the various steps which are necessary if you are to design training which is both efficient and effective.

So Package One provides a basis for the material which we are going to look at in Packages Two, Three and Four.

In these Packages we are focussing on **methods** of training and on the **implementation** of training. An overview of these topics was made in Component 8 of Package One and you should revise that now. This and the next two Packages will allow us to look closely at **how the trainees learn**, as well.

Let's refresh your memory of our design system by reproducing a Figure which we showed previously in Package One. You can see from the heavily outlined boxes which steps in this system we are dealing with now and in Packages Three and Four.

Methods of Training: Groupwork

THE DESIGN SYSTEM

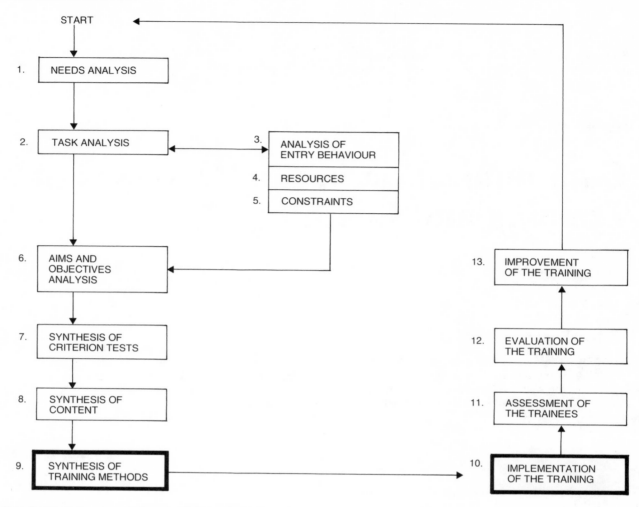

Note: Feedback lines are not shown in this figure. In practice, all of the boxes, each of which shows a step in the design system, feed back information to every other box.

FIGURE 1

▰▰▰ Checkpoint

Figure One is not a complete reflection of the work of this Package. Can you suggest why this is so?

Part of this Figure concentrates on the training aspects of the systematic approach, but this Package really deals with methods of **training** *and* **learning.** *Note the "and learning" bit. We are also going to examine more closely here just how the various training methods can affect learning by the trainees. Once again, we hope to offer a blueprint of how it is all done so that you can utilise various techniques and tactics to make your training more effective.*

First, we will have a look at the part which **communication** plays in training.

Communication in the Process of Training and Learning

All normal people communicate. You don't have to say anything necessarily to convey your meaning; a lift of the eyebrows can "say" a lot as we all know! Communicating is a fundamental activity in our lives, so it must be equally basic to our training.

So we are beginning with basics. Let's attempt to answer some questions about communicating in this and the next Component. We will try to answer these questions in Component One:

How do you define communication?

What are the aims of communication anyway?

Are there any models of communication?

So, let's see

4

* How do you define Communication?

Dictionary definitions say that to communicate is to share, transmit, impart information or ideas. Surely this is what training is about? Yes, but in training you have to communicate **successfully.** Another point is that communication in training should be an **exchange** because it isn't only one way, i.e. **from** one person to another, but **between** them. In a way, when you communicate, you are trying to influence somebody; in training you are attempting to influence the trainees so that they show a change of behaviour, generally by performing better at their jobs.

Has what we have just said reminded you of anything to do with specifying objectives?

Well, objectives identify the behaviour which you want to change, usually a job performance. That's why they are sometimes called behavioural or performance objectives, although we referred to them as specific objectives because of this function of specifying the desired behaviour or the level of performance needed.

So it looks as though an important part of achieving those objectives is by communicating well.

There are many, many ways of doing this of course and our next Figure shows a few different meanings of "communication".

COMMUNICATING TO BRING ABOUT A CHANGE
OF BEHAVIOUR

FIGURE 2

Now, what about sharpening up our definition? Try to write your own definition before you read ours, overleaf.

A DEFINITION OF COMMUNICATION

> "Communication in training is the successful sharing and interchange of information and meanings".

FIGURE 3

So what does this definition tell us about our next question which is

* **What are the Aims of Communication Anyway?**

We consider these to be:—

✱ The sharing and interchange of information such as knowledge, mental skills, motor skills and attitudes.

✱ Achieving success in this sharing and interchange by having our communication

received (heard or seen)

understood (we get the hearing across)

accepted (nothing is going to change unless the communication is accepted)

get some action (change of performance or behaviour).

What does a failure in meeting any of these aims mean?

It means that the process of communication has failed. And that suggests that the training has failed, too.

We will develop these aims in more detail as we go along through this Component. First, we will answer the next question, which is

* **Are there any Models of Communication?**
There certainly are, but before we examine them let us ask you a question.

What do you understand by the word "model" as used in this context?

What it certainly doesn't mean is some sort of model aeroplane or model steam engine, although all of us tend to think of that type of model when first meeting this use of the word in training. In a way though, there is some accuracy in thinking of a model almost as a toy model, as they are miniature replicas of the real thing: a model of a motor car may be a toy or a sophisticated device used by motor engineers to develop a new car. In this case, the model car has most of the elements of the real thing, very reduced in size. So have training, or communication models: they represent a simplified version of the real thing, or reality, on a smaller scale. Models help us to understand how the reality works as they concentrate on the elements of real life, showing their inter-relationships, or working parts.

MODELS HELP US TO UNDERSTAND THE REAL THING

FIGURE 4

So much for what a model is; now what are the main models of communication?

There are four main models which we shall look at. These are

* **One-way, two-way models.**
* **Shannon and Weaver model.**
* **SMCR model.**
* **Westley-Maclean model.**

One-way, two-way models

All human communication involves two people: one is a source who gives information and one at whom the giving is directed, the receiver. The next figure shows this simple model of a **one-way communication.**

ONE-WAY COMMUNICATION

FIGURE 5

The giver of information has been called by various names such as transmitter, emitter, encoder and **Sender.** We will use the last name. Usually the person to whom the sending of information is directed is called the decoder or the **Receiver.**

▨▨▨

What do you think the terms "encoder" and "decoder" mean?

"Encoder" is used because the sender often has to put the communication into some special form, using special symbols or a special vocabulary, using certain words, sounds or images. So the "code" of a mathematician is often that of mathematical symbols, the engineer uses a vocabulary of words which have special meanings in engineering, whilst the geographer uses code words such as "escarpment", "syncline", "metamorphic", "central business district", "peak land value intersection and so on.

These code words are a sort of shorthand, which the specialists use to express themselves clearly and which depends on the message being transmitted; if they overdo this, specialist codes deteriorate into jargon. All talk between people is a form of coding. So when somebody asks you to "put into words" they are asking

you to code something. Putting it into pictures, diagrams, dots and dashes (morse code) drum beats, gestures or bugle calls are all symbols of different codes which may be used to make up the message.

The "decoder" has to translate the word, image or sound code to make sense of it.

In this text, we are going to use the words "sender" and "receiver". Remember that all senders are encoders and all receivers are decoders.

So, if what we have described is one-way communication what does **two-way communication** entail?

Well, if you look back at our definition of communication, you will see that we said that it has to be **successful.** Now, how do you know if it is successful or not?

Similarly, if you glance at our aims of communication, you have to know if the communication has been **received, understood, accepted** and results in some **action.** If it does then it has been successful. Therefore, the sender has to find out his degree of success in communicating by taking **feedback** from the receiver.

▨▨▨

What is "Feedback"?

We have met this term before in Package One of this Programme. Although "feedback" has several meanings because it has several functions, in the sense in which we are using it here feedback is the communication of responses by trainees or the trainer.

Here, then we have **two-way communication**, shown in the next Figure.

TWO-WAY COMMUNICATION BETWEEN PEOPLE

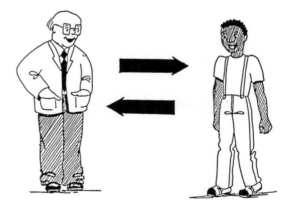

FIGURE 6

Now, before we go on to describe two-way communication in more detail, we are going to use certain code words, i.e. we are encoding our communication to you, so we must explain to you what our code words mean. Here they are:—

Message: what the sender is saying to the receiver. At this moment we, the senders, have a simple message to you, the receiver; this message is "read on!"

Medium: the carrier of the message. In this case the medium is the printed medium, i.e. we are using a book as a medium to convey or transmit the message to you.

Can you give us some other examples of media, or mediums?

Our examples are: film, records, audio and video tapes, slides, black and whiteboards.

Channel: the channel of communications provides the sender with access to the receiver. They are **systems of communications** through which communication takes place such as press, telecommunications, radio, television, face-to-face encounters of the receiver with the sender. Obviously, we have a mixture here of the mass-media, e.g. television and radio and smaller-scale channels like face-to-face discussion.

We now ask you to summarise what we have said in a code different from the spoken word which we have employed. So, using the diagrammatic code, illustrate two-way communication, using the terms which we have described so far.

TWO-WAY COMMUNICATION

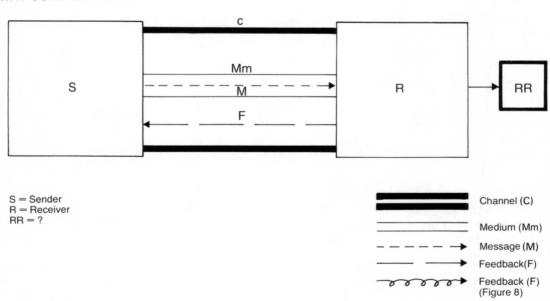

FIGURE 7

In Figure 7, What does RR stand for?

*RR is the **Receiver's Response.** Remember that in a successful communication one of the aims is to get some action, that is we wish the receiver to respond to our message. Hopefully, you will have responded to our message, which was a request to draw a diagram, by drawing your own illustration, but as we are involved in one-way communication, without feedback, we'll never know! However, two-way communication includes feedback so you can monitor the receiver's response, gauging the success of your communication by the accuracy by which, say, knowledge has been understood or a skill improved.*

Let's see if we can develop this communication to you by asking you to think of a simple, everyday example of two-way communication, using illustrations (diagram, cartoon, etc) to explain your example and to show different types of coding.

Here's our example: using the key shown in Figure Seven, suppose you send the results of a recently completed course to a trainee. Later, the trainee rings you up to make an enquiry about his marks. We can show this in the next Figure.

TWO-WAY COMMUNICATION IN REAL LIFE

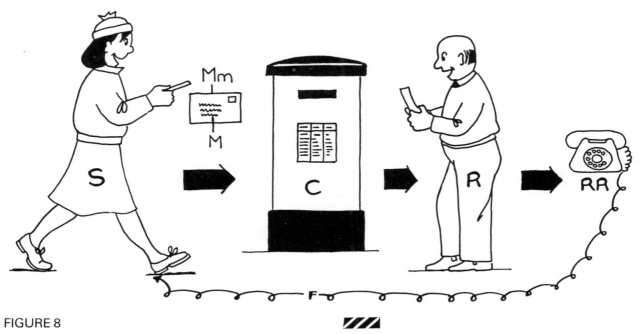

FIGURE 8

Did you notice how the message differs from the feedback?

Yes, we know they're going in opposite directions! That isn't the main point, which is that the feedback is using a different medium, (phone) from the medium of the message (post) but the same channel (telecommunications).

Now in Figure 8, we coded our message in the form of an illustration. We could have coded it as a diagram, which looks something like this:—

ANOTHER CODE, ANOTHER WAY

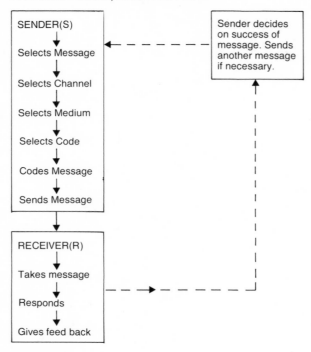

FIGURE 9

A final example of how we could have coded our message is shown in the next Figure, a "straight-line" or "flow" diagram. You will notice how each of the varying codes can be made to emphasise different parts of the message.

TWO-WAY COMMUNICATION: THE WHOLE PROCESS

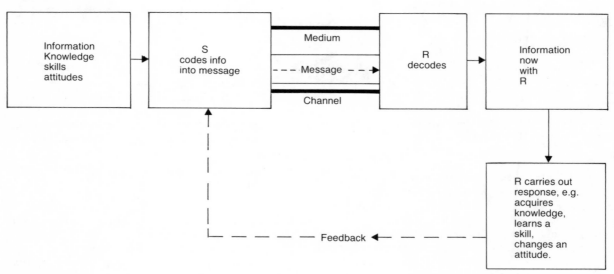

FIGURE 10

We are now going to look at the other models of communication. Each of them will give you a different view of communication, so that you will become familiar with the whole process before we examine how communication effects learning.

Incidentally, you should bear this question in mind all of the time when you are working through this Package; how does what I am reading relate to learning and how could it improve my training? Mostly we will point out how this can happen, but bearing this question constantly in mind will give direction to your thinking and help your memory. We will touch on this mechanism for remembering and understanding later in this Package.

The next model of communication is the

Shannon and Weaver Model
This model is very similar to the one-way model which we have been thinking about. Shannon was an engineer at the American Company, Bell Telephone and his original theory was extended by Weaver to cover all types of communication.

SHANNON AND WEAVER MODEL

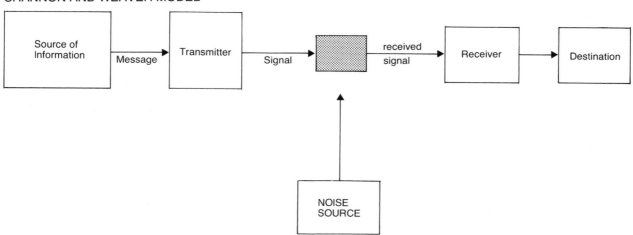

FIGURE 11

What do you notice is different in this model from the one previous?

Apart from minor changes like the use of the word "signal" (remember that Shannon was a telephone engineer) "transmitter" and "destination", this model introduces an important new concept, that of "noise", shown by the black box in Figure 11.

Noise is any interference with the message, e.g. in the case of a telephone it could be static interference and in the case of a trainer communicating to a trainee it could be any stimulus additional or unwanted in the learning message. Noise is a **barrier** to learning. We shall look at other barriers in the next Component.

The Shannon and Weaver model does not include feedback, i.e., it is a "linear" rather than a "loop" model.

Can you think of any other loop models?

*Package One gives the answer to this question: our design **system** is a loop model. Check this is in Figure 1 if you need to, remembering that loop models have **feedback** and therefore the advantage of **improvement** being inbuilt because of their cyclic nature. Our next illustration exphasises this.*

INBUILDING IMPROVEMENT

System
ONE

Feedback
TWO

Improvement
THREE

FIGURE 12

As Figure 12 shows, you have to evaluate what is wrong, as you do in a loop model, then improve it!

The SMCR Model
Devised by a man called Berlo, this model is a more sophisticated version of those which we have dealt with already. The next diagram shows how it works.

THE SMCR MODEL (after Berlo)

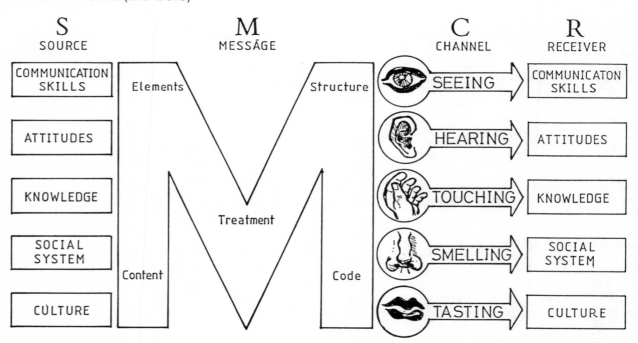

FIGURE 13

Berlo's model shows four major components of communication: source, message, channel, receiver. He shows the factors which can effect the **Source**, a person or group sending the **Message** and he identifies the main parts of the message, which you will notice is coded, after naming the attributes of the source including the social system and cultures to which it belongs. For Berlo, the **channel** is also the medium and he shows the channels available to the

Receiver who has the same range of attributes as the source, even if those attributes vary. Like Shannon and Weaver's model, this one is linear, showing no feedback, but it does illustrate part of the complexity of the process of communication.

Westley-Maclean Model
This model has two aspects: communication between two people and mass communication.

WESTLEY MACLEAN MODEL: COMMUNICATION BETWEEN TWO PEOPLE

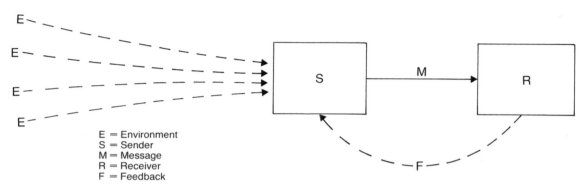

E = Environment
S = Sender
M = Message
R = Receiver
F = Feedback

FIGURE 14A

Obviously, this is a loop (or "looped") model, virtually the same as the two-way model with the exception that Westley and Maclean suggest that S focuses on a specific item of his or her environment (E) and creates a message (M) for transmission to the receiver (R). However, much the same happens in the two-way models where the information to be transmitted also comes from the environment and includes feedback (F). The next part of Westley-Maclean's model is different.

WESTLEY-MACLEAN: MASS COMMUNICATION

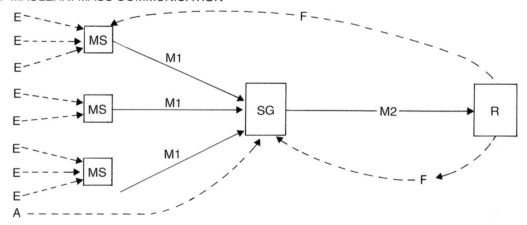

E   = Environment
MS = Mass communication source, e.g. mass media producers
SG = Sender - "Gatekeeper"
R   = Receiver
F   = Feedback
M1 = Message
M2 = Message

FIGURE 14B

Westley-Maclean are particularly concerned here with the effect of mass media (e.g. TV, radio) and show how material from the environment (E) is collected by the mass media producers (MS) who act as a "Sender — Gatekeeper". In turn SG filters out a second message (M2) which is sent to the receiver (R).

SG performs many of the roles of a trainer, who in addition to receiving information from the environment directly (A) focuses the attention of trainees on aspects of training which are the most important from the point of view of the Company and the trainees themselves.

We have described this second model by Westley-Maclean to emphasise the importance of the trainer's role not only as a sender of learning messages but additionally as a "gatekeeper". This "gatekeeping" role acts not only in the filtering of information from the mass media, which are significant sources of information for learning, but also from more immediate sources. For example, in most Companies, especially large ones, it is the trainer's duty to filter out elements of Company policy and concentrate the learner's attention on those which affect him most specifically. Needs Analysis is part of the trainers filtering mechanism and so is the writing of Aims and Objectives.

The gatekeeping trainer designs his training on what his filter tells him are the most important factors which will benefit the firm and the trainee most. This aids the Company's cost-effectiveness and efficiency by improving job performance where it is required most, as the next illustration shows.

Pick out what you consider to be the most important aspects of communication which we have discussed so far in this Component.

We think that these are important points:
* *Two-way communication is made when feedback happens.*
* *The sender knows what the receiver's response is to his message when he gets feedback.*
* *If the receiver's response is what the sender intended it to be, the communication is successful.*
* *You can only have communication when sender and receiver are connected by a channel, through which a medium carries a coded message.*
* *Messages must be coded and decoded.*
* *Trainers, in their function of gatekeepers, filter information to the receivers.*
* *Noise acts as a barrier to communication.*

Amongst other things, the points we've mentioned do emphasise feedback. Every time a sender dispatches his or her message, the receiver distorts it when it is accepted, because everyone perceives messages differently and often decodes them with variations. Immediate feedback allows corrections to be made by the sender quickly.

Does this surprise you? Perhaps you believed that if you expressed yourself clearly then the message was bound to be accepted and understood exactly as you meant it to be? Well, try this exercise with a group of trainees or colleagues; you'll need a video camera to do it properly, but this is not essential.

THE TRAINER AS GATEKEEPER

FIGURE 15

Passing a Message: Exercise 'MESSAGE SENDER''
1. Ask five members of your group to leave the room.
2. Show the **sixth** the following illustration for exactly
   one minute (we will call the sixth person, "S" in this
   text).

ILLUSTRATION

FIGURE 16

The sixth person (S) receives the illustrations, shown in Figure 16, from you. Tell him, very clearly and repeating this instruction once:

Look at these pictures for one minute. Try to remember as much of them as you can. After looking at them you are to describe them to the next participant as though they make up one picture, saying:—

"I am going to describe a picture to you. After I have told you about it once, I will repeat what I have said. You are then to describe it to the next participant who will be called in. You will not be allowed to see the picture at any time and when you have completed your description please sit down."

4. Then give the pictures for one minute. After one minute call in the first participant who left the room.
5. S then describes the pictures to the first participant whom you have just called in.
6. When S has finished tell him or her to sit down. (This prevents feedback).
7. Call in the second participant and have the first participant describe the picture to him or her.
8. Carry on until the last participant has been called in and given description and instructions. The instructions to the last participant are changed from that person having to describe them, to being told that the picture described is now to be drawn on a flipchart or a board, by him or her.
9. After the picture has been drawn, discuss the differences from the original eight pictures. Debrief the group by asking them to explain these differences as examples of failed or successful communication, explaining the reasons for success or failure. The video recording, if you have made it, helps to show where the transmission went right or where it went wrong. If you have had other members of the group observing rather than participating, ask them at the beginning to pinpoint examples of good and bad message sending, accurate and inaccurate responses by the receivers. They should report their observations to the whole group during discussion.

▰▰▰

What points do you think the debriefing discussion should bring up?

We think that exercise "MESSAGE SENDER" could show:

* *The importance of feedback for correcting transmission and receiving-faults during communication.*
* *The fact that however clearly you think you send your message it will not be received and responded to accurately in many cases.*
* *Further transmission can distort the message even more.*
* *Receivers tend to exaggerate things which are important to them and which arouse positive feelings.*
* *They often suppress things which offend them or clash with their personal experiences. Some parts of the picture disappear completely.*
* *Receivers tend to remember the bizarre, e.g. the elephant with the TV.*
* *All receiver's perceptions of messages differ.*

So remember that your clearest instructions to trainees will always become distorted and the clarity of learning messages is difficult to sustain. If you don't make the effort to make your message simple and lucid, your trainers have no chance of learning anything worthwhile.

We are now beginning to touch on barriers to communication and we shall examine these more closely in the next Component. First, we'll summarise this one. You should attempt to make your own brief summary of this Component before reading ours; outlining the major points will do.

Summary

Communication in training is the successful sharing and interchange of information and meanings and to be successful must be received, understood, accepted and result in some action on the part of the receiver, who is the trainee.

Models help us to understand how communication is carried out and the two-way model is especially important in training and learning.

The Sender, usually the trainer, who transmits the learning message, codes it suitably for an appropriate medium and sends it via a channel.

The Sender hopes that his or her message will result in an intended receiver response and in training these responses may result in the fulfilment of desired learning outcomes such as the learning of knowledge, skills and attitudes.

The Westley-Maclean model emphasises the role of the trainer as "gatekeeper" and of feedback which monitors the accuracy of the receiver's response and therefore the success of the communication.

Shannon and Weaver show how "noise" can distort the message and interrupt communication and exercise "Message Sender" emphasises what happens when feedback is absent and how receivers have different perceptions of messages.

Noise is the first of the barriers to efficient communication which has been considered; such barriers hinder communication. Because good communication is basic to effective learning they can also handicap the learning itself if they are inefficient.

Before you begin the next Component think of an occasion in which you feel you communicated successfully and one in which you failed.

For the first, write down what it was about the communicating which you feel made it successful.

For the second, failed communication, list the factors which you believe made it unsuccessful.

Send your conclusions to your Programme Tutor for comments if you wish.

Component 2:

Communication in the Processes of Training and Learning (2)

Key Words

 Barriers to effective communication; the Trainer; training environment; size of group; awful assumptions; the missing pre-test; forgotten feedback; psychological barriers; formal Freddie; "Learnermass"; comprehensive comprehension; non verbals; "pointing" and "blindering"; "polarizing"; mediums which miss; "slow quick-quick slow"; silly structures; generation gap; networks; symmetrical and complementary relationships; trainees' checklist; "Looking outwards" game; personal communication checklist.

Introduction

In the last Component, we asked you to think of a successful and of a failed communication which you have made. Towards the end of this Component we shall further consider those factors which make communication successful. Building on the basis of those points which you identified in your failed communication, we shall begin this Component with an examination of **barriers** to communication. In this Component we shall try to answer a couple of important questions and these are:—

What are the barriers to effective communication? How do you communicate effectively?

* What are the Barriers to Effective Communication?

We wonder what you decided that caused your failed communication and how far you considered that those barriers could be overcome? If your problem was one of communicating in a social context, was it something like our next illustration shows?

BARRIER TO COMMUNICATION

FIGURE 17

Figure 17 shows a situation which many have had the misfortune to experience. Most of us have also experienced training sessions where we felt adequately prepared, excited and ready to do the business for the trainees well. And it didn't work out that way! For some reason the session was not a success, the trainees didn't respond enthusiastically and we felt as flat as they did after it was over. Something went wrong and in asking ourselves what, we often realise that we failed to overcome some barrier. As Figure 17 shows, difficulties in communication often arise around people, so we will view the problems which arise through the **senders** first and **receivers** second.

As you will remember, in the training situation, the senders are the trainers and the receivers, or responders, are the trainees.

Barriers to Communication erected by trainers.
* Training Environment. There are many factors in the physical training environment which can create barriers. Whilst we can't expect to have an air-conditioned atmosphere with ideally comfortable seating, too often classrooms are full of poor quality chairs, broken tables and few facilities except a pitted blackboard and a couple of sticks of broken chalk. Often much more attention should be paid by trainers to the floor coverings, making for quietness, pleasant impact of the colour scheme, acoustic quality of the room and giving enough space for the trainees to move around in. Some of these items seem obvious, but do we all give sufficient care to them, or plead shortage of cash rather than our own lack of effort for the shortcomings?

* Size of Group. A poor teaching environment is emphasised by the trainer not selecting group sizes which fit the classroom. The physical problems in a classroom are all exaggerated if we crowd too many people into it. Apart from physical discomfort making for an unhappy audience, the noise of trainees shuffling around can go a long way to drowning out the attempt of the trainer to communicate.

THE SARDINE SYNDROME

FIGURE 18

"Sardines" may be O.K. as a party game but it isn't so good for training! So ensure enough comfortable space.

* Awful Assumptions. Sometimes trainers make awfully inaccurate assumptions about what the trainees know when they start a course. If the trainees haven't sufficient basic knowledge or skill to form a firm foundation, they may never catch up. However, a trainer who operates the systematic approach to training will have carried out a proper Entering Behaviour Analysis and he will be aware of any trainees who fail to meet the course pre-requisites well before training starts. You will find full details of these procedures in Component 6 of Study Unit One, Package One of this programme.

Any course member who doesn't have the necessary pre-requisite knowledge or skills must be brought up to scratch before training starts.

So don't make awful assumptions: work on facts!

* The Nursery Pre-Test. This point follows from the last: Entering Behaviour Analysis is carried out **before** the training starts and as "well-before" as possible. When the trainees have arrived don't forget to give them a Pre-test to find out more specifically what they know about the content of the course. The information which you will gain should knock any lingering assumptions which you have on the head. But make sure you do pre-test: sometimes it is a bit of a nuisance starting off a course with a test and nobody likes extra marking. However, Pre-tests do spotlight weaknesses instantly and you can set about remedying them from the beginning. A weakness undetected early is always damaging and is more so the longer it is not identified.

THE CASE OF THE MISSING PRE-TEST

FIGURE 19

If you make awful assumptions and indulge in missing Pre-tests you'll start communication at the wrong level, or, if the trainers don't know enough or aren't skilled enough, they will not understand what you are saying, anyway, so you won't communicate at all.

* Forgotten Feedback. We have seen how there can be no efficient communication without feedback. Remember that not only does the sender, or trainer, need feedback to monitor the responder, but the trainees themselves need the trainer's comments on their feedback so that they can establish how well they are doing. So an efficient communication looks like this:—

THE SECOND FEEDBACK

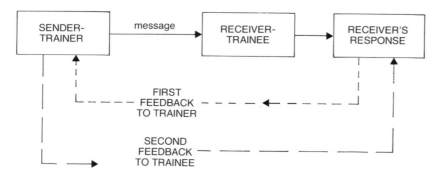

FIGURE 20

* Psychological Barrier. Trainers and taught often have a barrier between them because of their different roles. Unfortunately, this is often built on the barrier between someone who knows and is skilled and someone who isn't. Trainers will find this impedes the sending of their message and consequently of successful learning. You have erected a barrier without even knowing it.

Very positive efforts are needed from trainers if this psychological barrier, in the minds of the trainees, is to be overcome. We need to go out of our way to develop informal relationships with trainees and to offer help and guidance without them really knowing that we are so doing.

* Formal Freddie. That well-known trainer, Formal Freddie, builds psychological barriers higher by his formal, stiff approach to trainees. He widens the gap which we have just spoken about by keeping the trainees at arm's length at all times.

So, make your interpersonal relationships as informal as possible by being tolerant, relaxed, and patient in improving communication. We can even make friends of the trainees by getting on the same side of the fence as them, by enjoying trainees' company, by getting to know them on equal terms. Use the training as a lead-in to enjoyable relationships; don't try to act too differently or patronisingly.

FORMAL FREDDIE'S FENCE

FIGURE 21

* **"Learnermass".**Unfortunately, some trainers think of the **learners as an undifferentiated mass** of people and launch a single communication at them in the hope that it will hit their "Learnermass" target. There really isn't a Learnermass: trainees are all different from each other and every group is crammed with **individual differences** between each person.

We will talk more about this when we consider barriers erected by trainees next and in Study Units Four and Five of this Package. For now, remember to modify your learning message as far as possible so that it is likely to be accepted by each receiver to the fullest possible extent. Don't follow the percept of the next illustration.

LEARNERMASS LAIR

FIGURE 22

* **Comprehensive Comprehension.** As experts in their field, trainers frequently overestimate the comprehension of their trainees, which in the initial stages often isn't all that comprehensive. Things which we take for granted, are new to them and whilst it doesn't do to patronise the trainees by oversimplifying, trainees don't comprehend as much as we think, especially at first.

Sometimes trainers like to show off their superior knowledge because it makes them feel good. This doesn't make the trainee feel all that good, so no "Flash Harry" stuff!

FLASH HARRY RIDES YET AGAIN

FIGURE 23

Do remember, flashing can damage the health of your communication, so keep a low key until the trainees get to know you and feel more secure about their knowledge and skills.

* **The Non-Verbals.** There is a story of the trainer who said to a trainee, "When I crook my finger like this, it means that you are to come to me."

"And when I shake my head like this it means I'm not coming!" replied the trainee.

So there are ways of communicating by gestures which don't rely on words. This is called non-verbal communication. Indeed some gestures, facial expressions and body movements can actually contradict what we are saying. Others reinforce our words, whilst others relay messages of doubt, encouragement, or dismissal, sincerity or excitement without any words at all. People are particularly good at spotting insincerity.

So be very careful to ensure that your message is not clouded with ambiguity or contradiction by the language which your body uses. Obviously, you want to avoid personal mannerisms too, because trainees can become so engrossed in watching them that they miss the message. You think you haven't any? Try watching a videotape of yourself teaching!

* **Pointing and "blindering".** There are two lovely words used by communication experts to describe the quality of the words which we use to form our messages.

In "pointing" we use words in communicating which emphasise, consciously or unconsciously, part of the message which we are sending.

"Blindering" happens when our words camouflage our real meaning.

Blindering and pointing occur not just when we pick words to express ourselves, but also in the tones and emphasis of our voices.

We're all little blinders. If you want to know how you come across to your audience, try audio taping one of your lessons. You'll probably be surprised at how much more your voice is saying than you think it is! Obviously, your message will be affected in consequence.

* **"Polarizing".** Often parents will say to a child "Now, do you want to go to bed or would you like to do some more homework?" (or have a smack or some other unattractive alternative). So the child picks the lesser of the two evils and goes to bed, often believing it has made a free choice. You offered a polarized choice.

Be careful to avoid polarizing your communication. The trainees sense there is something wrong with the message and instead of concentrating on your message, spend time, concentration and attention on wondering what the **range** of alternatives is rather than the "black" or "white" choice which you offer.

POLARIZATION

FIGURE 24

Remember that most of us are not at either the North or South Poles of choice, but somewhere in between.

* **Mediums which miss.** If the sender picks the wrong medium he will not transmit the message successfully.

▰▰▰ **Checkpoint**
Consider a variety of messages and deliberately select transmitting mediums which are **wrong** for them.

Here is one example from us: your message is to convey to your trainees the conditions of poverty found in parts of Victorian England and you elect to show this by a series of graphs and diagrams (the mediums) which illustrate average wages, average food intake, amount spent on food and working hours. It's unlikely that your communication would carry an effective message.

However, suppose you picked a few suitable photographs and read the following passage:

"*I was only eleven when I first went to work. I got up at five in the morning and walked four miles to work. We began at six o'clock until eight when we'd have some breakfast for ten minutes. Usually I had a piece of bread and butter and a cup of tea.*

The steam presses were heavy and noisy to work and you had to watch you didn't get your fingers trapped. At twelve o'clock we had half-an-hour for dinner. Mostly I ate a cold potato pie my mother had given me.
When I got home my mother usually gave me some fried bread and tomatoes or bread and dripping. I could stay up if I wanted to, but I was usually so tired that I went straight to bed around eight or nine o'clock.
Saturday was a half-day and we had seven day's holiday a year, being paid 6d a week and no sick money!"
(This is a true account of working life in Lancashire towards the end of the last century).

If the message is to be effective then the medium must be efficient. We suggest that this narrative would convey the atmosphere of the times much better than cold facts and figures. So pick your medium carefully.

---

* **"Slow, quick-quick, slow".** We all do it: rattle on too quickly, or bore our audience with a slow delivery. The sad thing is that often we don't know we're doing it.

The speed of delivery of our message affects reception and the only way to check this is to attune yourself carefully to receiver reaction. Or, once again, have a look at a videotape of yourself teaching.

* **Silly Structures.** Sometimes in the middle of a training session you realise that you've missed out an essential ingredient of your training sequence because feedback shows that you've lost your receivers. So it's back to the beginning because you haven't sequenced your material properly and the consequent lesson or demonstration structures are unsound.

However, there is no excuse for silly structures if you have sequenced your content according to the methods we explained in Components Six and Seven of Study Unit Two, Package One.

MAKE SURE OF YOUR STRUCTURE BEFORE YOU START

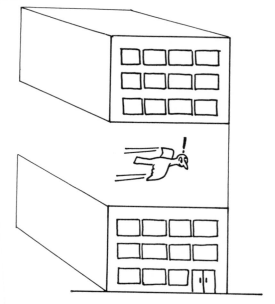

FIGURE 25

* **Generation G-p.** Often there is a large age or generation gap between trainers and trainees. This brings all the problems which we meet outside of training related to the varying perspectives which different generations have on life and learning. One aspect concerns us directly in training: many trainers did their learning from books and tend to base their communications in words and especially books. Trainees today, who often spend a lot of time watching television, have a more visual approach, basing their thought patterns on images.

The remedy is obvious: send your learning messages in visual form and use real objects for demonstrations as frequently as possible. However, putting this remedy into practice is easier said than done, because there is still a shortage of effective visual learning materials. Often this means that you will have to make your own resources and Packages Ten and Eleven of this Programme give a wider coverage on the presentation and making of suitable visual materials. Tape-slide sequences, overhead projector transparencies and video tapes are especially useful, but do take time, skill and money to prepare.

* **Networks.** There are several different forms of communication network related to the type of training which you can do. Have a look at the Figure which follows. It shows different methods of delivering the learning and we will discuss how these networks operate in some detail as we proceed through this Package.

COMMUNICATION NETWORKS: BASIC PATTERNS

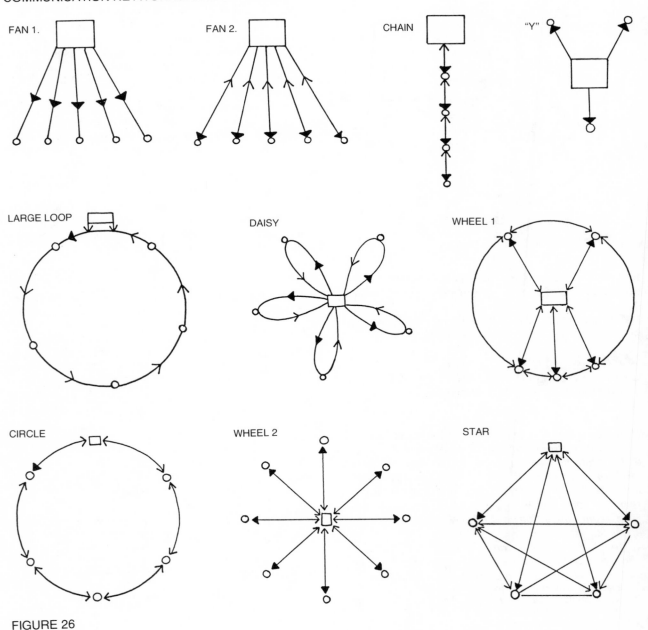

FIGURE 26

☐ Sender/Trainer
○ Receiver/Trainee
→ Learning message from Sender
→ Feedback to sender from receiver/messages between receivers

As these basic patterns represent **communication** networks they also represent basic patterns of teaching which a trainer may use to deliver the learning to the trainees, communication being basic to the learning process.

▰▰▰

Can you say how these networks represent these delivery-of-learning, teaching patterns (e.g. discussion group, lecture) naming the type of teaching and delivery which each network represents?

This is how we interpret the patterns:—
FAN ONE Represents a non-interactive lecture, where the trainer, the sender, talks **at** *the trainees and has no other interaction with them. Accurately, the diagram would show more than a dozen receivers/trainees, but space precludes an illustration of that size in this text.*

FAN TWO This is an interactive lecture, where the lecturer permits comment and discussion, i.e. feedback from trainees.

CHAIN Represents the situation found sometimes in games and simulations, where a hierarchical structure may be used as part of the game. LARGE LOOP and CIRCLE are also used in games and role-play exercises. You should notice that the traffic in the large loop is one-way but two-way in the circle.

Y AND Represent independent and distance
DAISY learning situations. In Y, the trainer sends out the material to the learners and receives no feedback. In Daisy, he does have material and comments returned from the receivers. This Training Technology Programme is a Daisy network, although there are many more receivers than we have shown in the diagram.

WHEEL 1 Represents a group-learning situation where there is interaction between the receivers and with the sender although the communication between the receivers is limited.

WHEEL 2 Shows an even more restricted group-learning pattern where the receivers are only allowed to communicate with the sender and not with each other.

STAR Is a group learning pattern such as a seminar or group discussion, where everybody talks freely to everybody else.

The trainer who is sending the learning message must bear in mind that he must suit his communication pattern to the type of learning which he is providing, having matched that learning to his objectives and content. As a sender, the trainer must also realise that selecting a method of teaching or delivering his material has implications as to which communication pattern is most useful for his purpose.

A failure to match methods, content, objectives and delivery with suitable networks will erect a barrier to effective communication.

Thus far, we have been concentrating on barriers to communication erected by **trainers**. We now turn to barriers erected by the **trainees**, but before we do so have a go at the Checkpoint which follows.

▰▰▰

In considering relationships between two people (often called a **dyadic** relationship) it is recognized that the process of communication may either be symmetrical or complementary.

In symmetrical relationships, the two people are of equal status, i.e. you have a sort of "mirror image". Where they are not equal you have a complementary relationship.

Now, how does this effect training and which of the barriers to communication which we have discussed does this remind you of?

We believe that the relationship between trainer and trainee is often complementary (unequal) and that this inhibits communication. Aiming for a symmetrical (equal) relationship creates better communication and therefore better learning during the training.

If we take an example, in a group discussion the trainer may have to begin with a complementary relationship when setting the scene for the ensuing discussion. Subsequently, he or she must encourage a symmetrical relationship with equal and therefore freer and more effective communication between the participants.

In answer to the second part of the Checkpoint, this barrier is most like that which we described as the "psychological barrier". There we explained the effect of a difference in roles; we could have called it a difference in roles and status. So try to establish symmetrical relationships with your trainees as soon as and as widely as possible.

OURS IS THE PERFECT RELATIONSHIP

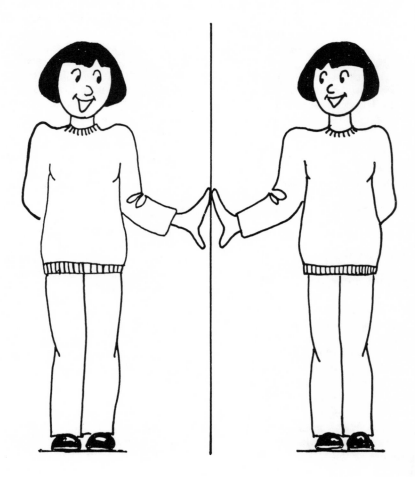

FIGURE 27

Barriers to Communication erected by trainees.
We have dealt with communication barriers caused by trainers comprehensively. None of us must forget that trainees themselves erect barriers, either consciously or unconsciously.

However, as we are talking to you, the trainer, or sender, then we will tackle trainee, or receiver barriers in a different fashion from the style which we have used so far in this Component.

Why are we doing this?

Well, we've given you some pretty 'solid' text to work through and we are going to change the stimulus; the stimulus to you, that is! Incidentally, a change of format will stimulate us, the writers, too. This is a useful point to remember when you are writing learning materials yourselves.

We are going to try to find out how sensitive you are to trainee, or receiver communication barriers, by asking you to work through the following checklist.

SOME QUESTIONS ABOUT COMMUNICATION.

Tick the appropriate box against each statement. By "appropriate" we mean the box which shows your feelings most accurately.

	TRUE	UNTRUE	DON'T KNOW

1. It is necessary for trainees to know the aims and objectives of training at the beginning of a course.

2. Each person invests any particular word with a different meaning.

3. Broadly speaking, trainees have the same vocabulary as trainers.

4. Most trainers attend to all parts of a learning message evenly and equally.

5. If you provide a large variety of stimuli for trainees at any one time then you improve communication.

6. Reception of the same stimulus by two trainees is uniform.

7. A trainee tends to remember messages which are favourable to him, more than unfavourable ones.

8. Trainees believe that everything the trainer says is true.

9. A well-prepared trainee will decode the trainer's learning message as well as one who isn't well prepared.

10. Every learning message is received by a trainee in the light of his or her previous experience.

11. The content of a message is more important than the relationship between the communicators.

12. Most trainees can remember the content of a message verbatim for a couple of minutes.

13. In any one group most trainees have a fairly uniform level of ability in communicating.

14. Differences in trainees' attitudes don't affect communication.

15. Differences in trainees' knowledge don't affect communication.

16. Differences in the cultural background and social system to which trainees belong don't affect communication.

17. Satisfactory communication is based upon a trainee's motivation to learn.

18. Receivers are as important as senders in the processes of communication.

Your answers should have a mixture of TRUE and UNTRUE. Let's have a look at how we think you ought to have replied.

Question 1 — **It is necessary for trainees to know the aims and objectives of training at the beginning of a course.**

TRUE: communication should be established within defined boundaries and should let people know where they are going. So define your aims and objectives to the trainees straightaway.

Question 2 — **Each person invests any particular word with a different meaning.**

TRUE: every trainee gives a different meaning to every word. In a way, all communication involves a compromise of meaning between people. So make sure that you define and give plenty of examples of your key words. This facilitates more accurate communication.

Question 3 — **Broadly speaking, trainees have the same vocabulary as trainers.**

UNTRUE: education and experience build up special types of vocabulary and choice of phrase; in a sense you see the world as you talk about it. Class differences also operate here; working and middle class methods of expression differ. So try to use the vocabulary of your trainees and train them to become proficient in the vocabulary which expresses best the job performances in your organisation. Then you'll speak a common language and communication will be much easier.

Question 4 — **Most trainees attend to all parts of a learning message evenly and equally.**

UNTRUE: they don't, but often the trainees must attend to (pay attention to) a message before they "see it" clearly. If they see it clearly then they have a chance of retaining it. Try not to let them select parts of the message only e.g. the parts which interest them the most are the easiest to understand. Every time a trainee selects one part of a message and ignores another, then a barrier to full communication appears.

Question 5 — **If you provide a large variety of stimuli for trainees at any one time then you improve communication.**

UNTRUE: the key words are "at any one time". We are capable of picking up only a limited number of stimuli simultaneously. That's why the coloured lights, moving lights, sound and movement of a disco are confusing: too many stimuli, causing dazzle. It is acceptable to spread a variety of stimuli over a period of time. So don't dazzle communication by overstimulating at any one time.

Question 6 — **Reception of the same stimulus by two trainers is uniform.**

UNTRUE: no two people receive, or perceive, the same stimulus in the same manner. Believing that they do causes a barrier in understanding. Obviously, this is not a conscious barrier to understanding communication, erected by a trainee, but it is there, nevertheless. So make sure that you try to find out how your learning stimuli have been received and reacted to. Try to bring about as uniform an interpretation and response as possible.

Question 7 — **A trainee tends to remember messages which are favourable to him more than unfavourable ones.**

TRUE: we are all in the business of building up our own self-image, i.e. what we think of ourselves and how we think others see us. Thus messages which are favourable to our self-image are remembered; unfavourable messages tend to be forgotten more quickly. So pump out as many favourable messages as you can.

Question 8 — **Trainees believe that everything the trainer says is true.**

DON'T KNOW: whether they believe what you say is always true doesn't matter too much, except that too many doubtful statements from you will obviously have a bad effect in the long run. The important point is that you must emphasise carefully which parts of your learning message are observed fact and which are inferences you are making and which may be open to doubt. If you express an opinion then say it's an opinion; that way you keep the lines of communication open and free from doubt.

Question 9 — **A well-prepared trainee will decode the trainer's learning message as well as one who ins't well prepared.**

UNTRUE: we talked about "decoding" in the last Component. However, an ill-prepared trainee, whether through his own idleness or an inadequate grasp of the pre-requisites for training, won't have the mental or physical equipment to decode what you are saying and your message will meet a dead-stop barrier. So do check on those pre-requisities and on the trainee's preparation for training.

Question 10 — **Every learning message is received by a trainee in the light of his previous experience.**

TRUE, very true. All messages arouse in the receiver a response based on his previous experience. Some of these feelings may get in the way of effective communication. So we and the trainees, all colour our interpretation and reception of a message by what's gone before.

RECEIVING A MESSAGE IN THE LIGHT OF EXPERIENCE

FIGURE 29

How the members of Moses' audience in Figure 29 will interpret his news must depend on their individual previous experiences. This arousing, by a message, of receivers' feelings on the basis of what has gone before is called "transference". So beware of the distortion of your message through transference.

Question 11 — **The content of a message is more important than the relationship between the communicators.**

UNTRUE: most types of communication have a **message content** and a **relationship** between the sender and the receiver. Surprisingly, it has been shown that the relationship is more important than the content. If a trainee is not in reasonable harmony with you, then he will erect a barrier to communication between you. And if the trainee misinterprets your message and is not in harmony with you, then the trainee will blame you. So try to generate efficient communication in an harmonious atmosphere.

Question 12 — **Most trainees can remember the content of a message verbatim for a couple of minutes.**

UNTRUE: they can't. This touches on the processes of memory and we will consider in Package 4. However, most people can only remember up to seven facts for a brief period. Longer retention requires the mind to store the facts and both quick and longer term recall are limited capabilities of the trainee's mind. So don't overload short-term memory fuses: give the message time to sink in and reinforce it by repetition.

Question 13 — **In any one group most trainees have a fairly uniform level of ability in communicating.**

UNTRUE: you will always have barriers to communication erected by the different capacities of trainees to communicate. For the poorest, remedial work will be necessary. For everyone, constant monitoring of the way your messages are getting across is essential; feedback again!

If you look at our SMCR model of communication in Component One, you will realise that this question and the next three are all questions about what Berlo calls the "source factors" and the "receiver factors". These are the personality, experiential and social aspects of the sender (the source) and the receiver (R). All differ from receiver to receiver and all of the differences can be permutated with each other to produce a vast array of individual receiver and trainee differences.

Clearly, every difference is going to cause the sender's learning message to be received and interpreted differently. Consequently, receivers' responses will vary. So you must recognise these individual differences and accommodate them in your communication by selecting flexible mediums of communication and of training styles which maximise the success your learning messages will achieve.

Incidentally, the answers to Questions 14, 15 and 16 are the same as for Question 13 and for the same reasons: UNTRUE.

Question 17 — **Satisfactory communication is based upon a trainee's motivation to learn.**

TRUE: very, very true. If there is little or no motivation to learn on the part of the trainee who is receiving your communication, then you have another dead-stop barrier. Motivation is probably the greatest positive force in learning and your communication with the trainees must encourage their motivation to learn. We are going to look at this one in greater detail towards the end of this Package, but remember our Golden Rule

No motivation = no learning.

Lack of motivation is one of the biggest barriers of all to communication.

Question 18 — **Receivers are as important as senders in the processes of communication.**

TRUE: receiver trainees, are what it is all about, as the next illustration shows. That's why you, the trainer and sender of the learning messages, must take so much care to ensure that you select the transmitting medium most suitable for a particular piece of learning and an appropriate teaching method. It is why you have to identify individual differences between each trainee so that you can ensure successful communication and an absence of barriers between your sending and their receiving. Remember, Learnermass ought not to exist, but does.

Taking care over these matters will ensure you appearing as a credible source, or sender, to your trainees. Source credibility, how far your trainees can rely on you and trust you, is a matter for examination when we describe individual training styles. For the moment, aim for those symmetrical relationships in training.

Incidentally, if you got all, or nearly all of the answers correct then you are a very sensitive communicator indeed.

ALL EQUAL IN THE EYES OF.

FIGURE 30

At the end of Component One we asked you to look at a couple of occasions, one where you communicated successfully and one where you did not. In the light of what we have considered in this Component, review those communications. List those barriers which you

were unable to surmount when your communication failed and those factors which accounted for your success. Check the lists which you have first written with your original answers.

There is no answer from us to this Checkpoint, except that we hope we have communicated well enough for you to have got our message!

Now for the last part of this Component.

* How Do You Communicate Effectively?

First, we would like to ask you to do an exercise about communication. It is quite a simple one, but shows some important aspects of communication very effectively.

The Looking Outwards Game

1. Sit your group, either of other trainers or trainees in pairs, each pair sitting back-to-back.
2. In each pair, person A tells his colleague, B, how to draw a simple diagram as shown in the next illustration Figure 31(a). You have distributed this diagram previously to half the group, telling them not to let anybody else see it.

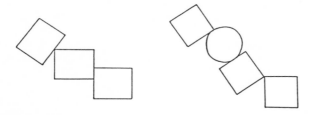

FIGURE 31(a)

Another example of a suitable figure is shown next.

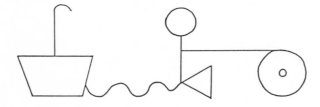

FIGURE 31(b)

3. There must be no checking or communication made by B back to A. B must remain silent.
4. Now reverse the roles, using the alternative diagram as shown in Figure 31(b) which you distributed previously to the other half (B) of the class.
5. A and B should be allowed about five minutes to draw each diagram.
6. Ask A and B to compare diagrams.

7. Ask A and B to join up with another pair and for the four of them to produce a list of Guidelines designed to improve communication. Tell them to do this by drawing on their experience of the Looking Outwards game.
8. Ask each group of four persons to write their guidelines on an OHP transparency or flipchart and to either show them to the whole group, explaining their findings, or pin them up on the wall.
9. Ask one group to consolidate the lists into a master list of guidelines for the next session when you are together.
10. Finally, display your own master list of guidelines which the groups can check with their own, discussing the similarities and differences.

Our suggestions for starting you off on your master list of guidelines are shown in the next Figure.

MASTER LIST FOR THE LOOKING OUTWARDS GAME

To Communicate successfully you should:—
1. Have a clear picture of what you want the receiver to understand.
2. Try to orientate the receiver to the learning by making clear to him or her what the task is, i.e. describe your objectives.
3. Make sure you have an idea of how skilled you are at sending and receiver is at receiving.
4. Make your message understandable to the receiver by using his or her own vocabulary and terms, i.e. code the message properly.
5. Whoever you are communicating with, try to keep your message simple.
6. Give your messages one at a time.
7. Repeat and reinforce where necessary.
8. Use analogies, metaphors and even anecdotes if necessary to make your message clear.
9. Decide which part of your message needs special emphasis.
10. Consider the use of as many media as suitable and make sure the media are appropriate.
11. Try to ensure adequate feedback.
12. Pace your message sending to the capacity of the receivers.
13. When giving learning messages follow the rules for sequencing i.e. PROCEED from
    — the known to the unknown
    — concrete to the abstract
    — observation to reasoning
    — simple to the complex
    — the whole to the detailed view
    — deal with first things first, i.e. follow a chronological order.
14. Try to understand the psychological state of the other person.
15. Sort out your own feelings about the subject of your communication and feelings of your receiver.

FIGURE 32

We hope that our master list gives you sufficient to go on. Not all the points we have made will arise from the drawing part of this exercise, but will come up in the subsequent discussion.

Of what type of communication is the drawing part of the Looking Outwards game?

One-way. If you want to include the idea of feedback then change it to two-way by allowing a limited amount of checking and questioning during the drawing. Alternatively, you can ask half of your whole group to do a two-way and half a one-way communication, when the result should be even more interesting and comprehensive.

Finally, we'd like to ask you to do an exercise which will show you how effective a communicator you are yourself.

We want you to prepare a Checklist covering the major aspects of communication, answering a simple "yes" or "no" to each question. Your "No" answer will show where you have weaknesses. We are only going to start you off with a few questions for you to ask yourself; it's up to you after that, but making out the questions should prove very beneficial to you.

Checklist: "How Good a Communicator am I?"

Can I define "communication" clearly?
Does my communication bring about a change of behaviour?
Can I state what are the objectives of communication?
Do I understand the differences between one and two-way communication?
Do I know who the Shannon and Weaver are?
Can I describe the role of a sender?
Of a receiver?
Can I list the major barriers to communication?
As we said, these are only example questions, but if you work through these two Components on communication then you can make up your own list.

Summary

There are many barriers to effective communication, erected both by the trainer who sends the learning messages and the trainee, who is the receiver. The successful communicator must be aware of these and a trainer must overcome them if his learning messages are to be responded to, in the way intended.

Each type of communication has a distinctive network which characterise different methods of delivering the learning.

Successful communication is based on many factors; establishing harmonious, symmetrical relationships with trainees is a good place to start.

Yes, we know this is the shortest summary on record so far, but your Checklist, "How good a communicator am I?", really provides you with a summary, doesn't it?

Remember, successful communication is sending, not sending up!

Have we communicated clearly?

Now, listen to an effective communicator on the radio, or watch a television programme where a group are communicating clearly. Decide why the communications are effective, sending your observations to your Programme Tutor for comment, if you want to.

Component 3:

Learning and Models of Instruction

Key Words

 "Learning"; training and education; Objectives Model; the OM approach and the traditional approach; criticisms of the Objectives Model; replies; the Process Model.

Introduction

If our memory serves us correctly, there is a line in "Pirates of Penzance" which goes, "I am a very model of a modern Major General". If we may paraphrase Gilbert and Sullivan, we'd like to say "I am a very model of a modern learner, in general".

The message which we wish to convey by this quotation is that, in this and the next two Components which comprise the rest of this Study Unit, we are going to look at learning and learners, in general, and at models of training and learning.

If we are to make our message clear then we must code it accurately and we must ensure that you know the code words which we are using. As our message is spread over the next two Components, we shall define our code words as we go along and we will begin with a definition of "**learning**".

However, before we do that, we'd like to have a short recapitulation (we'll call it "recap") of Components One and Two of this Study Unit. In the case of our Recaps we aren't going to provide the answers here: they are all to be found in the previous Components. If you know the answers, then good; if you don't, you are missing parts of the code we're using, so that the message won't be clear to you. So our first Checkpoint is only recapitulatory.

▨▨▨ Checkpoint

RECAP. Write down a brief explanation of the following terms:

Communication	Awful Assumptions
One-way	Learnermass
Two-way	Polarizing
Sender	Silly Structures
Receiver	Networks
Gatekeeper	Symmetrical relationships
Medium	Blindering
Channel	Advance Organiser

As we said, the answers are all in Components One and Two. You should have been able to recall the meaning of the words as a basis for our present discussion.

You'll have noticed that we cheated a little, because we popped in "advance organiser" which is from Package One. We have done this, because we want to offer an advance organiser for the next two Components, now as follows:

"In the remainder of this Study Unit, we are examining some further aspects of communication and its relationship with learning. We will then move on to consider the relationship between two major models of learning and training, giving examples of each. We will view learning and its definitions, showing where learning is successful and where it is not and deciding if there is any difference between "**training**" and "**education**". Finally, in Component Three we will distinguish between the Objectives and the Process models of planning your training and your curriculum."

Component Four will be concerned with the delivery of the learning, relationships between this delivery and our design system, whether the delivery is centred around the trainer or the trainee and how size of the groups, which we are training, affects delivery.

Examples will be given of each aspect and they will be contrasted with non-examples in each area.

So, for this Component, the plan is:
Another short look at communication
Learning
Training and Education
Objectives and Process Models

* Another Short Look at Communication

When we look at the role of trainers more closely later in this Package, we will examine choice of words and vocabulary to be used when you are putting your messages across in the classroom. For the moment, it is worthwhile bearing in mind a few tips about message-sending.

Write down a short list of points which you would check to ensure that the message which you are sending to the trainers is clear and efficient.

Here are our suggestions:—

MESSAGE CHECKLIST

1. What is it that I am attempting to say?
2. Does my message convey this purpose efficiently?
3. Which words express the message more clearly?
4. Could I say it even more briefly?
5. Have I used any words for which the receiver is not prepared?

FIGURE 33

Remember that Figure 32, Component Two, was about communicating in general. Figure 33 is about the message itself. Keep your messages direct.

EFFECTIVE MESSAGE TRANSMISSION

FIGURE 34

* Learning

We are now about to send a series of messages to you about learning, so we have to ensure that you and we have the same understanding of the codeword "learning".

Define the process of learning as you understand it in training.

As with everything else in training and education, most codewords are given a variety of meanings, each peculiar to the author who is making the definition. For example, most dictionaries say something like, "Learning is to get knowledge of a subject or a skill", or "to impart knowledge", or "to teach", or "to inform". There is a distinct flavour of one-way communication about some of those isn't there!

Other authorities talk about learning being a process of acquiring knowledge, exchanging attitudes and behaviour, the creation of the controlled conditions where learning occurs, or a change of knowledge.

All of these definitions have some truth, but we like definitions which are short; nobody ever remembers long ones, anyway.

Remember that when we talked about objectives, we called them "specific" objectives but a synonym was "behavioural" objectives. And objectives are what the trainees are trying to attain by learning. So we have to have the word "behaviour" in our definition, somewhere.

Therefore, our definition is shown in the next Figure.

A DEFINITION OF "LEARNING"

Learning is a change of behaviour

FIGURE 35

If you wanted to, you could say "behaviour and performance" in this definition.

We can go a little further here by suggesting that **the purpose of training is to promote learning**. Many of the books we consult talk about "education" rather than "training" in their definitions of learning. This leads us to our next topic.

* Training and Education

Trainers have been described as following a well-defined path leading to a destination, whilst educationists are those who wander in the fields on either side of the path, sometimes without a map. It is unfair to "education" to suggest that the practitioners do not know their goals or how they are to get there. However, there is an emphasis in training on using a systematic approach, a design System which tells you where you are going by the use of objectives and of proper evaluation which informs you of how far you and the trainees achieved the objectives and how the going was.

Are there any distinctions between education and training? Have a look at the following statements, which help to clarify the issue.

It's mainly **training** if
* The instruction is designed to help people perform specific tasks.
* The results of instruction are consistent.
* The procedures of instruction are about how to do something.

It's mostly **education** if
* The procedures which are learned tend to be generalised and can be transferred to other situations.
* The results of instruction vary.
* There is an emphasis on why something is done.

Probably most of us wouldn't disagree too strongly about these statements. They only point out the differences between education and training and don't suggest anything other than the truth, that education and training often approach learning differently. Neither is "better" than the other.

▰▰▰

Here are four statements. By commenting on them you will show your attitudes towards aspects of training and education.
1. Training belongs to business, the public sector and industry; education belongs to schools.
2. Training gives immediate results, education doesn't.
3. Training is practical; education is theoretical.
4. Education is more important than training.

Our comments are as follows:
1. We do not believe this to be an accurate statement. There are elements of training in schools especially where shorter-term objectives are to be realised, e.g. in chemistry and physics laboratories. However, training has a long-term nature too, e.g. training in policy and decision making, in improving staff morale and attitudes. Learning is a mix of training and education.
2. Often the results of training are either "pass" or "fail": you can either work a lathe or you can't; install an electricity supply properly or not at all; programme a computer accurately or fail to programme it properly. The results of training are often visible immediately, just as are success and failure, but sometimes the fruits of education are not apparent for a longer period, they are tempered by time and the outcomes may either be never known, or known years after the learning event. The really important point is that in both training and education, it is important that the learners receive feedback on their progress as quickly as possible. This reinforces each learner's development.
3. If not entirely true, this statement does make the point that education emphasises the "why" and

training the "how", although aspects of both education and training are concerned with both "why" and "how". Because of technological advances, the practices learned in training are sometimes short-term because they have to be up-dated continually. Hopefully, a person who is well-trained continuously over the years, develops the capacity to generalise wisely and transfer the advantages of being trained into other areas, to solve the problems thrown up by new circumstances.
4. This statement is completely untrue. You can learn the skill of operating a word-processor, but a well-trained person will also learn to appreciate the important part which word processors play not only in office procedures, but as part of an array of technological aids which will elevate the position of the word-processing person beyond that of secretary to that of decision maker. Secretaries have access to information of certain types more easily through word-processors and computers than do their bosses and now often possess more knowledge than anyone else when it comes to making decisions. Accordingly, in future, the boss's and the secretary's roles will not be so clearly defined, both tending to do work of a similar nature, but providing different inputs.

THINKING IN TANDEM

FIGURE 36

You can see from what we have written in the last few pages that we see some differences between training and education, but that we don't think one is better, or more efficient, or effective than the other.

▰▰▰

Look at Questions One to Four again. Do you notice anything about these statements which we talked about in barriers to communication?

Well, the statements are examples of "polarized" thinking and of the dangers inherent in it. Remember what we said: most of us live between the poles of thought and our thoughts and attitudes are "in between", too.

Methods of Training: Groupwork

We shall finish off our discussion of training and education with an illustration, which we hope encapsulates some of what we have said and directs your thoughts.

DIFFERENCES BETWEEN TRAINING AND EDUCATION

FIGURE 37

Now that the message of Figure 37 has got you thinking along the right lines, we will turn our thoughts to other aspects of learning.

* Objectives and Process Models

One valid distinction between education and training, which we've kept up our sleeves to introduce in this section, is shown in the next flow chart.

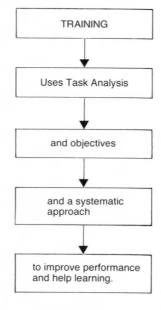

Objectives Model

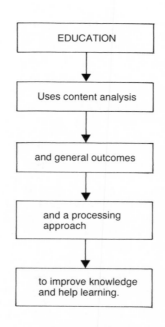

Process Model

FIGURE 38

Now, from what you've read in this Programme so far and in this Component, you know that Figure 38 is over-simplified and not completely accurate. Nevertheless, it does highlight the difference between two models of planning the training and the curriculum, which we propose to examine. Incidentally, we consider the "**curriculum**" to be "**the skills and subject areas covered within a training course**"; the "**core curriculum**" consists of "**the key elements of the training curriculum and those basic elements which must be taken by all trainees**".

We have talked about "**models**" before. Can you remember how we defined them?

A "model" is a "simplified version of real-life", or of "reality". In this case, "real life" is the system for designing the training which we had in Package One. The model which we described then is called the Objectives Model for the obvious reason it is based on the use of General and Specific Objectives. No doubt you recollect the Figure which we employed to illustrate specific objectives.

THE SPECIFIC OBJECTIVE

FIGURE 39

However, as Figure 38 shows there is another model of designing courses and this is called the **Process Model** and we shall have something to say about that later in this Component.

At this stage, it is worthwhile to have a closer look at our way of designing and implementing training which uses the Objectives Model and comparing it with traditional, or conventional methods to see what are the advantages of using the Objectives Model. We shall gain an even fuller understanding of our systematic approach by doing this and of the concept (an idea or general notion) of the design system. Make out your own comparison before you read ours.

Remember that the Systematic approach to designing training, which we explained in Package One of the Programme, is based upon the Objectives Model. The traditional approach is the conventional one which is still used widely and was employed by most of us before we were introduced to the Objectives Model.

IMPLEMENTING AND DESIGNING TRAINING: A COMPARISON BETWEEN USING THE OBJECTIVES MODEL APPROACH AND THE TRADITIONAL APPROACH.

OBJECTIVES MODEL APPROACH (OM)	TRADITIONAL APPROACH (TA)
*This approach is **systematic** using a variety of system Activities and System Functions which are inter-related logically.	*This approach is not necessarily systematic, often using **intuition** instead of logic.
*OM requires an Entering Behaviour Analysis of the knowledge, discrepancies in performance are identified and needs prioritised.	*A Needs Analysis is not usually conducted so that discrepancies may not be identified accurately.
*OM requires an Entering Behaviour Analysis of the knowledge, skills and attitudes so that the trainer understands the human material he or she is to work with.	*Entering Behaviour Analysis is not usually made in a systematic fashion, so that there are "grey" areas where the trainer does not know about the trainees fully.
*Particular care is taken to establish whether or not trainees fulfil the course pre-requisites when their Entering Behaviour is analysed. Remedial action is undertaken before the training begins when weaknesses are identified.	*In TA, attention is sometimes not paid as to whether or not trainees have the pre-requisites necessary to begin training.

*Pre-tests further highlight trainee's entering knowledge, skills etc. The results of these pre-tests offer a basis for comparison with post-tests showing the degree of progress which each trainee has made.	*Pre-tests are not usually given. Neither are post-tests for comparative purposes.
*Resources Analysis is made showing clearly where there are resources deficiencies, how it is proposed to remedy them and who is to take the action necessary.	*Usually, the practitioners of TA have an idea of the way in which resources available can meet the demands of training, but unforseen deficiencies do occur.
*The constraints on training are examined fully in OM and an analysis explains how they are overcome.	*Constraints are recognised, but such recognition may be late and leads to expedient, "off-the-cuff" reaction when the constraint becomes tangible.
*Detailed Task Analysis provides the trainer with an analysis of the task or job for which the training is organised. The Task Analysis provided comprehensive information of the training task down to lesson level.	*Task Analysis is not generally undertaken. As a substitute, the content of the course is broken down into topics without a further examination being made of the training content until each lesson arrives.
*Objectives are used as a basis for OM.	*Objectives are not used.
*Objectives are linked to Aims and are structured and selected from the information made available to the trainer from all of the previous analyses made in OM.	
*Objectives offer some guidance as to which methods of training and learning may be used.	
*Trainees are told what their objectives are, so that they know where they are going, and when they get there.	*Trainees often have only a general idea of where they are going from their gleaning information from the training syllabus.
*Trainees can concentrate on those objectives which benefit them most, so they can organise their work more fruitfully.	*The trainees usually give all parts of the course content equal attention; it is difficult for them to have a perspective on the training and they cannot decide what will benefit them most.
*Criterion tests are linked to each objective and offer checks on how training is succeeding as it goes along. Therefore, assessment is formative based on how successful trainers are in achieving certain criteria.	*Tests cover some aspects of training, but not all. Most assessment is normative, i.e. it is for grading purposes, based on competition between trainees.
*Because of the close-knit system of criterion tests, the trainer has a great deal of feedback from the trainees.	*Feedback is patchy and not always organised on a systematic basis.
*Comments by the trainer in feedback, help trainees to gauge their progress, identify their strengths and begin the process of remedying weaknesses.	*Inadequate feedback mechanisms mean that weaknesses can continue undetected.
*Content is carefully sequenced and presented in a logical order.	*Content may not be sequenced and sometimes "backtracking" is necessary to cover vital ingredients which might have been missed.
*Detailed System Functions and both analysis and synthesis which yield pertinent information to the trainer, allow him the best possible chance of effective and efficient implementation.	*Implementation is not based on an adequate supply of information and may be uncertainly effective.
*Evaluation is always carried out and gives vital information to the trainer which allows him to have a finger on the "pulse" of training, identifying weak parts of training, which are replanned and strengthened and strong areas, which are built upon.	*Often evaluation is not carried out at all. Consequently, weaknesses in training are not identified, dissatisfaction with the course abounds, complaints are not heard. Eventually, the whole of a course collapses, in extreme cases.
*Review and revision leading to the improvement of training are standard. OM courses get better all the time.	*There is little review or revision. TA courses improve little, or only very slowly, over long periods.

FIGURE 40

You may have thought that we have exaggerated the benefits of the objectives model and been over-critical of the traditional approach. This is not so; let us give you a single example. Recently, in a well-known institution, a large course had no evaluating mechanisms whatsoever. It wasn't so much that there were danger signals flying, as the course trainers hadn't any way of ensuring that the signals were put up. So they were not alerted to the failings in the training. When the crash came, the course collapsed so badly that it had to be closed down.

This is a heavy price to pay for a lack of system and a lack of evaluation as part of that system.

Write down what you consider to be the most significant characteristics of the Objectives Model.

Our points are that the Objectives Model
* *is systematic.*
* *uses analysis and synthesis to provide information for the trainer.*
* *uses formative testing.*
* *evaluates, reviews, revises and improves training.*
* *uses feedback (a "loop" model) and, of course,*
* *is based on objectives.*

The nature and advantages for training of the Objectives Model are numerous, which is why we recommend its use.

OBJECTIVES GET YOU THERE!*!

FIGURE 41

However, if you read more widely in the literature, you will find criticisms of the Objectives Model and we will view these now. Before we do so, revise our design system and the Objectives Model upon which it is based and see if you can make out any possible criticisms.

We will also answer the criticisms, pointing out where they are sufficiently accurate for you to take care when using the model.

CRITICISMS OF THE OBJECTIVES MODEL AND REPLIES

CRITICISMS	REPLY
*Nobody knows where objectives come from and where they are derived. This is always a major criticism in the literature.	*This objection has no grounds at all if our design system is used. Needs Analysis shows clearly where needs are to be met and we have shown in Package One how objectives are organised so that each objective is related to and deals with each need which has been identified. Task Analysis supports Needs Analysis, so using our systematic design system makes this a non-problem giving us a well-defined prescription for deriving objectives.
*If you use OM you can't go on a "Voyage of Exploration" and some spontaneity and initiative may be lost in training.	*In training, you don't want to go on voyages: deficient performances have to be remedied and there is no time for wandering. However, if you want to explore new avenues, then objectives make sure that your exploration is relevant and make it easy for you to keep a sense of direction. In these circumstances spontaneity and initiative can be encouraged not discouraged.
*OM does not help trainers deal with unpredicted events in the classroom.	*OM gives such a thorough-going structure and offers so much valuable information to the trainer that unpredicted events are fewer in number. If the occurrences are unpredictable, then objectives offer an "anchor" which allows the unpredictable event to be held in perspective and improves the chances of the Trainer deriving some relevance and benefit from the event. In any case, classroom events are related to teaching techniques rather than to a design system.
*Objectives can be ambiguous.	*Our design system shows how objectives are written clearly and task analysis pinpoints much of the material which objectives deal with. Such precision makes it easy to write unambiguous objectives.
*Many objectives are trivial.	*This is a criticism which has elements of truth and which you must guard against. It is easy to write low-level objectives, e.g. in the cognitive domain the knowledge and comprehension levels are easier to write to than producing objectives at the levels of synthesis and evaluation. So when you produce your objectives, make certain that you also write to the higher levels of each domain. Your Test Specifications will show the spread of your objectives, at a glance.
*There are many paths through any body of knowledge.	*Yes, there are, but objectives do help to indicate those paths which will be most fruitful. Your design system gives you so much information on your trainees that you can match their knowledge, skills and abilities to the path which is most suitable for them. In any case, learning a skill usually has an obvious best route and often only one way in which it may be learned.
*Objectives can become too specific and there are too many of them consequently.	There is a danger here: how specific they are depends on which deficiencies your Needs Analysis shows and what details you put into your objectives to ensure that deficiencies are removed by training. However, these can be a problem in that an extensive training course does demand numerous objectives. So you must be careful not to overdo the number of objectives which you write. It's a matter of commonsense really, but keep your objectives to a minimum.

*Objectives and the whole objectives model take up too much time to produce.	*They do take time, but this is not really the point. Using a design system gives information to the trainer which is invaluable; using objectives gives direction to the training. As such information and direction are essential to good training, the point is that you aren't wasting your time. You've got to put the effort in sometime.
*Lists of Behaviour do not represent the structure of knowledge.	*Well, they certainly represent the structure of a skilled performance and the careful sequencing of content used in our design system gives a logical sequence and structure to be followed when training is concerned with learning knowledge. In any case what other structure of knowledge is there?
*Objectives, when written in a mass at the beginning of training, or parts of a course, put the trainees off.	*True, they do. So try using key words, which look less formidable and place the objectives at the end, where they will seem familiar to the trainee who has received the learning message and knows the code. End placement can also be a useful revisionary exercise: the trainee reading through them can really check how well he or she knows the material.
*The use of behavioural objectives and of OM suggests a poverty-stricken model of trainee-trainer interaction.	*The criticism fundamentally misunderstands the use of objectives which are to provide direction and of the systematic approach, which is to give structure to and information for training. Interaction between trainer and trainee is about what happens in a classroom and neither objectives nor the design system of OM prevent effective relationships between people.
*Writing objectives and using a design system doesn't suit certain types of subjects.	*Using the design system causes no problems whatever you are teaching. As a structure of training and provider of information about content, the trainees and the efficiency of the course, it is unbeatable and works for any subject. Writing objectives for skills is effective, but some subjects like history and philosophy do not lend themselves to easily written objectives. These are not the subjects dealt with in training, so the criticism applies more to education as distinct from training. Writing objectives to direct attitude change can be difficult, but if you have objectives you at least have it clearly in mind which attitudes you are attempting to change.

FIGURE 42

What general point do you notice about the criticisms of OM?

They are mainly critical of the use of objectives themselves. We think we have answered most of the criticisms and we have tried to show how OM and the use of objectives is particularly suitable as a system which produces efficient and effective **training**.
However, don't **overdo** *the writing of objectives.*

AH! A BAD CASE OF OVERDOING OBJECTIVES

FIGURE 43

At the beginning of this Component we mentioned the **Process Model** and showed this in Figure 38. Here are the **characteristics** of this model:—

> *The model is not systematic. The supporters of this model suggest that the variables in training are so numerous that it is difficult to deal with them systematically. By '"Variables" they mean environmental factors like the physical character of the classroom; other factors like tradition and custom; training styles; constraints which are administrative, occupational, legal and financial; differing subjects, curricula, methods of assessment and evaluation and teaching; differences between trainees.
>
> If you look at that long list carefully, you will see that our design system actually does deal with most of those variables, by means of our different System Functions.
>
> *The Process Model does not specify outcomes. It does require that there is a detailed explanation of what the trainer is to do by following certain **principles of procedure** when he or she is teaching.
>
> These principles are very useful when training and they will be examined in the next Component.
>
> *Indeed, the Process Model suggests that the large number of variables makes behavioural outcomes unpredictable. This is a sort of "set them off and see what happens" approach.
>
> *Assessment is flexible and so is evaluation in the sense that it arises naturally and is not designed automatically as part of the system.
>
> *Usually, practitioners of the Process Model follow the procedures outlined in Figure 38. They begin with their training content, divide it into teachable chunks, have general outcomes only in mind and concentrate on providing learning experiences for the trainee, especially by following certain "principles of procedure".

Certainly, the Process Model provides an alternative way of approaching training. You will have noticed, however, that the Objectives Model, if used flexibly, covers some of the ground of the Process Model, anyway. As we described in Package One, you can begin to design your training by starting with content; this is one example of overlap.

Nevertheless, we are convinced that the Objectives Model is superior to any other and is especially effective in the training context. In training, especially skills training, precision is required and you have to know where you and the trainees are going, when you've got there and how good the going was. Our design system, based on the Objectives Model, gives a trainer so much help, in the shape of rational procedures to follow, the information needed to ensure efficiency and guidance as how to make the training effective, that it is a uniquely valuable tool and blueprint.

Summary

Message checklists help you confirm the efficiency and clarity of your learning messages.

Learning is a change of behaviour, or performance following training, the purpose of which is to promote learning.

Whilst there are differences between "training" and "education", these are overlaps and training is found in education and vice versa. The differences are partly based on the concentration in training on "how" and in education on "why", but both are fundamentally processes which help the learner to learn.

The major models of training are the Objectives Model and the Process Model. Our design system is based upon the Objectives Model which, although criticised, is an invaluable tool, a blueprint for the trainer, providing a logical and systematic approach which gives the trainer a mine of information about discrepancies in job performance and the needs which arise from them, about the task, resources and constraints, about dealing with the content of training, criterion tests, effective implementation and assessment.

The Objectives Model emphasises the importance of learning outcomes, the provision of feedback on which the evaluation of training, its strengths and weaknesses, is based and of training review, revision and improvement.

The Objectives model is a loop, or cyclic model, which allows training to improve as it goes on.

Finally, the Objectives Model is based on the judicious selection, derivation and writing of General and particularly Specific Objectives, which give the trainer and the trainees a clear direction in their training.

You'll recollect that we said, at the beginning of this Component, that we proposed to examine "a very model of a modern learner, in general". Well, we have examined two models and in the next Components we will consider the "modern learner" as part of our paraphrased quotation. At first, our consideration is to be "in general", leading into a detailed examination of methods of teaching and learning in the Study Units of the next two Packages.

State the advantages and disadvantages of using the Objectives Model in an actual course which is part of your training. Dispatch your comparison and conclusions to your Programme Tutor for comment, if you wish.

Component 4:

Strategies for Delivering the Learning

Key Words

 Delivery models, strategies, methods and tactics; trainer-centred and trainee-centred strategies; "Learnerface", flexibility and the Mixed Strategy; methods and Group Size; number of group relationships; Larger, Smaller Group and Individual methods of delivery; delivery strategies and types of training; learner activity.

Introduction

Our "modern learner" mentioned in the last Component has to be taught by "modern" methods and in Packages Two, Three and Four of the Training Technology Programme we show you some of those methods.

The shape of this Component, which sets the stage as a sort of advance organiser for the remainder of these Packages, is as follows:
Some Explaining to do.
Training and Delivery Strategies.
Group Size and Delivery.

* Some Explaining to do

We are sending you messages about training and learning and those we must encode. As we learned in Components One and Two of this Study Unit, we must make certain that you can decode our messages, so we will begin by explaining some of the most important terms and meanings of our code.

As we have said before, when anyone communicates in a special area, such as a subject discipline like mathematics, or engineering, geography, or education, certain words have specific meanings and convey the message in a sort of "shorthand". All geographers know what "escarpments" and "peak land value intersections" are with a high degree of precision. Unfortunately, in education and training the use of many words and phrases is ambivalent and different authors give the same terms varying meanings.

We remember, for example, a textbook which says of Berlo's SMCR model of communication, that "the channel is the medium". This, you'll recollect is not at all how we interpreted "channel" and "medium", but we hope our messages on communication were clear, because we took the trouble to explain what **we** meant by "channel" and "medium" and all of the other terms which we used.

So let's do some explaining now.

In the last Component we said that one use of the word "**model**" was a "simplified version of reality, or real life". The next codewords we want to examine are "**delivering the learning**". To us, this means the way in which the trainer gets the learning, i.e. information, knowledge, skills and attitudes, across to the learners, who are the trainees.

Put another way, you, the trainer are the sender of learning messages (which we've described before) to the receivers, who are the trainees.

This Component is about delivering the learning and the various ways in which you can do this.

These ways of making your delivery involve a choice
  of model
  of delivery strategies
  of delivery methods
  of delivery tactics

Well, we've considered "model", so we will explain what we mean by "**delivery strategies**". This is a phrase borrowed from military usage, where "strategy" is the system of the commander who directs the **large** operations and military movements of a campaign. So for our usage:

"**a delivery strategy is the system which the trainer uses to plan and direct the broader aspects of delivering the learning, considered in general terms**".

▨▨ Checkpoint

Can you give an example of this system which we have considered already?

Using the design system is part of this art.

From our point of view, as trainers, there are three training strategies which the trainer can use to deliver the learning; these are the:—

  Trainer-Centred Strategy.
  Trainee-Centred Strategy.
  Mixed Strategy.

We shall look at these later, but remind you that we have already gone into detail about them in Component Eight, Study Unit Two, Package One. You would find it an advantage to revise that Component now.

Carrying on with our definitions we come to "**delivery methods**". A "Method" is explained in dictionaries as a systematic arrangement or procedure for attaining an objective. In training, we follow certain methods of delivering the learning such as the lecture method, group discussions, projects, using a-v media etc. So "**a delivery method is an arrangement or procedure for delivering the learning in practice**".

Finally, we come to the phrase "**delivery tactics**". This is a continuation of the military analogy: tactics are what happens on the ground where the actual fighting is going on. The commander-in-chief and the generals decide on strategy: the unit commanders decide on tactics, the infantry do the fighting, using various **techniques** and with types of **support**.

STRATEGY, TACTICS AND TECHNIQUES

FIGURE 44

Thus, in training terms "**delivery tactics are how you put training strategy and methods into action, using various techniques and supported by various means**".

We have used a military analogy to explain training terms. From our point of view, as trainers, this analogy can give a wrong impression. Why is this? Figure 44 gives you a clue to the answer.

There are three types of person in Figure 44: the General, the unit commander and the infantryman, each carrying out a different role and different tasks.

In training, often one person does all three jobs, as you know, by deciding a strategy, choosing methods and carrying out tactics.

The theme underlying what we have been saying is that you focus more and more closely on the action in training until you reach what happens when you are facing the trainees. We call this face-to-face situation the "**Learnerface**". Often, when blackboards were to be always found and were used in every classroom. this was called the "chalkface". As the "chalk and talk" method isn't so popular these days, we think Learnerface is a better description of where the actual training goes on. The Learnerface can be in a classroom, at the workbench, in a laboratory or removed from them to the page of a book, as in distance learning and this Programme, where part of the Learnerface is what you are looking at now. The other part is when you talk to us on the telephone and send in work for comment.

LEARNERFACE

FIGURE 45

Now, draw a diagram which shows the relationship between model, strategy, method, tactics, techniques and media.

Our diagram is shown in the next Figure.

DELIVERING THE LEARNING

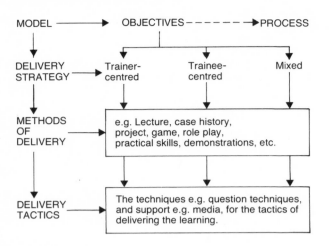

FIGURE 46

One of the trainer's main jobs is to **choose** the most effective strategy, method and tactic and the "how" and "why" of this selection process is to occupy us largely in this Package and the next two Packages.

However, before we go into further detail can you suggest why it is that our discussion so far has been somewhat one-sided?

Well, delivering the learning is a form of communication, between the trainer and the learners. You'll remember our definition of communication which is that, "communication in training is the successful sharing and interchange of information and meanings". To that definition we could have added, "which leads to learning".

Now, we haven't said much here about the learning and the learners. We have talked about ways of delivering the learning, which is looking at the training from the trainer's point of view only; this is what we mean by "one-sided". So we must make sure that when we describe ways of delivering the learning, we also examine the learner's part in making the communication, or delivery, successful by accepting the delivery and responding to it.

So we could have called this Package, "Methods of Training and Learning". Incidentally, you'll note that we used the word "methods" only. A truer title would have been "Models, Strategies, Methods and Tactics of training and learning", but that would have been a bit too much for a title!

We have discussed models of delivery in this Package already, considering both Objectives and Process Models. Whilst we recommend usage of the Objectives model, we were careful to suggest that the Process model has its place and that there is an overlap between the models anyway. Ingredients of both can be used in training and the mixture is a profitable one, attractive to the learners.

SOME INGREDIENTS OF LEARNING

FIGURE 47

We showed a couple of "learning ingredients" (objectives) in the last Figure and perhaps we should have called them "learning delivery ingredients". Let's now go on to consider some more of these ingredients, that is the three training strategies shown in Figure 46.

* Training and Delivery Strategies

We have already considered trainer-centred and trainee-centred strategies extensively in Component Eight, Study Unit Two, Package One and you will have had time to look at that again. It is appropriate for us to revise that Component now and add both new material and a different perspective by comparing the characteristics of the two strategies of trainer-centred and trainee-centred training, as we do in the next Figure. Make out your own outline list before you read ours, which is not in any particular order of importance.

DELIVERY STRATEGIES: CHARACTERISTICS

TRAINER-CENTRED STRATEGY	TRAINEE-CENTRED STRATEGY
*Trainer may or may not involve the trainees in high degree of verbal participation.	*Trainer always involves trainees in verbal interaction.
*Trainer may or may not accept erroneous or irrelevant trainee contributions.	*Trainer always accepts all contributions, without negative evaluation.
*Trainer uses "I" a lot, consequently he and the group are not always cohesive.	*Trainer uses "we" in a cohesive group.
*Trainer lays down syllabuses, assignments etc., giving step-by-step instructions.	*Trainers vary from those who do lay down syllabuses and guide discussion to those who ask questions like, "What should we talk about today?". The latter is a strategy rarely found in training and is more typical of some forms of education which are sometimes undirected and frequently misdirected.
*Trainer sees himself as an "expert", believes training content to be of first importance.	*Trainer may see himself as an expert, believes content to be important but places activity by the trainees as most significant.
*Trainer usually makes well-organised presentations, frequently as an exposition of the facts or skills.	*Trainer tends to offer looser presentation, not so much expository as experiential, i.e. offering a learning experience to the trainee and then seeing how it develops.
*A-V media used are either self-instructional or one-way and are highly structured and managed by the trainer.	*Media are two-way or self-instructional. However, such media are difficult to obtain.
*The trainer decides on how fast the learning will go.	*Trainees are given the chance to pace their own training.
*The trainer is working within a system which everyone understands so that it works smoothly and efficiently.	*The trainee-centred approach may be resisted by some members of staff because it is "new" and causes insecurity.
*Trainer-centred strategies cover the ground efficiently although they may not always be effective.	*Sometimes the trainee-centred strategy lacks coherence and loses both efficiency and effectiveness.
*Trainer can offer strong leadership, although this can become authoritarian.	*Trainer is more of a "facilitator" helping the trainees to learn by providing resources and learning materials.
*Trainer has a big advantage in designing training situations and in pitching them at a suitable level for the average trainee. However, if you're not an average trainee you may be unlucky.	*Trainer allows trainees to find their own levels and to work accordingly. May have a problem in holding it all together as so many different levels of learning are going on at once.
*Trainer uses training methods which he has tried, understands well and can be carried out successfully. However, if the trainer's repertoire of techniques is small then the training becomes boring, repetitive and the techniques used are not the best available.	*Whilst the trainer uses tried and trusted techniques, he is always "game" for attempting to use new methods of delivering the learning. This gives variety, but also results in some failures.
*The trainer actually does a great deal of the work and the trainees may become passive. This can be a big drawback.	*The trainees are usually very active; they do all the work, but sometimes they are doing the wrong work and waste time until they get on course again.
*Timetabling is often a standard 45/60 minute period.	*Flexibility of time tabling is utilised, but the strategy runs into difficulties if adequate time is not available.
*Little use is made of other trainees (peers or proctors) in the training.	*Peer group help (i.e. help from trainees) is used widely.
*The trainer organises most of the training. If efficient, he does this effectively; if not?	*The trainee organises much of the training. Some may not do this well.

*Trainer usually offers little or less personal guidance to the trainees, although this is not by any means always true of this strategy.

*An effective trainer using the trainer-centred strategy can motivate his trainees to learn. If the trainer is not effective, then trainee motivation is low. Often the degree of motivation of the trainer is reflected in the degree of motivation of the trainees.

*The trainer decides on the accessibility of the learning materials.

*This strategy tends to expository training methods (see Component Eight, Study Unit Two, Package One). These involve the trainer frequently talking **at** and **to** the trainees.

*Difficulties can be experienced in achieving objectives in the higher cognitive domain e.g. synthesis, analysis and evaluation.

*Higher order objectives in the psychomotor domain are easier to achieve by this strategy as they usually involve a demonstration by the trainer and/or a competent or master performer, followed by practice by the trainees under supervision.

*Higher order objectives in the affective domain (e.g. Organising and Characterising) are difficult to achieve unless the trainer makes a point of developing strong feedback from the trainees.

*Social skills may be difficult to teach by the trainer-centred strategy.

*Assessment is well structured and often grading is made on a competitive basis following the "curve of normal distribution". Sometimes trainers following a set syllabus on an award bearing course have no choice about methods of assessment, anyway.

*The trainer often offers little personal freedom to trainees, although the best trainers do offer elements of choice to trainees within set structures. If the training leads to an award this situation of limited freedom is difficult to avoid.

*Learning is most frequently in the form of larger groups except in skills training where it is usually on an individual basis.

*Extra time for learning is usually not provided, unless enrolment for remedial classes is allowed.

*The trainer makes subject matter presentations, administers tests and manages the "housekeeping".

*Evaluation may or may not be carried out thoroughly, although effective trainers using the trainer-centred strategy are careful to evaluate.

*Often media presentations are expanded and explained by the trainer and are thought of as "enrichment".

*Revision of the learning material is most frequently made when a subject expert wishes to change a treatment or when old content is considered out-of-date.

*Personal tuition and guidance on a large scale is essential if this strategy is to work although this places very heavy demands on trainers' time and this requirement often simply cannot be met.

*Motivation tends to be personal to each trainee and consequently varies across a wide range. If the trainee is not motivated to learn then this strategy fails, but adequately high levels of motivation to learn are usually achieved.

*The learning materials are usually easily accessible. Indeed, they have to be: if not, the strategy fails and availability of trainers' time for preparation, as well as lack of funds, may act as serious constraints.

*This strategy involves mainly discovery training methods. (See Component Eight). These methods involve talking **with** the trainees and the trainees talking **with each other**.

*Higher order objectives in the cognitive domain achieved effectively by this strategy.

Higher order objectives in the psychomotor domain (e.g. Precision Articulation and Naturalisation in Figure 187 in Component Three, Study Unit Two, Package One or Complex Overt Response, Adaption and Origination in Figure 188) are difficult to achieve and in practice may be unsafe.

*Higher order objectives in the affective domain are always difficult to achieve however the trainer sets about it, but this strategy offers a reasonable chance of success.

*Social skills are improved by this strategy as the trainees have to work together much more.

*The problem of grading is sometimes a difficult one using the trainee-centred strategy. This strategy is often unsuitable when employed in entirety for award-bearing courses.

*The trainees have a greater degree of personal freedom if they are on non award-bearing courses, or if they are on training which is cognitive or affective rather than psycho-motor. When the training is in physical skills, little personal freedom can be permitted to the trainees.

*Learning is generally in smaller groups or on an individual basis.

*Extra time is frequently provided, if it can be made available.

*The trainer's role is not primarily to instruct but to manage the learning environment, diagnose trainee problems, facilitate the use of resources and co-ordinate information.

*Evaluation is usually a strong point of this strategy and measures are taken to relate the effectiveness of the instructing and materials to their cost and effectiveness.

*Media presentations are usually followed up by discussion between the trainees, this discussion frequently not being led by the trainer.

"Whilst new content must be incorporated the trainer reviews the material continuously by judging its efficiency in relation to the performance of the trainees. Where performance is deficient then ineffective material is removed, whether the replacement material has the virtue of being new or not.

FIGURE 48

If given the choice, which strategy of training would you use, the trainer-centred or the trainee-centred?

If you said trainee-centred, you would be wrong.
If you said trainer-centred, you would be wrong.

The whole point is that you pick the strategy which suits best the training which you are delivering and you mix the strategies, to achieve the best results. For example, if you are training in skilled job performance, then the trainer-centred strategy is basically better; if you are training for a change in trainee attitudes, the trainee-centred has the most advantages.

*However, whichever style you adopt, you can always mix your strategies as you go along, to achieve the best results from any particular piece of training. This is why we recommend the use of the Mixed Training Strategy where you switch from strategy to strategy, picking the one which suits your training and delivery of the learning most. So, "**Be flexible in your choice and use of training strategies**" another of our Golden Rules.*

We can use a useful example here from the Components on communications, where you mix styles.

Can you bring an example of this mixing to mind?

*You recollect symmetrical and complementary relationships? Well, often in a single training session you will begin with a complementary relationship when you organise the session, giving out introductory instruction, guidance and valuable information. Subsequently, having given your exposition, or presentation, you switch to a symmetrical relationship. In a way, you are changing here from a trainer-centred style to a trainee-centred, **in one lesson.** If you can change like that in one lesson, you can certainly switch around between strategies when planning training by using the Mixed Training Strategy. Consequently you have the best of both worlds.*

There is a tendency for the trainee-centred strategy to be described as an approach in which the trainer stands in front of a group of trainees, laying down the "law" about the work and assignments which are to be done, talking **at** them and often lecturing, to a bored group who are receiving information like passive receptacles, not doing much actively.

TRAINER-CENTRED LEARNING?

FIGURE 49

On the other hand the trainee-centred strategy is shown to be a learning situation in which the trainer is part of the learning group, his role being to facilitate the learning. The trainees are active, finding out for themselves and learning by doing rather than by watching or hearing.

Are these pictures true?

The first picture of the trainer-centred strategy is true of that strategy at its worst. Lecturing away at passive trainers is ineffective, if carried out for long spells without variation. But not all trainer-centred training need be like that.

*Similarly, the illustration of the trainee-centred strategy is also true of that strategy at its best. So both pictures represent extreme views. However, the most superior training, as we said, combines the best of both strategies. **Frequently**, a short exposition used judiciously is effective; **always** making the trainees as active as you can is the best way of learning, as we stated before in one of our Golden Rules.*

So where you can, try to achieve maximal trainee involvement and activity, put the trainees and their needs first and try to facilitate learning and discovery rather than presenting information.

Just for the record, you'll find in the literature of training that different names are given to the trainer-centred and the trainee-centred strategies. These are:—

    Trainer—Centred: didactic, expository, presentation, instructor-centred, reception learning.

    Trainee—Centred: discovery, inquiry, learner-centred, experiential.

Remembering the information in Components One and Two on communication can you think of another pair of names?

We suggest that the trainer-centred strategy could be called "sender-centred" and trainee-centred is "receiver-centred." You'll remember that the efficiency of the receiver's response is what decides on the success of the communication and the effectiveness of the learning.

We can now show you a couple of diagrams which illustrate the differences between trainer-centred and trainee-centred strategies. The diagrams are simplified statements and show the systems which underline these two approaches.

THE TRAINER-CENTRED STRATEGY

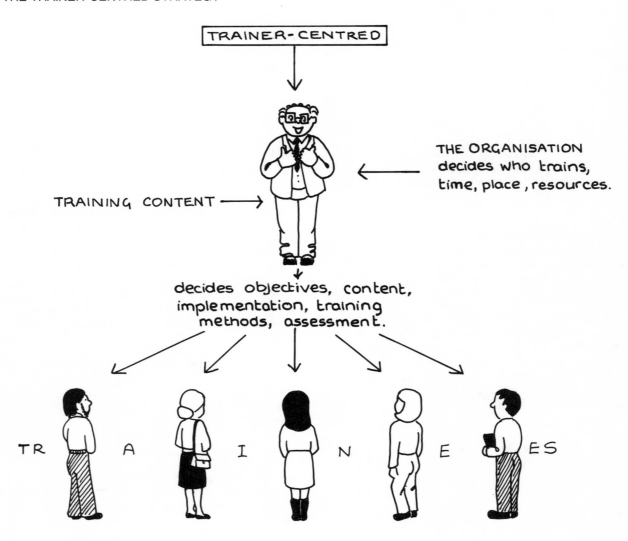

FIGURE 50

THE TRAINEE-CENTRED STRATEGY

FIGURE 51

Certain methods of delivering the learning lend themselves to the trainer or sender-centred strategy, e.g. lecturing. Others are more appropriate for the receiver or trainee-centred, e.g. group discussion.

From this, you can see that another factor now enters our consideration of the delivery of learning: the size of the group which is doing the learning.

* Group Size and Delivery

Training groups vary in size, just as what goes on in them changes in accordance with the purpose of the training. For example, you can have one large group who are watching a video, the whole audience doing the same things: watching, listening and thinking. You could also have an equally large group working in a trainee hair salon all of whom are doing different things: dealing with shampoo, cutting by thinning and tapering, clubbing, layer cutting, using re-agent, winding curlers, tinting, drying etc.

So when we talk about group size and the delivery of learning, we have to bear in mind that the distinctions we make are a little crude. Nevertheless, some delivery methods suit larger groups, some are best for smaller groups and some are used for delivering the learning to individuals.

Before we can look at delivery methods more closely, we will have to define what we mean by "larger" and "smaller" groups.

The most important consideration here is the number of relationships which are possible between members of a group and these are shown in the next table.

GROUP SIZE: NUMBER OF POSSIBLE
RELATIONSHIPS WITH ONE TRAINER

Number of Trainees	Number of Relationships possible
1	1
2	6
4	44
6	222
8	1,080
10	5,210
11	11,374
12	24,708
18	2,359,602

FIGURE 52

▰▰▰

What important fact does Figure 52 tell you?

It seems to us that the very steep increase in the number of relationships between ten trainees and the trainer make it difficult for there to be much in the shape of interaction on a personal level beyond that size of group. Certainly, when you increase the group size beyond eleven trainees, you have certainly moved from a **smaller group** *to a* **larger group** *in terms of possible relationships and your method of delivering* **the learning has to be modified correspondingly.** *More relationships = less personal contact.*

So for the purposes of this Package we shall recognise that "larger group" delivery is made to twelve or more trainees, "smaller group" from two trainees (plus the trainer) to eleven trainees. Where only one trainee is present with the trainer, that is individualised delivery or "individualised instruction".

Subsequently, we shall consider methods of delivery roughly in accordance with those group sizes, but do remember that the limits which we have chosen are **arbitrary** ones.

We can now extend Figure 46, to include the material which we have considered since then, as shown in the next flow diagram, Figure 53.

FROM MODEL TO TACTICS

OBJECTIVES **MODEL**

TRAINER-CENTRED **STRATEGY**	MIXED **STRATEGY**	TRAINEE-CENTRED **STRATEGY**
LARGER GROUP **METHODS**	SMALLER GROUP **METHODS**	INDIVIDUAL **METHODS**

Box 1 Larger Group only

Lectures

Non-interactive lesson (OWL)

Some TV/Video/ Film presentation

Box 2 Smaller Group only

Group discussion

Syndicates

T. Groups

Triads

Action learning groups

Quality Circles

Leaderless Groups

Encounter Groups

Clinics

Box 3 Individualised only

PSI

Keller Plan

Programmed Learning

Mastery Learning

Open Learning

Distance Learning

Resource-based Learning

In-basket

Theses

Computer-based Learning

Interactive Video Learning

Action Maze

Dyads

Box 4 Larger and smaller Group

Panels. Buzz Groups. Colloquy.
Pyramids. Practicals.
Juries. Symposiums.
Interactive Lessons (2WL).
Role Play. Brainstorming.
Simulations. Games.
Simulation Games. Workshops.
Wilson Quadro. Seminars.

Box 5 Smaller Group & Individualized

Projects. Assignments.
Problem-solving. Tutorials.
Case-studies. Workshops.
TV/Video/Film.

IMPLEMENTATION AT "LEARNERFACE".
Delivering the Learning using
TACTICS

FIGURE 53

The last **important** Figure is fundamentally about the choices which face the trainer when delivering the learning. Initially, the first selection is made between the Objectives **Model**, or a Process Model. The trainer decides on a delivery **strategy** next and then has to choose between a large variety of **methods** of delivery, sometimes using only one method and sometimes combining several. This selection often depends on the size of group which is to be taught, as particular methods are more suitable for some trainers than others.

Finally, the trainer delivers the learning to the trainees in the classroom, workshop or laboratory, using various **tactics**, which we have not examined in detail yet.

How suitable is the Objectives Model as a basis for the different strategies of delivery?

There are two main aspects to this model: the use of behavioural or performance objectives and the systematic approach to design of training. Clearly, you can use the design system with any delivery strategy as you can incorporate objectives into trainer-centred, trainee-centred, or mixed delivery strategies.

At the extreme positions you can have training centred very much on the trainer, who issues a list of objectives to be attained by all learners, or you can have a trainee-centred approach which allows the trainee to select objectives from a list, freely. Even further towards centering the training on the receiver, it is possible for the trainees to develop their own selection of personal objectives either with or without consultation with the trainers.

It all depends on the sort of training which you are carrying out, but the Objectives Model is generally useful and applicable.

We now show an expanded version of Figure 271 from Component Eight, Study Unit Two, Package One to show the relationships between our strategies and the type of training.

GENERAL SUITABILITY OF DELIVERY STRATEGIES FOR DIFFERENT TYPES OF TRAINING

Suitability shown as High, Medium or Low. These categories will vary according to the purposes of your particular training.

TYPE OF TRAINING	TRAINER-CENTRED STRATEGY	TRAINEE-CENTRED STRATEGY
SKILLS High level Medium Level Low Level	HIGH HIGH HIGH	LOW LOW MEDIUM
KNOWLEDGE AND INFORMATION High Level Medium Level Low Level	LOW MEDIUM MEDIUM	HIGH HIGH HIGH
ATTITUDES Major Change Lesser Change	LOW MEDIUM	HIGH HIGH
MENTAL SKILLS e.g. Problem Solving	LOW/MEDIUM	HIGH
CREATIVITY	LOW	HIGH
LEARNING HOW	HIGH/MEDIUM	MEDIUM/HIGH
LEARNING WHY	LOW/MEDIUM	HIGH
INTENSIVE TRAINING (Time restricted)	HIGH	LOW
WORKSHOP SKILLS	HIGH/MEDIUM	LOW
PRACTICAL	HIGH/MEDIUM	MEDIUM/HIGH
LARGER GROUP	HIGH	LOW
SMALLER GROUP	LOW	HIGH
INDIVIDUALISED	LOW	HIGH

FIGURE 54

▨▨▨

This Component has described various choices of model, strategy and methods open to the trainer. Remembering the Components on communications, what possible pitfall must the trainer bear in mind when making a selection?

*Try to avoid "polarizing" your thinking: the choices are **not** between using either an Objectives or a Process Model, they aren't between picking either the trainee-centred or the trainer-centred method and sticking to your choice rigidly. Select the parts which will best serve the training which you are doing and switch around in a flexible fashion to meet the requirements of the trainees most effectively.*

However, you might forgive us for adding the following illustration.

OBJECTIVES REACH THE PARTS OTHER MODELS CAN'T REACH

FIGURE 55

Summary

A model is a simplified version of reality and we considered here and in the previous Components two major models (there are others) namely the Process Model and the one which we recommend for use in training, the Objectives Model.

In considering models, we began to look at how the trainer is delivering the learning to the trainees and the ways in which this delivery involves a choice not only between models, but also of effective delivery strategies, methods and tactics.

There are three major strategies: Trainer-Centred delivery, Trainee-Centred delivery and a combination of both which we have called a Mixed strategy.

All **delivery strategies** have optimal uses and the trainer wishes to pick the best strategy for training in hand, switching around between strategies to obtain the best learning.

The same principle of choosing extends to **delivery methods** of which there is a large variety. Most methods tend to be particularly useful for certain sizes of group, with choice of method varying according to the number of trainees.

For the purposes of this Package, we distinguished between delivering the learning to larger groups consisting of the trainer plus twelve or more trainees, smaller (not small) groups of from two to eleven trainees and individualised delivery, where one trainer is mostly concerned with only one trainee at a time.

Delivery tactics are about what happens at the Learnerface, where a range of techniques is used, supported by the media, to encourage and engender learning.

Whichever strategies, methods and tactics are used, or whatever combinations are made, the trainer must always strive to ensure that the trainees are involved actively in the learning. The trainer-centred strategy, implemented at its least effective where the trainer transmits knowledge or skills for long periods, without giving the trainees a chance to practice and be active, must be avoided. So too, should a completely undirected trainee-centred strategy, which is entirely unsuitable for much skills training.

Therefore, when we look at delivery methods and tactics, we shall be very concerned to show how they can motivate the learners to be active in directions which lead to learning.

This Component completes Study Unit One. Before you go onto the next Study Unit, you might wish to try the following exercise.

Examine a current course which you are running and decide if it is trainer or trainee-centred. List the advantages and disadvantages of the strategy, or strategies which you are using and say how effective you believe your courses are in encouraging trainee activity.

Suggest any ways of improving your training, bearing in mind what we have said in the last four Components, particularly.

Send your work to your Programme Tutor for comment if you wish.

Study Unit 1. Objectives.

On completion of this Study Unit, trainers will be able, for training in their own place of work, to effectively:
1. Define "Communication".
2. Describe the aims of effective communication in training.
3. Evaluate the main models of communication.
4. Analyse barriers to effective communication.
5. Communicate effectively, both orally and in writing.
6. Evaluate the part which efficient communication plays in learning.
7. Compare the processes of training with those of education.
8. Apply the Objectives Model to training.
9. Contrast the Objectives Model with the Process Model.
10. Compare the implementation of the Objectives Model with a traditional approach to training.

11. Criticise the Objectives Model by examining its strengths and weaknesses.
12. Show how the learning may be delivered by different delivery strategies.
13. Compare the characteristics of a trainer-centred strategy with a trainee-centred.
14. Explain how group size affects learning.

(Note: this is a list of the more important Objectives. It is not comprehensive. Add other objectives for yourself.)

Study Unit 2

Methods of Training: Groupwork

Component 1:

Methods of delivering the learning to Larger Groups: Lessons and Lesson plans

 Key Words

Planning the training; scheme of work and lesson plans; structure of a scheme including delivery methods, learning activities and key events; formats.

This Study Unit examines methods of delivering the learning to Larger Groups

Introduction

In this Study Unit we shall be concentrating on methods and tactics for delivering the learning to **Larger Groups**. We show a selection of these methods in Boxes 1 and 4 in the next figure, a copy of Figure 53, Component 4, Study Unit 1. We also mentioned the fact that whilst we considered larger groups to consist of 12 or more trainees, this is an arbitrary limit and that some delivery methods are suitable for both larger and smaller groups.

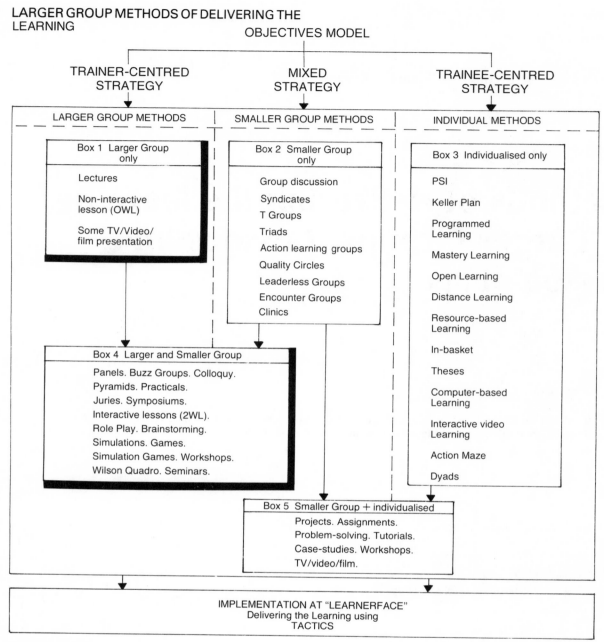

LARGER GROUP METHODS OF DELIVERING THE LEARNING

OBJECTIVES MODEL

TRAINER-CENTRED STRATEGY	MIXED STRATEGY	TRAINEE-CENTRED STRATEGY
LARGER GROUP METHODS	SMALLER GROUP METHODS	INDIVIDUAL METHODS

Box 1 Larger Group only

Lectures

Non-interactive lesson (OWL)

Some TV/Video/ film presentation

Box 2 Smaller Group only

Group discussion
Syndicates
T Groups
Triads
Action learning groups
Quality Circles
Leaderless Groups
Encounter Groups
Clinics

Box 3 Individualised only

PSI
Keller Plan
Programmed Learning
Mastery Learning
Open Learning
Distance Learning
Resource-based Learning
In-basket
Theses
Computer-based Learning
Interactive video Learning
Action Maze
Dyads

Box 4 Larger and Smaller Group

Panels. Buzz Groups. Colloquy.
Pyramids. Practicals.
Juries. Symposiums.
Interactive lessons (2WL).
Role Play. Brainstorming.
Simulations. Games.
Simulation Games. Workshops.
Wilson Quadro. Seminars.

Box 5 Smaller Group + individualised

Projects. Assignments.
Problem-solving. Tutorials.
Case-studies. Workshops.
TV/video/film.

IMPLEMENTATION AT "LEARNERFACE"
Delivering the Learning using
TACTICS

FIGURE 56

One such method is the **lesson**, which we all know can be delivered to six or sixty trainees. Lessons delivered to smaller numbers of trainees are usually very interactive, which means that there are many interactions between the trainer and the trainees. Those delivered to big numbers cannot be so interactive, certainly not so far as individual trainees are concerned.

Generally, we shall consider the lesson to be a typical method of delivery to larger groups and after we have looked at that method we will consider others, such as lectures and panels. Of course, lessons may also be regarded as slices of training time, using a combination of training methods and sizes of groups. So let's begin with the

* The Lesson

Any visitor walking through a training establishment or a school, would see lots of activity, with trainers or teachers working away in classrooms, supervising activities on workbenches, setting up laboratory experiments, demonstrating skills and surrounded by active trainees. Sometimes there will be hubbub and on other occasions the groups will be working quietly, or alone.

TRAINING: THE TEACHING ACTIVITY

FIGURE 57

Someone unused to training, might come away with the impression that this activity **is** training and that's what it is all about. What visitors don't see, or see very little of, is the **planning** which goes on to the training activity.

MISTAKEN IMPRESSIONS OF TRAINING: THE TRAINING ACTIVITY

FIGURE 58

As we can see, the trainer in the last Figure is thinking about his courses. Planning and thinking is hard work, like writing distance-learning materials and much less enjoyable than the actual teaching which is usually stimulating and exciting, certainly to the trainer and hopefully to the trainees.

So in our consideration of lessons, we are starting with what has to be done first: planning the lessons. Planning is time-consuming and trainers may often spend half of their workdays in planning alone.

The ability to plan instruction and thorough planning itself are essential for effective training. We spent most of our time in Package One in explaining a systematic approach which acts as a basis for planning. In a way, a trainer's instructional plans are like an architect's plans in which the building is designed as a whole (the design system of the trainer) then important pieces of the structure (the modules or parts of the course) using various methods, then the specifying of the small details of construction (the planning of lessons by the trainer).

Certainly, neither in training, nor architecture, would a sound and stable structure result if planning was made on a day-to-day basis.

So, in looking at lessons, we shall show how training plans, like architectural plans, cover the design of the whole, the structure of each part and then the details of each part. These can be shown like this:

Design as a whole   = **Design System**
Structure of each part = **Scheme of Work**
Details of each part   = **Lesson plans**

By pre-planning, the trainer can see the training as a whole, making sure that every trainee is actively involved in learning activities and that in every lesson, assessment and evaluation lead towards the attainment of the learning outcomes which are desired.

Pre-planning helps the trainer to establish well-defined objectives, to ensure an adequate supply of resources and to select various and effective learning activities which will promote learning. So let's get on with, first, the planning of lessons and next their implementation.

We begin with the structure of each **part**, the **Scheme of Work**. Now, "part" is rather a vague word; here, we mean it to be the modules, or sections of which a long course is made up, or even the whole course, where the course is a short one.

* The Scheme of Work

 Checkpoint

Can you define a scheme of work from what we have said and by drawing upon your own experience?

SCHEME OF WORK: DEFINITION

> "A scheme of work is a plan which shows the arrangement and general structure of a series of lessons, designed to meet important objectives."

FIGURE 59A

That's a basic definition, which we can expand on later.

Draw a simple diagram which illustrates this definition.

THE SCHEME OF WORK: A FRAMEWORK FOR LESSONS

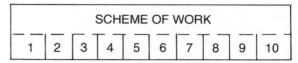

SCHEME OF WORK									
1	2	3	4	5	6	7	8	9	10

'1-10 Lesson Plans'

FIGURE 59B

We will take a dose of our own medicine now and plan out how we are going to examine the structure of a scheme of work.

Bearing in mind our design system and the information which we have given you, write out those elements which you think might make up the structure of a scheme of work.

Our structure is shown in the next diagram.

THE STRUCTURE OF A SCHEME OF WORK

1. GENERAL INFORMATION
   ↓
2. AIMS, GENERAL AND SPECIFIC OBJECTIVES
   ↓
3. CONTENT AND SYLLABUS
   ↓
4. DELIVERY METHODS
   ↓
5. LEARNING ACTIVITIES, LEARNING RESOURCES
   ↓
6. ASSESSMENT
   ↓
7. EVALUATION
   ↓
8. KEY EVENTS
   ↓
9. FORMAT OF THE SCHEME OF WORK
   ↓
10. CHECKLIST

FIGURE 60

So a scheme of work is a framework into which we slot lessons and lesson plans which are to be formulated once we have planned the scheme itself.

Let's begin with the first of the elements in our framework.

1. General Information

What sort of information do you consider should be used to "set the scene" for a scheme?

A scheme of work begins with general information about the training itself; here you write in the details such as:—
> *Course Title*
> *Awarding Body*
> *Training Staff*
> *Length of Course and dates*
> *Duration of Sessions*
> *Day and Time*
> *Venue*
> *Target Audience*

Much of this is routine information and does not present any problems, but we might say a little about "Target Audience".

Perhaps **you** might say something about the target audience, first, as we covered this topic in the previous Package. Who, what, is the target audience?

This is the group of trainees whom you are training. Information about them is available from your Entering Behaviour Analysis (See Package One) and you should have a clear picture of them at the beginning of the course. In the scheme of work, however, you would only have a very brief statement about the group, mainly an outline for the use of other trainers, who would have to refer to the Entering Behaviour Analysis for details.

2. Aims, General and Specific Objectives

These are provided by Aims and Objectives Analysis. An important aspect in that they are sequenced properly, so that the lessons themselves follow a logical pattern. Instructions on sequencing are given in Package One, Study Unit Two, Components Three and Figure 175 of Component Two gives the procedure for writing specific objectives which forms the basis of your checklist of objectives. Certainly, in working through your objectives checklist, **you'll need to know if the objectives:**

> * Are based on the trainee's personal needs.
> * Provide for recognition of the individual differences in ability and goals.
> * Are known and understood by the trainees well ahead of their use in training.
> * Are feasible and can be achieved in the time available.
> * Were developed using trainee input, where appropriate.
> * Allow the trainer the chance to make objective assessments of the trainees, rather than subjective.
> * Take cognizance of all the information provided by the design system functions.
> * Are written in accordance with the correct procedure.
> * Are derived from the Aims of the course.

3. Content and Syllabus

Often your training content is laid down in the form of a syllabus, especially when you are following an award-bearing course. Nevertheless, you still have discretion to concentrate on certain sections more than others and this can be reflected in your scheme of work by covering selected topics with more lessons.

Components Six and Seven of Study Unit Two, Package One, show you how to synthesise your training content and the latter Component tells you how to sequence your content.

In preparing schemes, the content is usually divided into topics or skills to be mastered and it is worthwhile to examine your topic/skills carefully and critically to see if they should be changed or modified.

You have a topic/skill which it is proposed to include in a course. Suggest a checklist of important points which you might wish to bear in mind when considering the worthwhileness and structure of that topic/skill.

Our checklist is shown in the next diagram.

TOPIC/SKILL CHECKLIST

1. **Is the topic/skill relevant to the trainees?** Here you are asking if the topic is important to their efficiency in their jobs and if the skill is a really necessary part of the whole skilled process of their becoming competent operatives?
2. **How significant is the topic/skill?** Here you are ensuring that you have a proper perspective and that you do not spend too much time and effort on a topic or skill which, although significant, is less so than others.
   Needs Analysis (Package One) will have shown you the need for training in certain areas and the Needs Index information together with the Need Statements will have prioritised the needs. These priorities will make clear both the significance and relevance of the topic/skill.
3. **Is the topic/skill precise?** Task Analysis and your specific objectives help to make the topic/skill well defined and show the extent to which it leads into other ideals and understandings.
4. **Has the topic focus and continuity?** Linking your objectives carefully to each topic/skill will ensure focus and a sensible lead on to the next topic/skill.
5. **Is the topic/skill feasible and practical?** Analysis of Resources and of Constraints (Package One) will show if you have the wherewithal to complete training in the topic/skill and indicate how much training time you can allocate to it.
6. **Will the topic/skill motivate the trainees?** Certainly if they have a clear-cut objective to be attained by studying the topic or practising the skill then they will be motivated to achieve it.
7. **Is the topic/skill adequately covered?** We suspect that this may be another way of asking you if you've done your job properly? One way of ensuring adequate coverage is check with Component Six, Study Unit Two, Package One, which shows sources of content. Make certain that you use as many sources as possible. Ensure that sufficient time has been allocated to each topic.

FIGURE 61

Write down a list of commonly used sources of content regarding skills and topics.

Here are some which we suggest:—
* *Syllabuses and all of the information from the design system.*
* *Other trainers.*
* *Experts in the topic and master performers of the skill.*
* *Textbooks and manuals.*
* *Current events: always try to add a touch of what is happening in the topic field right now or what are the latest advances in the skilled procedure. Even a touch of the exotics, foretelling the future, will help maintain interest.*
* *Job descriptions and Task (Topic) Analyses are useful sources.*

YOU MUST GIVE YOUR TOPIC/SKILL A DECENT COVERAGE

FIGURE 62

4. Delivery Methods

In your scheme of work you won't be able to do much except indicate the method of delivering the learning. However, you have to make certain that you are familiar with the full range of methods of delivering the learning and that they are suitable for helping the trainees **acquire, assimilate, apply,** and **develop** new knowledge, mental and motor skills and attitudes, if necessary.

You'll need to check that your methods will motivate the trainees to learn, generate as much trainee activity and independence as possible and that each method will deliver each topic and skill efficiently and effectively.

5. Learning Activities, Learning Resources

Definition of "Learning Activities" could be that:

Learning Activities are what the trainees do and experience in training. The trainees learn through these activities which help them achieve the objectives of training.

As we have said before, the more active the trainee then the better the learning. So ensuring that your scheme indicates profitable activity is very important. Here's another Checklist which should help you focus on learning activities and their vital significance in ensuring effective training:

■✓✓✓

Write out your list before studying the next Figure, which shows our suggestions.

LEARNING ACTIVITIES: CHECKLIST

1. Do the learning, activities provide relevant experiences related to the objectives?
2. Do they provide a variety of experiences?
3. Do the trainees know which activities are essential, which are recommended and which are optional?
4. Have the trainees reasonable choice and flexibility in selecting between the options which are provided? This assumes that a choice is possible, of course; this may not be the case in some skills training.
5. Do the learning activities cover the background knowledge and skills necessary and have the trainees enough information, knowledge and skills initially in their repertoires to benefit from the activities?

THE RIGHT REPERTOIRE?

FIGURE 63A

6. Do the learning activities offer the chance for trainees to practise, practise and practise again the behaviour or performance specified in the objectives? And is it appropriate practice?

PECULIAR PRACTICES

FIGURE 63B

7. Is the purpose of the activity (which may be stated as an objective or achieving part of an objective) clear to the trainees? If it isn't clear to them, is it clear to you?
8. Do the learning activities reflect the individual interests and preferences for ways of learning of the trainees?
9. Do the learning activities give adequate feedback both to the trainer about how well the trainees are progressing and then to the trainees themselves, giving them knowledge of their results and success or failure in the activities?
10. Do the learning activities match, or replicate the performance required by the job?
11. Do the activities reinforce the learning by giving practical opportunities to carry out the skilled procedures which have been demonstrated, use the knowledge taught or consider their attitudes in the light of new information?
12. Do the learning activities give the trainer the role of facilitating the learning rather than acting as a presenter, or expositor, of material?
13. Do the learning activities involve the trainer beneficially in offering assistance to the trainees, in making learning diagnosis, asking questions and in the process of making evaluations? Is the trainer fully involved in these activities?
14. Are the learning activities linked to the process of assessing the trainees and do they know what the links are?
15. Are the learning activities generally adequate in producing the desired learning outcomes, or end products, of the training?
16. Finally, are the learning activities truly active in producing learning by the trainees?

FIGURE 63

That is a formidable list, isn't it?
Why do you think this is?

*The length and strength of this list emphasises the **key role of learning activities in the training and learning process.** Getting them right is absolutely fundamental to the success of your implementation of training.*

Incidentally, it is time to say that learning activities are the ways in which you put your delivery methods into practice, so that they give a background to the **tactics** which you use in the learning situation. Therefore the learning activities are what happens at the Learnerface.

Whilst we have discussed learning activities in a general sense, let's have a look more closely at how they may be used as tactics in training. Really, we should concentrate on the tactics when we are discussing the methods of delivery in more detail, but we shall use this opportunity to put in an advance organiser for the tactical scene.

Make some suggestions, of a general nature, describing a variety of learning activities which you could use in your training. Remember that learning activities are what the trainees do and experience. Make sure you have adequate **Learning Resources** for the activities to take place.

Our suggestions for activities are shown in the next table.

SOME SUGGESTIONS FOR LEARNING ACTIVITIES

✱ Solving practical problems in skills procedures e.g. welding a broken pipe joint.

✱ Viewing, evaluating and commenting on audio-visual materials.

✱ Answering set exercises on a technical manual or textbook.

✱ Observing skilled operatives and answering a series of questions in a handout which emphasise the main cues in the skilled procedure.

✱ Observing a trainer demonstrating an operation.

✱ Taking part in an exercise which simulates the real thing, e.g. dealing with an awkward customer, hair styling on a model.

✱ Listening to guest speakers and answering or asking questions during and after the presentation.

✱ Working through programmed text, e.g. a fault-finding chart.

✱ Solving theoretical problems using a list of references or data given by the trainer, e.g. stresses on a roofing structure.

✱ Using models or "mock-ups", e.g. model of a steam engine, practice key boards, electrical circuit boards.

✱ Watching videotapes of trainee performance and evaluating their own, or somebody else's performance, e.g. interviewing.

✱ Practising skilled procedures with certain limits in time and materials, e.g. making ten buttonholes in one hour with no waste.

✱ Reading information sheets and picking out the main points.

✱ Memorising information, e.g. a list of technical terms, or the formula for lathe speeds.

✱ Taking part in a case study or a simulation, e.g. deciding on the best solution in a social-care problem involving several trainees; chairing a committee meeting.

✱ Evaluating materials, e.g. computer software, or making a critique of a finished product, either a sample from your own firm or another trainee's finished work.

✱ Writing reports for discussion by the group, e.g. on the performance of an engine, or preparing a balance sheet summary.

✱ Carrying out laboratory experiments and reporting on the findings, e.g. calculating the breaking point of a beam.

✱ Taking part in scaled-down performances, e.g. building a model of a roof-truss system, a central heating system, or building a brick wall.

✱ Collecting samples, e.g. of building materials and gathering examples, e.g. of good writing in newspapers.

✱ Preparing graphic materials, e.g. maps, charts, schematic drawing, layouts, design sketches.

✱ Working as a team where co-operative effort is needed, e.g. jobs which require heavy lifting, team problem-solving and production techniques.

✱ Planning jobs, designing set procedures, costing materials, explaining safety procedures.

✱ Producing a project, e.g. make working drawings of building footings, or a garden shed; organise a service, e.g. a complete beauty treatment for a client or fellow trainee.

✱ Communications exercises, e.g. writing a clear memo to the boss or to a client.

FIGURE 64

Obviously, we could go on describing a huge variety of learning activities, because there are many for each job and for each trainer, so that the permutations are almost endless. Nonetheless, we felt it important to give you the flavour of what we mean by "learning activities" and have spent some time on this because of their **fundamental importance in achieving successful training.**

The usefulness and quality of your learning activities is a measure of your success as a trainer in actually delivering the learning, by whatever method you believe to be optimal. It also shows the accuracy of your taking account of the information which you have gleaned from entering behaviour, resource and constraint analysis, etc.

So, having ensured that your learning activities give your trainees a chance to achieve competency in each performance for which they are being trained, let's move on to consider the next part of the structure of a scheme of work shown in Figure 60, i.e.

6. Assessment of the trainees
Well, we had a good "go" at this in Package One, Study Unit Two, Component Nine, so we are only going to emphasise a few important matters here.

DON'T OVERDO THE TESTING

From the point of view of developing a Scheme of work, can you say which aspects of assessment you would select as being of particular importance, in a general sense?

Here are our suggestions:—
* *Always keep your objectives before you when developing assessment items and don't overdo it! By this we mean that you should only write as many items, or tasks, as will tell you how far each trainee is meeting the objectives and achieving a grasp of the information you are delivering, or developing a skill.*

FIGURE 65

* *Try to be objective: your assessment should be free from personal judgement and bias. Achieve this by using objective tests, rating scales, performance checklists, multiple-choice questions and give model answers, where possible.*
* *Make the test fit the training: ensure that the kind of trainee performance which is assessed is the same as that required by the objective and in which the students have been trained. If the objective is the achievement of a skilled performance then let the trainees show their skills on a machine. If it is about knowledge of facts then a paper-and-pencil test is likely to be suitable. If trainee attitudes are being assessed then testing should be by observation of their behaviour.*
* *Timing is important: set the tests at those times which best indicate progress and give quick feedback to the trainees about their performances and how well they have done. Don't test long after the training events as this won't tell you much about trainee performance, except their powers of recall, nor will it help them.*

7. Evaluation

The key here is to evaluate as you go along, as well as at the end of training. If evaluation shows successful trainee accomplishment of the objectives, assume your training and the objectives themselves are valid. If not, then re-think, review your training and make immediate adjustments for current and future use.

Monitor the results of evaluation carefully: observe the trainees; develop feedback through questionnaires; talk to the trainees.

Keep your evaluation hot!

EVALUATE THEN REMEDIATE

FIGURE 66

If assessment, evaluation and observation show your training to be inadequate, put it right as soon as possible. Fork-lift drivers please note!

Remember too, that much valuable evaluation takes place well after training, when you check how successful your trainees are on the job, at the workbench, in the laboratory or wherever it is that they carry out their work. **"Follow up" evaluation** must be done if you are to get a proper depth of perspective on the success of your training.

8. "Key Events"

It is always a good idea to note certain "key events" in your training. In a way, these are "anchors" to which your training is attached, cannot be changed and are events around which the training has to be fitted.

Making reference to a course which you are running currently, write down a list of **key events.**

As we don't know what your courses are and they will cover a great range, we only offer some suggestions:—
Visits: *usually these are on set dates for prescribed times which you cannot change, so you have to organise the training around them. If the visit is to show certain fundamental aspects of training, you'll have to pace your own course so that the trainees know enough*

to benefit from the visit before it takes place.

Visiting experts: *much the same as for visits, you must make certain that the visitor has a good-sized audience and that all arrangements have been detailed for smooth operation when he arrives.*

Exams and holidays: *need timetabling carefully, especially as the trainees must be paced in their training so that they are "on the boil" when they take the examination. Don't let them go "off the boil" before they are tested.*

FIGURE 67

Resources: *make sure that you complete your Resources Checklist well before training begins so that the appropriate actions can be taken to ensure adequacy of resource provision. Remember repairs always take twice as long as the repairers estimate!*

"REPAIR TIME" EQUALS "ESTIMATED TIME FOR REPAIRS × 2"

FIGURE 68

Icebreakers: *did you introduce your trainees to each other and help them to get to know their colleagues by using "icebreaking" games at the very beginning of the course?*

Deadlines: *for coursework, and for exams; are the trainees ready to meet deadlines and are they prepared well enough? Have they been able to obtain the necessary reference books, tools and the like? When did you give out your bibliography, list of essential tools, anyway?*

Revision: *Did you leave enough time for the trainees to revise without thrusting new material on them at the last minute?*

Personal Contact *between the trainers and the trainees. Have you given the trainees an opportunity to "get at" the trainers on a personal level, to discuss problems both within and outside of the training? Are tutorials scheduled? Do the trainees know when you are available for discussion?*

We could go on, but you'll have the idea of key events, by now. It's always worthwhile jotting down a list, before you begin the actual training.

We'll now finish off our discussion of **planning** your scheme of work by examining the **format** of the actual scheme.

9. Format of the Scheme of Work

Taking into account all that we have said so far about the structure of a scheme of work, make out a suitable draft format, for yourself.

We will give several formats as examples, so that you can choose on which suits you best or modify any of them. Before we do this, we'd like to give you a tip by mentioning that you should **number** *your objectives. Following our design system, you will have arranged them in a suitable sequence: if you now number each one — and you may have done this already — then you can refer to them easily in the scheme.*

SCHEME OF WORK: FORMAT ONE

GENERAL INFORMATION   Course title:

Awarding body   Names of training Staff

Length of Course and Dates   Duration of sessions   Days and Times

Venue   Target Audience

WEEK NUMBER	OBJECTIVE NUMBER	TOPIC/ SKILL	DELIVERY METHOD	LEARNING ACTIVITY	RESOURCES	ASSESSMENT	EVALUATION	COMMENT
1	1	1		1	1	1		
2	2	2		2	2	2		
3	3	3		3	3	3		
etc.								

FIGURE 69

SCHEME OF WORK: FORMAT TWO

WEEK NUMBER	OBJECTIVE NUMBER	TOPIC	DELIVERY METHOD	TRAINEE ACTIVITY	AIDS	ASSESSMENT

FIGURE 70

SCHEME OF WORK: FORMAT THREE

SESSION AND TIME	GENERAL OBJECTIVE, NUMBER	SPECIFIC OBJECTIVE, NUMBER	TOPIC/ SKILL	TRAINING METHOD AND LEARNING ACTIVITY	ASSESSMENT AND EVALUATION	ROOM NUMBER
1	1	1a 1b	1	1a 1b	1a 1b	14
2	2	2a	2	2	2	14
3	3	3a	3	3a	3a	}22
etc		3b 3c		3b	3b	

FIGURE 71

SCHEME OF WORK: FORMAT FOUR

TOPIC/SKILL	OBJECTIVES	TRAINING METHOD ACTIVITIES AND RESOURCES	ASSESSMENT AND EVALUATION

FIGURE 72

SCHEME OF WORK: FORMAT FIVE

TRAINEE PERFORMANCE OBJECTIVES	CONTENT	LEARNING ACTIVITIES	RESOURCES	EVALUATION

FIGURE 73

SCHEME OF WORK: FORMAT SIX

GENERAL INFORMATION		

OUTLINE		

OBJECTIVES

Terminal		Enabling
1		1a 1b 1c 1d 1e 1f 1g
		2a 2b 2c 2d

TOPICS
1
2
3
4
etc

METHODS	LEARNING ACTIVITIES	RESOURCES
1	1a ⎫	1a
	1b ⎬ for Topic 1	1b
	1c ⎭	1c
2	2	2
3	3a	3a
	3a	3b
4	4	4
etc	etc	etc

ASSESSMENT
1
2
etc

FIGURE 74

You'll recollect that we have explained the use of enabling and terminal objectives in Component 2, Study Unit 2, Package One.

As an example, we'll fill in part of a scheme of work, using some of the material from Component 2 mentioned above.

First, we write out our objectives for the full scheme of work. Space precludes our doing this, so we are selecting one topic only and we list the objectives for this beneath, imagining that this is the third session, or week, of our course.

COURSE: "WORKSHOP PRACTICE".
Topic 5: **"Safety in the Workshop"**
General Objective 8 "The trainee understands the dangers which are present in the workshop".

Specific Objectives "After training, the trainee will be able to

8a Label the workshop dangers, on a plan of the workshop provided, to 100% accuracy.

8b List the workshop safety rules in 25 minutes, identifying all twelve rules.

8c Identify the reasons for observing safety rules in a gapped handout, with 90% correct responses.

8d Explain the reason for the presence of machine guards, in the workshops, on the machinery, comprehensively and naming five out of the six reasons.

8e State the dangers associated with moving parts of machinery, pointing out the dangers to the instructor on two selected machines and stating correctly six out of eight major points.

8f Describe suitable clothing for the workshop, to the instructor and the group, with a clear idea of appropriate clothing.

8g Suggest types of unsuitable clothing, hairstyles, etc., in group discussion, giving four apt examples.

8h Give reasons why jewellery is not worn in the workshop, to the instructor and the group, with a clear knowledge of the dangers.

8j Check out a diagram of workshop electrical hazards, to the instructor in the workshop, with no more than two errors.

8k Demonstrate a positive attitude towards avoiding dangers when in the workshop, at all times.

8l Value the importance of safety measures which are used in the workshop, generally and at all times."

GENERAL INFORMATION

Course title: "Workshop Practice"

Awarding Body: Lancashire Polytechnic

Names of Training Staff: B. Wilson and W. S. Churchill

Length of Course 4 months. 23 March
and dates to 20 July

Duration of 2 hours
Sessions (4 hrs/week)

Days and Mondays and
Times Thursdays 0815
to 1015

Target Audience: Steam pressing operatives: 20 trainees

Venue: Workshop and L319

WEEK NUMBER	OBJECTIVE NUMBER	TOPIC/ SKILL	DELIVERY METHOD	LEARNING ACTIVITY	RESOURCES	ASSESSMENT	EVALUATION	COMMENT. VENUE
2								
3	8a	Labelling Dangers	Description of dangers, point out on plan. Relate to workshop.	Listen, question and answer (Q and A)	OHP — One large scale plan of workshop.	Time allocated too short.	Extra half-hour required	(In workshop).
	8b	Safety Rules	Paper and pencil after showing rules board. Discussion.	Complete labelling of dangers on individual plans.	20 plans for individuals.	To 100% accuracy	Several major dangers missed	Spare plans: revise
				Look at rules board, complete list. Discuss.	Rules board	List all rules	Most missed rule II	Revise rule II (L319)
wsc	8c	Reasons for rules	Explain reasons. Use gapped handout.	Complete handout. Q and A. Discuss.	20 handouts	By handout; 90% correct	Poor, most got 60%	Revise (L319)
	8d	Machinery guards	Demo in workshop by supervisor. Discussion after demo.	Watch demo. Take notes. Q and A. Then discuss with trainer and supervisor.	Machinery available in free time.	Q and A then listing. Workshop supervisor to comment.	O.K. but difficult for some to see demonstration which was a little fast.	(Workshop) Speak to Supervisor.
4	8e	Dangers of moving machinery	By two operators. Discussions with trainer	Observation, note taking, pointing out dangers to trainer. Q and A with operators. Discuss.	Machines 4 and 5 to be free. 2 operators.	Informal	O.K. very effective. Operators very good.	(Workshop) Use 3/4 machines next course.

WEEK NUMBER	OBJECTIVE NUMBER	TOPIC/ SKILL	DELIVERY METHOD	LEARNING ACTIVITY	RESOURCES	ASSESSMENT	EVALUATION	COMMENT. VENUE
4 WSC	8f 8g 8h	Clothing	Q and A Show human figure dummies	Trainees describe clothing, answer questions Identify unsuitable clothing worn on dummies. Discuss.	Clothing Dummies	Informal	Needed a lot of coaching.	(Workshop) Use graphics next course. Point out unsuitable clothing on trainees.
5	8j	Electrical Hazards	Tour of workshop showing possible hazards. Models of bad wiring, frayed, etc.	Note taking and discussion Drawing models, checking out with trainer and electrician.	Workshop machinery Models Electrician	Informal	Very effective Models very successful, but insufficient models to show all major faults; too much time taken.	(Workshop) (L319) Prepare OHP's as reserve and have more models made.
	8k	Attitude to dangers and safety	Course - also describe accidents in shop. Reports. Discussion with Safety Officer	View accident reports and make notes. Discuss with Safety Officer.	Safety Officer	Observation and informal comments from Safety Officer	Effective: general improvement noted on course, especially in dress	(Place of work).
	8l	Attitude	Questionnaire	Complete questionnaire	20 questionnaires	Mark questionnaire	Improvement during follow-up evaluation after course.	Follow-up after training shows improvement maintained with only 2 exceptions — refer to Workshop Manager or Supervisor for further training.
	All	Workshop dangers	Multiple-choice questionnaires	Answer and revise subsequently by discussion	20 questionnaires 40 multiple-choice questions	Final topic test.	17/20 passed (85%) pass mark 90%; average mark 92%	Remedial revision with 3 who failed; re-test end of Week 8. (L319) retest by WSC.

FIGURE 75

Having looked at our specimen schemes of work, what do you notice about the Evaluation and Comment/ Venue columns? And the scheme of work in general?

You complete the Evaluation column **after** *the rest of the scheme and in it you make your evaluation of the training when the particular event is over. Your Comment column gives an indication of what you are going to do about remedying weaknesses in the future.*

Evaluation on a scheme of work tends to be critical, but you should note the successes as well as the failures, perhaps on a full evaluation report of the training. You will wish to build on the strengths next time around.

For clarity, you may wish to put the location of your training (e.g. workshop L319) in the "Week Number" column, where it shows up well and leaves the last column for remarks only.

A general observation which you could make is the helpful manner in which properly written objectives help you to fill out your scheme by providing much of the information necessary before you start.

"WSC" shows where your co-trainer, W. S. Churchill is operating.

A scheme of work takes time to complete, but it is an invaluable guide to your training. By completing it carefully, you are not doing more work, but less: this detailed thinking has to be done sometime and by doing it before rather than later you will keep your training on the right lines from the outset. Rectifying mistakes at a later date is costly in both time and effort and you can often find you've got yourself "up the creek" entirely.

UP THE WRONG CREEK

Summary

In this Component we began the study of delivering the learning to Larger Groups and we started by looking at the lesson method, pointing out that lessons can, however, be given to a big range of groups, effectively.

Whilst much of the activity in training takes place at the Learnerface, this is preceded by careful planning. For lessons, the first stage of planning is organising and completing a scheme of work. This is a plan showing a structured framework within which can be slotted a series of lessons.

Making out a list of general and specific objectives before you begin on your scheme greatly facilitates the writing of the scheme itself.

An enormously important part of any scheme of work is that which deals with learning activities. The more active a trainee is, then the more he will learn.

Formats of a scheme can vary, but they are all of a general nature and offer both guidance to the trainer and direction to the training.

They are also extremely useful for conveying the structure of the training to another trainer. All training managers should ask to see schemes of work produced by their staff before the training, for which they are responsible, begins.

Before you go onto the next Component, which deals with lesson plans, make out a scheme of work for a course which you are to run in the future, or for training in which you are involved presently, but for which there is either no scheme or one which is not adequate. Design a Checklist for your scheme, then examine ours in the next Component. This Checklist is the last item in Figure 60, the structure of a scheme of work.

Send your Scheme of work to your Programme Tutor for comment, if you wish.

Component 2:

Methods of delivering the learning to Larger Groups: The Lesson Plan

 Key Words

Scheme of Work Checklist; key events; advantages of planning lessons; styles of lesson plan; lesson plan formats; trainee activity and learning activity; timing; events of instruction and lesson plans; knowledge and skills lesson plans; "whole-day" lesson plans as a vehicle for learning.

Introduction

In this Component, we are moving on from the organisation of the scheme of work to the writing out of **Lesson plans.** However, before we do this, we must formulate a checklist for our scheme of work as we promised to do in the last Component.

Checkpoint

Before examining our suggested Checklist, try making out one for yourself. You can carry out this procedure by first revising Component One of this Study Unit. When you do so, pick out the major items for checking only; should you attempt to select all of the minor and major items in the material which we presented, then your Checklist would become exhaustively long.

Your Checklist is an attempt to ensure that the direction, rather than the detail of your scheme is accurate.

GIVE DIRECTION, NOT DETAIL

FIGURE 76

Keeping the main points in mind, our Checklist follows.

SCHEME OF WORK CHECKLIST

PLANNING	YES	NO	MAYBE
1. Did I ensure that I used all the **sources of information from the design system?** a) Needs Analysis b) Task Analysis c) Entering Behaviour Analysis d) Resources Analysis e) Constraints Analysis			
2. Are the **topics skills and attitudes** a) relevant to the trainees? b) important to their jobs?			
3. Are the **objectives** a) stated in terms of behaviour or performance? b) constructed properly? c) sequenced properly? d) covering the whole topic or skill? e) sufficient to provide a basis for objective assessment?			
4. Does the **training content** a) correlate with the objectives? b) provide for a variety of topic and skills levels? c) give enough significant and relevant material? d) follow a logical sequence?			
5. Are the **delivery methods** a) suitable for the topic or skills? b) varied?			
6. Are the **learning activities** a) based on the objectives? b) encouraging of trainee activity? c) varied? d) providing of a wide range of activities covering trainee interests and abilities? e) providing of adequate trainee application and practice? f) giving quick feedback and reinforcement of trainee performance? g) relevant to learning the skill or topic? h) attainable within the time limits of training? i) stimulating and motivating?			
7. Do the **assessment procedures** a) give objective measurement? b) come directly from objectives? c) include adequate criterion tests? d) test the same trainee performance as required by the objectives? e) give feedback to the trainee? f) test terminal performance?			
8. Does the **evaluation** a) give information on all parts of the scheme and of the training? b) indicate clearly where remedial action is required for the training? c) provide for follow-up evaluation on the job, after training is finished? d) include information on trainee reaction to the training?			

	YES	NO	MAYBE
9. Does the **"General Information"** section include all of the essential and routine detail?			
10. Are all the **key events** covered?			
11. a) Does the **format** of the scheme do the job properly? b) If it doesn't have I altered it?			
12. If I **dropped dead** today would this scheme provide enough information for my successor to carry on efficiently?			

LAST WRITES

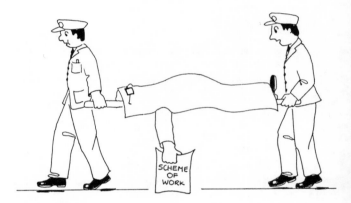

FIGURE 77

This checklist is the last item shown of Figure 60, structure of the scheme of work.

That just about covers our initial stage of planning for lessons, i.e., the scheme of work. Following the idea of Figure 77, we had better lay our scheme to rest now, before going on to look at the next stage, which is, **planning the lesson.**

Producing a lesson plan for each lesson is essential so that what goes on at the Learnerface is organised efficiently. In the rest of this Component, we shall examine this planning under the headings

The advantages of planning lessons.
Styles of lesson plan.
Lesson plan checklist.

* The Advantages of Planning Lessons.

We spent a fair amount of time examining the usefulness of planning schemes of work. Using that material as a basis, give some time now to considering what the advantages are of planning lessons, before looking at our suggestions, which are shown in the next Figure.

THE ADVANTAGES OF PLANNING LESSONS

✽There is always a time which comes when you have to organise what happens between you and the trainees in the classroom, or workshop. It isn't easy for any of us to get down to planning and there is a temptation to just start doing whatever it is that we are involved in without giving it too much thought. Almost always the penalty for this approach, or lack of proper approach, is severe: distance learning materials have to be rewritten, lessons get halfway through and have to be restarted because some essential piece of information or a step in a skilled procedure has been omitted. In the end, time is lost by unplanned effort.

✽ Once experience has been gained at writing carefully thought-out lesson plans, the amount of actual writing can be reduced because more of the plan can be carried in the trainer's head. But the plan has to be somewhere, so that the trainer's efforts are efficient enough to use time, resources and effort to the best advantage.

✽ Lesson plans form a record of your past training and a basis for subsequent improvement. The record of your previous efforts must be written, so that what went well and what didn't can be recalled easily.

✽ Much time is saved by carefully maintained plans: every time you come to the same topic or skill in future training, you will not have to think it all out again.

✽ Don't run away with the idea that "born" teachers do not use lesson plans. They do; even the most gifted trainer works on an organised, planned basis. Much of the reason for the success of "star" trainers, of whom there are few in training and teaching, anyway, is their capacity for planning and thinking out the action at Learnerface before they start.

FIGURE 78

* Styles of Lesson Plan

As you would expect, there are as many styles of lesson plans as there are trainers. We will give you a variety, from which you can choose or modify a plan which suits your needs best.

* Planning Format, A.

Perhaps the simplest plan of all is shown here, but it is one which is used widely, especially by teachers.

LESSON PLAN ONE

GENERAL INFORMATION
(Place information here of the type which you would
include for the scheme of work, Figure 73).

CONTENT	METHOD
BEGINNING	
MIDDLE	
END	
COMMENT	

FIGURE 79

You can see that this simple plan is only an outline of your lesson.

What would you include under "Content", "Method" and "Comment"?

*Content is **what** you are going to teach, the topic or skill or attitude, or a combination of all three.*

*"Method" is **how** you are going to teach the Content. You should also include here an indication of how the trainees are going to be active.*

*"Comment" is an **evaluation** of how you thought the lesson went and you indicate in this box strengths that can be built upon and weaknesses to be remedied. Include a lead in to the next lesson, based on this evaluatory comment. The next plan is a more sophisticated version of Plan One.*

LESSON PLAN TWO

GENERAL INFORMATION:

TITLE OF LESSON:

GENERAL OBJECTIVE NUMBER THREE:

SPECIFIC OBJECTIVE	CONTENT	METHOD
	BEGINNING	
3a	MIDDLE	
3b	END	

ASSESSMENT

EVALUATION

FIGURE 80

You should notice that both Plans One and Two have the Content, dealing with a topic or a skill, divided into a "Beginning", "Middle", and "End".

Two Specific objectives are to be dealt with in this lesson, i.e. 3a and 3b, both of which are derived from General Objective Three.

The "Assessment" information shows you how you are to carry out a formal assessment of the trainees, but you will not always require this box, should assessment not be intended for this lesson.

The "Evaluation" box has the same function as the "Comment" box of Plan One.

How long do you believe a lesson plan should be?

Generally, you should try to keep the plan for each lesson to about one page of A4 paper.

This makes for easy filing and handling during the lesson and it is important that you keep your plans of a reasonable length so that this preparation does not become too time-consuming.

Planning Format B
This format is more closely related to the schemes of work shown in Figures 74 and 75 and gives more detail than Plans One and Two.

LESSON PLAN THREE

GENERAL INFORMATION

TOPIC/SKILL	TRAINER ACTIVITY	TRAINEE ACTIVITY (LEARNING ACTIVITIES)	LEARNING AIDS

FIGURE 81

LESSON PLAN FOUR

GENERAL INFORMATION

LESSON TITLE

KEY WORDS	TOPIC/SKILL	TEACHER ACTIVITY	TRAINEE ACTIVITY (learning activities)	RESOURCES	EVALUATION
BEGINNING					
MIDDLE					
END					

OBJECTIVES

FIGURE 82

81

LESSON PLAN FIVE

GENERAL INFORMATION

OBJECTIVE CUES	TIMING	TRAINER ACTIVITY	TRAINEE ACTIVITY	RESOURCES	ASSESSMENT
BEGINNING	0915				
MIDDLE 6a ☐ ☐	0925				
b ☐ ☐	0940				
c ☐	10.00				
END	10.20				
EVALUATION	10.30				

FIGURE 83

Lesson Plan Five is a favoured format for training.

▰▰▰▰

What do the columns "Trainer Activity" and "Trainee Activity" relate to in the Scheme of Work format?

"Trainer Activity" equals "Delivery method" in the scheme and shows the way in which the trainer proposes to deliver the learning.

"Trainee Activity" relates to the "Learning Activity" box in the scheme of work and shows what the trainees will be doing during the lesson.

If you prefer, these columns in the Lesson Plan can bear the same title as in the scheme of work.

Once again, the "Evaluation" box is completed **after** the lesson is finished. The observations entered here are much more detailed than in the scheme of work evaluation column and include recommendations for future action in succeeding lessons. A useful addition to Plan Five can be taken from Plan Four, where "key words" or "cues" are included. Key words encapsulate the concept of a topic in one word, rather in the manner in which key words are used at the beginning of each Component in this Training Technology Programme.

In a lesson on a skill, the key words used are actually **cues**, which indicate when one part of the skill sequence is terminated and when another part of the skill is beginning. You'll recollect that we talked about cues in Package One, when we looked at Task Analysis in Study Unit One.

The "Timing" column gives an indication of the pacing of the lesson. In Figure 83, the lesson begins at 0915 hours and ends at 1030 hours. The approximate time when you should be reaching each section, in this case based on a specific objective, is shown. An alternative method is to show the number of minutes from the start of the lesson given to each section of it, e.g. Beginning, ten minutes; objective 6a, fifteen minutes; and so on. Whilst this technique shows the balance of the lesson in time, very well, it isn't so clear to you where you are supposed to be at, say, 10.05 hours. Use a combination of both methods if you like:

We might seem to be emphasising this timing business overmuch, but it really is important, not just as a guide to how accurately the lesson is going in practice, but also in the planning stage. Frequently, you will find that you had anticipated covering, say, three objectives and the topics associated with them, or elements of a skilled process, but when you get down to the fine tuning of the lesson, you simply haven't the time to do it all. You have to postpone dealing with part of your material to the next, or even a later lesson.

Don't be too strict about the timings, however; a minute or two's variation either way won't matter when you are actually giving the lesson, as you can always adjust the pace as you go along. You don't need the accuracy shown in the next illustration, for example.

OBJECTIVE etc	TIMING	MINUTES
	0915	
Beginning	0915-0925	10
Middle 6a	0925-0940	15
b	0940-1000	20
c	1000-1020	20
End	1020-1030	10
	1030	

THIS IS TRAINING NOT WAR

FIGURE 84

* Planning Format, C

In Component Eight, Study Unit Two, Package One, we described the important **events of instruction** and these are laid out in Figures 279, 290 and especially 289. Have a glance at that material now. It is possible to lay out a lesson plan in the manner shown in Figure 290 and such a plan would look like the next diagram, with some modification and additional material added to make it more suitable and informative for the purposes of a lesson.

LESSON PLAN SIX

GENERAL INFORMATION			
OBJECTIVES		TITLE OF LESSON	
TRAINER ACTIVITY	LEARNING ACTIVITY	RESOURCES	EVALUATION
GAINING ATTENTION			
INFORMING TRAINEES OF THE OBJECTIVE			
STIMULATING RECALL OF PRE-REQUISITES			
PRESENTING THE STIMULUS MATERIAL			
PROVIDING LEARNING GUIDANCE			
ELICITING THE PERFORMANCE			
PROVIDING FEEDBACK			
ASSESSING PERFORMANCE			
RETENTION			
TRANSFER			

FIGURE 85

There is enough information in Figure 289, for you to make out a lesson plan, of the type shown in Figure 85, for either a knowledge or a skills lesson.

In the column headed "Training Activity" you would be guided by the heading in each box, e.g. "Gaining Attention", as to your major activity and you would then write in your actual activities for the particular lesson, using the second and third columns of Figure 289 as a guide. We give an example of this in the next diagram.

LESSON PLAN SIX: EXAMPLES

TRAINER ACTIVITY	LEARNING ACTIVITY	RESOURCES	EVALUATION
GAINING ATTENTION Take the trainees on a conducted tour of the workshop.	Trainees take notes of main points and complete a gapped hand-out as they go round.	Workshop machinery Gapped handout	
INFORMING TRAINEES . . .			

TRAINER ACTIVITY	LEARNING ACTIVITY	RESOURCES	EVALUATION
GAINING ATTENTION Show trainees ten minutes video of sales person dealing with a client.	Trainers watch and make notes of salient points of salesperson's techniques, identifying each point, both good and bad. Discuss after video.	10 minute video	
INFORMING TRAINEES			

FIGURE 86

We should like to explain the Figure 289 box for "retention" and "transfer" (sometimes called "generalisation") further.

In **"retention"**, the trainer is giving learning activities which reinforce the material which has been learned, asking them to carry out similar activities to those which they carried out in the eliciting the performance stage. These repeat activities aid retention. In the case of a skills lesson, the trainees would carry out the skilled performance several times again.

In "**transfer**" you would be setting out activities which prove whether or not the trainees can use what they have learned in other areas, e.g. using instruments with which they have just located one type of fault in an engine, to find a different sort of fault or to make a similar but different product.

Can you think of other examples of generalisation, or transfer?

To take an example from Figure 86, the trainees have seen how a salesperson makes a deal with clients and would have some idea of how to relate to customers and the sort of skills which are required, e.g.

listening carefully; being sympathetic; making your point clearly; remaining polite at all times, assuring the customer that suitable action will be taken. These skills could be transferred to another situation by asking the trainees to show how they would deal with an awkward customer, or one who is making a complaint. This generalisation exercise could be carried out by a role-play, for example.

The transfer of a skill could take the form of using a tool with which the trainee had become familiar during training, in another situation, or for a similar but different purpose as we suggested previously.

TRANSFERRING (GENERALISING) KNOWLEDGE AND SKILLS

FIGURE 87

Planning Format, D.
We shall now view another couple of lesson plan formats which are useful alternatives to those considered previously.

LESSON PLAN SEVEN

GENERAL INFORMATION
LESSON TOPIC

OBJECTIVES
  a)
  b)
  c)

INTRODUCTION (5 minutes)
METHOD
LEARNING ACTIVITIES (45 minutes)   Objective a)   Objective b)   Objective c)
RESOURCES
SUMMARY (10 minutes)
EVALUATION

FIGURE 88

Clearly, Lesson Plan Seven deals with a topic and the conveying and learning of knowledge and information. Particular emphasis in this type of plan is laid on the Learning Activities. A more suitable format for a skills lesson would be as shown next.

LESSON PLAN EIGHT

GENERAL INFORMATION	
JOB/OPERATION OBJECTIVES TOOLS MATERIALS RESOURCES	
DEMONSTRATION (20 minutes) Stages of operation/process	CUES
1. 2. 3. 4. 5. 6.	
PRACTICE BY TRAINEES (40 MINUTES)	
EVALUATION	

FIGURE 89

Methods of Training: Groupwork

Planning Format E
Our lesson formats so far have shown you plans which are suitable for lessons of 45 minutes or an hour in length. When faced with a whole day session you'll require something half-way between a scheme of work and the lesson plans of which you have some already. Such a plan is shown next.

LESSON PLAN NINE: WHOLE DAY SESSION

GENERAL INFORMATION	
LESSON TITLE	"FORMING PROCESSES: INTRODUCTION"
OBJECTIVES	After the lesson trainees will be able to a) describe the raw materials used for basic, forming processes. b) state the special properties of the raw materials. c) explain the basic steps of forming processes. d) list the advantages, limitations and disadvantages of the products of primary forming.
METHOD	Mainly discovery and demonstration with trainees handling and using materials and watching basic steps of process.
LEARNING ACTIVITY/TRAINER ACTIVITY (full-day training session)	
Objective a) ($\frac{1}{2}$ hour)	Display of raw materials used for sand casting, rolling, extrusion, drawing, forging. Trainees handle materials individually.
Objective b) (1 hour)	Statement of special properties of materials used, including plasticity, ductility, toughness, malleability, fluidity. Trainees make notes of properties of materials whilst viewing and handling them. Compare results with statement of properties made by trainer. Draw up an agreed list.
Objective c) (5 hours)	Trainers and operatives demonstrate basic steps of sand casting, rolling, extrusion, drawing and forging in the workshops. **Trainees work in groups on one activity, under supervision of trainer and operatives.** Main activity is watching and noting main points and assisting where required.
Objective d) (1 hour)	Display of components and metals produced by primary forming processes. Trainees examine materials first, considering and listing characteristics of metal and component products, suggesting advantages and limitations of component usage. Then they discuss products with trainer and draw up agreed lists of characteristics, advantages and limitations. Receive summary handout.
SUMMARY ($\frac{1}{2}$ hour)	Discuss and evaluate day's work in plenary session.
RESOURCES	Raw materials, operatives, workshop equipment, handouts.
NEXT LESSON	Break into groups and practice and assist in one other process, under supervision.

FIGURE 90

When actually using Lesson Plan Nine, you'll need to go into further detail in most of the sections. For example, you would want to support the sections on each objective with a lesson plan such as we have shown in Lesson Plan Eight or Five. As we said, Lesson Plan Nine is a mixture of a scheme of work and a normal Lesson Plan; once again it emphasises the all-important learning activities.

From what you have read, describe the relationship between delivery methods, learning activities and lesson plans.

Delivery methods are the ways in which you communicate the learning messages and materials to the trainees, who use selected learning activities to apply and to experience the learning. Lesson plans are the vehicles which carry the delivery methods, the learning messages and the learning activities.

Finally, we examine a series of checks which determine how efficient our lesson plan is:

* Lesson Plan Checklist

Much depends on the plan which you have chosen as to what your checklist will look like, but the following salient points should be checked. We use Lesson Plan Five as our basic example for this Checklist.

A LESSON PLAN CHECKLIST FOR LESSON PLAN FIVE

The General Plan	YES	NO	MAYBE
1. Is it written clearly?			
2. Is it practical enough to be carried out in training?			
3. Does it show the time allocated for each part?			
4. Is it pitched at a suitable level for trainees?			
5. Does it fit in with the rest of the course?			
6. Is there sufficient time to cover the material?			
7. Is the allocation of time sufficiently flexible to cover any difficulties which arise?			
Objectives			
8. Are they stated clearly in terms of trainee performance or behaviour?			
9. Are the performance conditions specified?			
10. Are the criteria for measuring performance specified?			
11. Are the lesson's specific objectives all based on the relevant general objectives?			

	YES	NO	MAYBE
12. Is each objective stated separately?			
13. Are these statements precise, clear and accurate?			
Beginning			
14. Do the trainees know the objectives?			
15. Do they know what they have to learn through the objectives?			
16. Do they understand how the objectives relate to their previous experience?			
17. Do they know how they are going to achieve the objectives in this lesson?			
18. Are motivational and attention-getting techniques used?			
19. Is provision made for active student involvement?			
20. Is an advance organiser/preview used?			
Middle			
21. Are the delivery methods, tactics and learning activities selected to achieve the objectives?			
22. Are the delivery methods, tactics and learning objectives selected, suitable for the performance required?			
23. Are the delivery method, tactics and learning activities chosen with regard to trainees' needs, interests and abilities?			
24. Is the content related to the objectives?			
25. Is it sufficiently detailed?			
26. Do the learning activities allow for full trainee participation, including questions, practice and discussion?			
27. Are the learning activities varied and will they generate trainee interest and motivation?			
28. Do the trainees know which learning activities must be mastered?			
29. Is it clear how far the learning activities will be trainee self-paced?			
30. Are there any learning activities "in reserve" for the more able trainees?			
31. Is it clear what part audio-visual materials and presentation will play in the learning activities?			
Resources			
32. Are all of the necessary tools, materials, equipment and media listed in the plan?			
33. Are they all available?			
34. Do they all work?			

	YES	NO	MAYBE
End			
35. Is adequate provision made for revising objectives, drawing conclusions, making generalisations, reinforcing the content and learning activities and for "tidying up"?			
36. Are the trainees still involved?			
37. Is there adequate time for issuing coursework?			
38. Is it clear how this lesson links with the next?			
39. Is it clear how this lesson links with the coursework?			
Assessment			
40. Is assessment based on the objectives and is it couched in the type of performance specified?			
Evaluation			
41. Are the trainees involved in evaluation?			
42. Did you remember to evaluate after the lesson?			

FIGURE 91

JUGGLING WITH YOUR CHECKLIST

FIGURE 92A

▰▰▰

We have introduced a new item in this Checklist which we have not considered in this Component so far. What is it?

The item concerned is number 20. We have discussed advance organisers before, and you may wish to incorporate one in your Beginning Section. As an alternative to an advance organiser, which contains examples and non-examples of the material, you may prefer to use a simple overview, which gives a brief outline of what is to come in the Middle Section of the lesson itself.

The Checklist which we've described will suffice for all types of lesson plan with some modification. It may seem formidable at first sight, but after using it half-a-dozen times you'll find that you will be able to run through it in your head, juggling the checks around with ease.

Summary

Properly planned lessons permit the trainer to make the most efficient and effective use of time, resources, materials and consequently lead to cost-effective training.

Lesson plans come in a variety of forms, dependent on the topic or skill which is being taught and an important part of each is the detailing of the learning activities. Lesson plans should indicate how the trainees are to participate and how they are to be active. They provide a structure within which the learning is planned to take place.

Careful checking of the lesson plans should be undertaken to ensure that this learning has every chance of being successful.

Looked at from a different viewpoint, lesson plans are a vehicle for the delivery of learning through the use of objectives, training methods and tactics and learning activities.

THE LEARNING VEHICLE

FIGURE 92B

Before you begin the next Component we suggest that you select one of the Lesson Plans One to Nine which we have discussed and write out a few actual Plans for current or future lessons. Send the plans to your Programme Tutor for checking if you wish.

In the next few Components we shall concentrate more closely on the tactics which you may use during the implementation of the lesson itself.

Component 3:

Methods of delivering the learning to Larger Groups: Beginning and Ending a Lesson

Key Words

Beginning a lesson; gaining attention; lesson context; expectations and objectives; motivating; instant involvement; time limits; bearings; First lesson; generation gap; problems and reassurance; introductory games; warmth, enthusiasm and humour; covering the "mechanisms"; Ending a lesson; summarising; trainee involvement; lesson context; keeping up the pace; feedback and evaluation.

Introduction

As we suggested at the end of the last Component, we are now going to examine some of the tactics which the trainer can use in lessons. We are focusing more closely on what happens at the Learnerface. **We began by looking at General Planning and now consider specific skills.**

We shall start by looking at how you begin and end a lesson, in this Component, and then move on to consider the middle of the lesson and tactics such as questioning, in detail.

So for this Component, the plan is to view:

How you start a lesson
The very first lesson
How you end a lesson.

* How You Start a Lesson

Very often lessons carry on as they started: if you excite and interest the trainees from the beginning they will remain involved. However, if you bore them, or start low-key, it is difficult to pick up the pace later.

In a way, your lesson beginning is an appetiser for what is to follow.

MAKING AN INTERESTING START

FIGURE 93

Incidentally, Figure 93 would make an interesting start to any lesson, wouldn't it? It certainly emphasises the fact that you must catch the trainees' attention from the outset.

▨▨ Checkpoint

Before you carry on, think about the beginnings which you have made to some lessons recently. Ask yourself how you think they went and whether or not they were successful. Then make out a list of the things you feel you ought to be doing at the beginning of a lesson to ensure that you have made a good start.

Here is our list, shown in Figure 99.

BEGINNING A LESSON

1. Plan your introduction so that you orientate your trainees in the direction which the lesson is going to take.

ARE YOU GOING IN THE RIGHT DIRECTION?

FIGURE 94

2. One of the best ways of "getting your bearings right" is to inform the trainees of the specific objectives of the lesson. Either write your objectives on a black or whiteboard, use an OHP or issue a handout describing the objectives themselves.

FIGURE 95

Don't just spout out the statements of the objectives, but explain them and use question and answer (QA) techniques to ensure that the trainees know what is going on.

3. Ask the trainees how the lesson reminds them of what they learned before, whether this is previous skills, knowledge or experience.

4. Carry on the process of putting the lesson in context by showing the trainees that what they are going to do is directly related to their jobs, interests and experience. When we say "show" them, don't just tell them, but draw the relationships from the trainees themselves with questions like, "Now. Can you tell me how this lesson is going to help you in your job?" and "Where does this lesson fit in with that sales technique I was telling you about yesterday?" and "We had a couple of problems over using a micrometer last week. If we have another go today, where would you like me to start?" You'll have a good idea of where you're going to start, anyway, but give the learners a chance to become active, let them think about the problems, identify them and feel involved in their solution.

5. Make sure that the trainees know what is expected of them before they start, what they should be doing both during and after the lesson, e.g. "Now this is important stuff. Do you think we can get through it all by 11 o'clock?"
   They then have a sense of pace and urgency and are orientated to getting started and keeping up the pace.
   Very importantly, of course, you have to gain the attention of the learners and persuade them to stop talking about Manchester United or the latest fashions in clothes.

6. Another important activity is that of motivating the trainees to want to learn and to want to take part in the lesson's activities. If you catch their interest, show them the relevance of what they are doing, then you have made a good start.
   Let's have a look at this business of gaining attention and motivating the trainees, more closely.
   First, it is useful to give them a vivid, everyday example of what the lesson is about. If you are describing safety rules, show them examples, show photographs of what happens when a safety rule has been broken. If you are to discuss wastage rates, then bring in some badly made products, comparing them with properly finished materials.

WHAT'S WRONG HERE THEN?

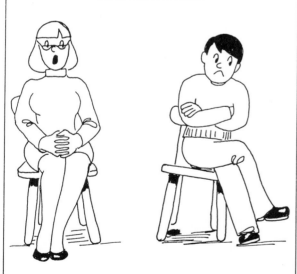

FIGURE 96

You can ask a provocative question, like, "If we continue making our product at ten units per hour, which is what we're doing now, how long will it be before you're all made redundant?" or "How many of you are going to be injured on the shop floor before the end of this year at our present accident rate?" or, "Why is Column's Mustard four pence cheaper per jar than ours?" or, "Why was the last car we rustproofed only 96% covered?"
   However, do make sure that your introduction uses material which is relevant to the lesson objectives and not too far out. If you use an anecdote, for example, keep it simple and to the point.

HAVE YOU SEEN THE LIGHT?

FIGURE 97

The dialogue for Figure 97 goes something like this:
Woman: "What are you doing?"
Trainer: "Looking for my glasses"
Woman: "Where did you lose them?"
Trainer: "In the classroom"
Woman: "Then why are you looking here?"
Trainer: "Because the light's better here"

Now, this is a sophisticated little story, but it certainly hasn't got the impact you need for most lesson starters: so pitch your material on the right level for stimulating interest immediately. Trainees have both a need and a right to know what you want them to do, why they're doing it, how they set about it, when they have achieved the requirement by learning the skill or knowledge adequately and by applying, evaluating or analysing the material or procedures, or whatever activity it is that they are about.

Don't let them feel that you are hiding something from them and make certain that your introduction grows naturally from your lesson plan.

A NATURAL GROWTH

FIGURE 98

7. Don't forget that you have to bear in the back of your mind all of the information which you got from Needs Analysis and the Entering Behaviour Analysis of your trainees. If you know them and know about them well enough, your lesson beginning should encompass and accommodate what you understand of the needs, abilities, previous knowledge, skills and interests of the trainees. Accordingly, you can make those necessary variations which help you to motivate different classes, e.g. one time you may show a photograph or video, whilst in another lesson beginning may use real objects, although you are dealing with basically the same topic or skill.

8. Finally, ensure maximal trainee activity and involvement right from the start. If you are making nuts or bolts or blancmanges, let the trainees feel, see (or wobble) them right at the beginning; if it is a verbal message, let them talk; if it is a skill let them have a go as soon as possible; if it is knowledge let them see it, or recall it, or be told that they have a problem to solve.

FIGURE 99

Consider a lesson which you are about to give soon and decide how you are going to involve the trainees quickly and actively.

We don't know what you have chosen to do, but your key should be activities which result in "instant involvement".

Usually, we include a Checklist in this part of our text, for you to decide whether or not you have covered all of the things which you need to do in your lesson beginning.

Have a look at the next Figure, feel involved and then go on to write your own Checklist before scanning ours.

INSTANT INVOLVEMENT

FIGURE 100

CHECKLIST FOR THE BEGINNING OF A LESSON

Ask yourself these questions:
1. Have I stated the lesson objectives specifically?
2. Is the behaviour/performance expected of the trainees made clear to them?
3. Have I included any learning activities?
4. Do the trainees have the chance to become active and involved?
5. Will they realise how the lesson relates to them?
6. Do they understand how it fits in with previous lessons?
7. Have I explained accurately what the trainees have to do and accomplish in the lesson?
8. Can they fit in this lesson with what they know and experienced previously?
9. Have I taken full notice of Needs and Entering Behaviour Analysis, i.e. do I know what the trainees need, what are their interests and capabilities?
10. Will they be likely to be motivated by the lesson beginning?
11. Will the lesson beginning be likely to gain their attention?
12. Is my time limit for the beginning indicated and is it reasonable?
13. Are the trainees likely to be correctly orientated to the lesson, it's direction and to the objectives?

FIGURE 101

How can you change this checklist to an instrument which evaluates how the beginning **went**?

Just change the tense of the verb, e.g. "Do the trainees have the chance to become active and involved?" changes to "Did the trainees have the chance to become active and involved?"

* The Very First Lesson

The very first lesson which begins a course is perhaps the most important one of all. In it, you and the trainees set much of the tone and establish the climate of trust which is necessary if learning is to take place. Or you do not do this, between you, and that's a really bad start.

There are several reasons why you have to be especially careful about that first lesson.

What do you think these reasons are?

We reckon that they could be:—
* Generation Gap. *There is usually a generation gap between trainers and trainees and this can lead to misunderstandings unless handled carefully. Try to make sure that your assumptions about training match theirs.*

* Our problems. *We've all got problems of our own. We are all concerned with our own performance on the first day of a course and what we expect; we may even be quite nervous not knowing the trainees and being in a new situation ourselves. So the first lesson can be a little tense and if we have problems they tend to make the levels of anxiety — ours and the trainees' — higher. However, remember that you are primarily concerned with **their** problems and needs, not yours.*

KEEP YOUR PROBLEMS BEHIND YOU

FIGURE 102

* The way you learned *may not be the way your trainees learn. Learning is much more active these days; most trainers were taught when less was known about methods of learning. Methods and tactics have changed; try to keep-up-to-date and innovative in your approach and remember that trainees today are very active visually as they watch so much television. They like pictures and real things. You may prefer books and manuals. Remember these differences and that you were and are a successful learner, which some of them will not be.*

* Collaboration *is important between you and the trainees if they are to learn. You haven't had much chance yet to establish this when the first lesson starts.*

* Remember *that what the trainees want to know in that first lesson is:—*
   a) Is this training going to meet my needs?
   b) Is this guy competent?
   c) Will he be fair?
   d) Is there a good chance that he will look after me well?

The first lesson is the beginning of your answer to these questions. So beware! That first lesson is of vital importance.

How can you ease this first-lesson situation and begin to establish a co-operative and trusting environment? Try some of these activities and techniques:—

Introducing Yourselves. Begin by stating your name and say a bit about yourself. Then have each trainee do the same.

Introduce your neighbour. Pair off the class (include yourself if you need to make an even number) and give them ten minutes to find out about each others' interests, history, expectations and experiences. Then they introduce each other. As we are talking about the delivery of learning to larger groups, you may well have to split down into two or three sub-groups to save time.

Circle Icebreaker. Everyone sits in a circle and the first person gives his name. The second person gives his name and the name of the first person; the third, their own name and of the previous two, and so on. People do forget, but the game is quite a lot of fun and personal details of dress, etc. are remembered. The trainer should be included in the game.

Why did you volunteer? Here trainees give their names and reasons for joining. It is useful to have them record this information in writing, if you haven't done so already (Entering Behaviour Analysis) in a quiet ten minutes set aside for that purpose.

Apart from exercises of this nature, what else will help relieve that first day tension? Try some of these techniques and convey some of the attitudes.

Be enthusiastic and tell the trainees how much you enjoy the topic or skill. Don't try to impress them with how clever, or knowledgeable you are, but describe some of your own shortcomings and even foolish mistakes you have made in the subject, or anywhere else for that matter. Look human.

Be humorous, even tell little jokes. "Now let me see, I've lots of faults as a trainer, I'll try and remember what they are!" Or, "You'd better forgive my faults as a trainer now. I may have forgotten what they are, tomorrow."

Be a confidence builder: trainees, especially adults re-entering training after a long while, need a boost to their confidence. Tell them they can really do it and that your prime interest is to make sure that they are successful.

Cover the "mechanics" of the course: make sure the trainees know their way around the training department; issue timetables and course Regulations; give a short presentation on matters like grading, coursework, deadlines, even previous pass rates. Don't overdo this. You are better off asking them to read the regulations at home and asking questions next week, than talking overlong on the first session, when trainees may not be at their most receptive, because they are anxious, or may be intimidated by detail. Do make them feel at home, at their ease.

EASY DOES IT

FIGURE 103

Give out a syllabus. Don't let too much of the first training session, or even day, revolve around the **process** of joining. Give the trainees a look at the course content in your first lesson, so that they go away with something "solid" to look over at home. So deal with **product** as well as process.

Make certain that the trainees leave the first lesson absolutely sure that you are on their side, that you are approachable and warm and care about them. Make sure, too, that each one believes that the course will be of use to them personally and looks interesting.

Oh yes! The pre-test! We recommend the use of pre-tests, but it is a little miserable to land a pre-test on the trainees during the first session. Why not hand out the pre-tests and ask the trainees to do them at home, putting them on trust not to use reference books or ask anyone what the answers are? Explain the use of the pre-test, saying that it is not a test at all really, doesn't count towards grading, only lets you know what you have to concentrate on in teaching and they'll get them back next week, anyway. You create trust by trusting them with their pre-tests.

So remember, a warm co-operative, trusting and active atmosphere for their first lesson. Be an OK guy!

GIVE 'EM A LITTLE WARMTH!

FIGURE 104

* How Do You End a Lesson?

Some of you will know the joke about the trainer who says to the group "I don't mind if you look at your watches, in class, to see how the time is passing, but it upsets me when you shake them to see if they are still going!"

Sometimes, towards the end of a training session, we all have the feeling that the trainees might just be shaking their watches, in their minds if not in reality, to see if they are still keeping time, so slowly does the lesson seem to have gone. There are techniques and tactics for avoiding trainee boredom in lessons and we are focussing on these more closely, but we do want to avoid the situation shown in the next illustration.

TIME OUT?

FIGURE 104A

So, to avoid this situation, we must give our lessons a final flourish and make the End of the period stimulating enough to retain the trainees' attention. At this stage it is not appropriate to introduce new material which might confuse the trainees, as it is too late for them to absorb and use such information. So we must retain attention by making it obvious that the end of our lesson is an important stage containing activities which are worthwhile to the trainees.

Ending a lesson is mainly about **summarising** what has gone before.

What are the main points of making a good summary?

We believe these to be as shown in the next table.

A Summary should:
* ✱ Form a conclusion to the lesson's activities.
* ✱ Condense the lesson to most basic and important points.
* ✱ Present these points quickly so that pace and interest is maintained.
* ✱ Allow time for the trainees to present their own conclusions and points of view, briefly.
* ✱ Give time for them to raise questions of doubt or asking for clarification.
* ✱ Be an "inviting" period, when the trainees are invited to tie up any loose ends, with the trainer.
* ✱ Aid retention of the lesson material by reinforcing important points and perhaps giving a slightly different and more memorable view of them, or perspective on them.
* ✱ Avoid the inclusion of absolutely new material, but could offer a different slant on the ground already covered.
* ✱ Not be boringly reiterative.
* ✱ Use a variety of effective tactics like "quickfire" questions and answers, quizzes asking direct questions of the trainees then concluding with an open-ended question which makes them think about the lesson after it has finished.
* ✱ Give the trainer the chance of making an OHP or whiteboard summary and then comparing it with the trainees' own summary.
* ✱ Show how this lesson links with the last one and the next.
* ✱ Allow feedback. Many of the points which we have mentioned already provide feedback of a two-way nature: from the trainees to the trainer to show how well the lesson has gone and how far the material has been absorbed, or the skill learned and from the trainer to the trainees to inform them how well they have done.

The trainer wants to know - must know — how well the lesson objectives have been achieved. So do the trainees.

Feedback should also show if the trainees can apply that new knowledge and skills and is an extension of the lesson in this sense.

This enhancement of the lesson is the beginning of your own evaluation as a trainer about how well it has gone.

Feedback provides the information needed for evaluation and allows you to modify your plans for the next lesson to accommodate the information which you received.

FIGURE 105

THE LESSON FEEDBACK CYCLE

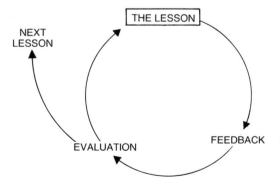

FIGURE 106

So that's how we believe you should end a lesson. By now, you'll be expecting that we are going to check on whether or not you have accepted the material which we have been communicating to you during this Component. We are trying to find out if our receivers' response is what it should be and what we hoped.

How do you think we are going to do this?

By using a Lesson Summary Checklist. You probably realised this before, but we use Checklists extensively because we are asking you to summarise our Components by this device. As this Training Technology Programme is largely based on distance-learning, we cannot ask you questions face-to-face as we would like to do in a normal training session. Our Checklists are one way of us getting around this problem. In a way, we are asking you to ask questions of yourself, so providing a discovery method of giving feedback. Write down your Checklist before reading ours.

ENDING A LESSON: CHECKLIST

Did I
1. allow enough time for the end of the lesson?
2. involve the trainees actively in making a summary of the lesson?
3. encourage them to state their views, ask questions and make observations during the ending of the lesson?
4. go over all the most significant points?
5. tie up all of the loose ends?
6. sequence the important points logically?
7. use what the trainees said to reinforce and make clear the key points so aiding retention?
8. show how this lesson related to past lessons and provides a "bridge" to the next?
9. develop feedback from the trainees to determine if they understood the lesson and can use the information or skills which were covered?
10. check how far the trainees fulfilled the lesson's objectives?
11. let them know what they achieved and how far they reached the objectives?
12. set about evaluating the lesson, possibly in writing, as soon as it was finished?

FIGURE 107

Summary

When beginning a lesson it is important that you stimulate the trainees, catch their interest and even excite them about what is to come during the middle part of the lesson itself.

Make sure that you state the lesson's objectives clearly to trainees; let them know what is expected of them; keep them active and involved; show how they are going to achieve their objectives; stimulate their attention and give them their bearings for both this lesson, past lessons and the next.

The very first lesson is the most significant in any series and has special problems and opportunities. Above all you have to satisfy the trainees that you are a warm, approachable person and that you are competent enough to look after their needs, which you understand. After this lesson they should be well-informed about the training and confident not only that they can do it well, but that they will benefit both in their job and as people.

Ending the lesson is mainly a process of Summarising what has gone before and should reinforce the main points in a logical fashion; aid retention; avoid reiteration; invite the trainees to participate actively; give their own point of view and condense the material into memorable form.

Above all, the lesson ending should provide feedback which tells the trainer how far the objectives of the lesson have been achieved and tells the trainees how successful they have been on as individual a basis as possible. Finish on a crest!

FEEDBACK: ON THE CREST

Component 4:

Methods of delivering the learning to Larger Groups: Questioning in Lessons

Key Words

 The Pause; aims of questioning; what questions can and cannot do; questions about questions; pre-packing cue or key questions; pitching questions; higher and lower order; trainees responding; pausing; prompting; clarifying; refocusing; trainees participating; redirection, level of questions; dealing with trainees' questions; question checklist.

Introduction

Before we even begin an examination of "questioning" as a tactic used in delivery of the learning, let us show you a diagram which we think is fundamental to this topic.

QUESTIONING: THE BASICS

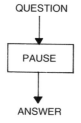

FIGURE 108

We want you to look at the diagram, think about it and consider what it means. We'll go into details later when you've had time for reflection.

By "questioning" we mean oral questioning and not the type of questions which appear in written form in assessment questions, handouts and manuals. Oral questioning is a lesson tactic which has numerous techniques, with four fundamental aims.

▨▨ Checkpoint

What do you think these are?

We believe the basic aims to be
* *Providing feedback*
* *Engaging trainees' attention*
* *Assisting trainees to participate and respond*
* *Helping trainees to think*
The first three speak for themselves; the last includes assisting the trainees to think critically and with a focus on the topic or skill which is the subject of the lesson.

Questioning, as a training and teaching tactic, has a very long history and goes right back to Socrates, who used questions almost to the exclusion of all other ways of teaching. Indeed, the "question-and-answer" tactic is sometimes just described as "Socratic" and plays a vital part in much training and teaching. Even skills training often relies heavily on questioning techniques and questioning may well be the most important activity in which trainers and teachers participate.

Research shows that teachers ask about 400 questions each day of their working lives. Unfortunately, this has given rise to a style of teaching and training where about three-quarters of the talk in a classroom is from the trainer and only one-quarter from the trainees. Obviously, if you want trainees to be active in the learning, then this isn't a healthy situation. Recent trainee-centred strategies which emphasise trainee involvement are slowly changing this balance, or lack of it.

A LACK OF BALANCE

FIGURE 109

Efficient questioning can undoubtedly lead to effective training and learning, therefore, in this Component we are going to examine:

What questions can and cannot do
Where you pitch your questions?
Effective questioning techniques
Dealing with trainees' questions

* What Questions Can and Cannot Do

In this particular Component it seems sensible to use questions themselves as a way of delivering our message. So let's begin with a series of questions about what questions can do well, what are their limitations in generating learning and what qualities are typical of a good question.

Don't just answer "yes", "no", or "maybe" to the following queries, but try to give a reasoned answer. But be careful, these questions are not always what they seem!

QUESTIONS ABOUT QUESTIONS

Write down your answers to the following:—
1. Why should questions aim to involve trainees?
2. Why is it difficult to stimulate trainees by questioning?
3. How can questions show up individual differences between trainees?
4. Why is it that repeating questions is poor practice?
5. How does it happen that some trainees are keen on question-and-answer sessions and some aren't?
6. Can questions "highlight" trainees special interests and experiences?
7. What reasons make questioning important at the beginning of a lesson?
8. What reasons make questioning important at the end of a lesson?
9. Are there any reasons for considering that questioning is important to feedback and if there are, what are they?
10. Why do trainees have little chance to practice self-expression in question-and-answer (Q and A) sessions?
11. Why should effective questions include as many ideas as possible?
12. Why is it that longer questions are usually more efficient than short ones?
13. Why is it that repeating questioning in a lesson produces variety?
14. How may questions be directed to different levels of knowledge?
15. What is the importance of coding questions carefully?
16. Why should an efficient question give the trainee a chance to guess correctly at the answer?
17. Why is it that distributing questions around the class is more important than getting the correct answer?
18. Why should an efficient question always hint at the correct answer?
19. How can you cover all of the key points of a lesson with questions?
20. Where and when should you set about sequencing your questions in a logical order?
21. Why do the best questions always permit a "yes", "no", or "maybe" answer?
22. Why are short questions inefficient?
23. How is it that questions can usually be disposed of quickly in a lesson, so that you can all then get down to the "real" work?
24. Are questions a resource for the class?
25. Do you always ask thought-provoking questions in class?

FIGURE 110

In the list shown in Figure 110, there are three inefficient questions. Pick them out and say why you think they are not likely to be effective.

Questions 6, 24 and 25 are the guilty ones. They are capable of being answered by "yes" or "no" and are not thought-provoking. Most effective questions begin with "what", "where", "when", "how" or "why", because any reply must include reasons which support it.

Let's have a look at our answers to the questions in Figure 110. We did warn you that some of the questions are not what they seem: by this, we mean that they take incorrect, or partly accurate standpoints. We use this device to encourage you to view each query critically.

1. **Why should questions aim to involve trainees?**
This is the main requirement that the questioning tactic has to fulfil: ensuring trainee participation, focussing their attention on the topic or skill and getting them thinking.

2. **Why is it difficult to stimulate trainees by questioning?**
Another primary objective of questioning is to be stimulative. In groups of up to, say, twenty trainees, the trainer can usually provide this stimulus to each satisfactorily, but this becomes increasingly difficult as the numbers get larger. Obviously, the more trainees there are, then there is less question time for each one.

However, the techniques of questioning themselves, if used properly, present no difficulties in creating stimulation, but don't forget that variation in your way of asking questions creates further stimulation.

3. **How can questions show up individual differences between trainees?**
Careful individual questioning spotlights different trainee attitudes, abilities, interest, knowledge and skills. Finding out about the latter should be combined with the trainer's observations of the trainees actually carrying out the skilled procedure.

4. **Why is it that repeating questions is poor practice?**
Well, it isn't poor practice necessarily. If the class is a large one some may not have heard the question distinctly. If it is a difficult one, then the trainees may want to hear it again. If you suspect attention is wavering, a repeat will re-focus their attention on the subject.

5. **How does it happen that some trainees are keen on question-and-answer sessions and some aren't?**
This is another aspect of the individual differences between trainees; some are forthcoming and confident, others are shy and quiet. For the quiet ones, answering a question may be a bit of an ordeal and it is always so for those who often don't know the answers. Those who don't prepare themselves properly will always dislike Q and A, but the tactic should eventually persuade them to do something about that situation.

6. **Can questions "highlight" trainees' special interests and experiences?**
You could just answer "yes" here, which is why it is a poor question. The point is that questioning can first identify trainee interests and then judiciously follow them up with further questions.

7. **What reasons make questioning important at the beginning of a lesson?**
The answer to this question lies in the last Component and should include the use of questions as a way of gaining attention, putting the lesson in context, motivating and involving the trainees and helping them get their bearings.

8. **What reasons make questioning important at the end of a lesson?**
The all-important function of questions at the end of a lesson is that of summarising by drawing the information directly from the class.

9. **Are there any reasons for considering that questioning is important to feedback and if there are what are they?**
During the lesson, questioning is the most important way of providing feedback. By constantly asking questions the trainer can ensure that the material has been grasped successfully and the tactic is quick, flexible and gives immediate feedback on how well the lesson is going. Effective questioning is a basically significant provider of feedback information.

10. **Why do trainees have little chance to practice self-expression in question-and-answer (Q and A) sessions?**
This question poses a query which is false. Questions provide considerable opportunities for the trainees to practice self-expression and that's why the tactic gives them such useful and confidence-building experience.

11. **Why should effective questions include as many ideas as possible?**
They shouldn't; a good question is always concise and should deal with one idea or concept or part of a skill only.

12. **Why is it that longer questions are usually more efficient than short ones?**
They aren't: an efficient question is short, sharp and precise.

13. **Why is it that repeated questioning in a lesson produces variety?**
The more the questions then the greater the variety of points which are put to the trainees and the more the different topics which they have to consider. Patches of lesson where the trainer only talks and fails to ask questions are usually sterile, unless the trainees are involved in doing something themselves like carrying out an exercise, completing classwork or working on a machine.

14. How may questions be directed to different levels of knowledge.?

This requires planning before the lesson to ensure that your questions are balanced in that they are directed towards higher levels of thinking, e.g. analysis and not just at the lower, e.g. repeating facts. More about this later.

BALANCING YOUR QUESTIONS

FIGURE 111

15. What is the importance of coding questions carefully?

Very important, this: use language and a vocabulary with which the trainees are familiar, otherwise your learning message will not be successful.

16. Why should an efficient question give the trainee a chance to guess correctly at the answer?

A question which allows the trainee to guess at the answer is not efficient. Why ask it if any shot-in-the-dark response will do? Trainees must consider the pros and cons of their replies and they won't do this if they can guess instead.

17. Why is it that distributing questions around the class is more important than getting the correct answer?

"Dodgy" question this is. Why? Because it's "polarized" your thinking quite wrongly. You must try for correct answers, but you have to ensure that you deploy your questions so that each trainee has had his chance to answer one or two by the end of the lesson.

18. Why should an efficient question always hint at the correct answer?

It should not: "hinting" or "leading" questions are weak because they cut down on the thinking which the trainees have to do to achieve the correct reply.

19. How can you cover all of the key points of a lesson with questions?

Again this is a question of pre-planning. It is good practice to cover each of your key topics, or cues in skills lessons, with at least one question that you have "pre-packaged" by thinking it out carefully before you start, during your lesson planning.

PRE-PACK YOUR CUE OR KEY QUESTIONS

FIGURE 112

20. When should you set about sequencing your questions in a logical order?

Simple answer: right from the beginning. If you link your questions to your objectives, or content, closely, you won't have a problem. The questions will follow a logical, orderly sequence and should build-up nicely.

21. Why do the best questions always permit a "yes", "no" or "maybe" answer?

They don't: these are the worst type of question, because they reduce trainee need for thought to a minimum and they can always guess!

22. Why are short questions inefficient?

They aren't: the short question is usually the most efficient. If you can't ask concise questions then you are not sure what you want and the trainees will certainly become confused.

23. How is it that questions can usually be disposed of quickly in a lesson, so that you can all then get down to the "real" work?

They can't be disposed of quickly, nor should they be. As we suggested previously, questioning is a basic tactic to a successful teaching-learning process and they are "real" work.

24. Are questions a resource for the class?

A poor question; the answer is "yes" because this is the way in which you find out more about class interests, previous experience, knowledge and skills. Exchanging this information is a valuable resource, especially with older trainees.

25. Do you always ask thought-provoking questions in class?

Another badly asked question, but your questions in class certainly must be thought-provoking. Ensuring that you ask your questions in such a way that the trainees have to think about their answers is a basic skill of the trainer's questioning technique.

So you should now have an idea of what questions can and cannot do. There is now one little matter to be cleared up concerning Question 14 in Figure 110; read it again, then read on.

* Where do you Pitch your Questions?

The easiest questions to formulate and answer are those which merely require the trainee to recall a fact from memory. Consequently, research has shown that half to two-thirds of the questions which trainers ask in lessons are of this type, called "lower-order", or "lower level", questions.

By contrast, "higher-order", or "higher level" questions demand much more thoughtful responses of the trainees. They are more difficult to formulate, but they are much more effective in encouraging learning.

▰▰▰

Define "higher order" and "lower order" questions more closely.

The key to the answer lies in the work which we did on sequencing specific objectives by domains in Component Three, Study Unit Two, Package One. If you glance at Figure 186 again in that Component, you'll be able to see the difference between higher-order or higher-level and lower-level categories.

Simplifying that material, we can show the type of questions you could ask in each domain, by the table which follows:

LEVEL OF QUESTIONS

> **LOWER-LEVEL QUESTIONS**
> **Knowledge:** requires only recall or recognition from memory to make an answer, e.g. How do you define communication? What types of still projector are there? How many categories are there in Bloom's Taxonomy? What ingredients are in a Maderia cake mix?
>
> **HIGHER-LEVEL QUESTIONS**
> **Comprehension:** asks trainees to compare and contrast, explain describe, e.g. how can you explain the sequencing of the objectives? Describe how you would make a Madeira cake. How would you compare two different techniques for perming hair? What does this pie graph show?
> **Application:** asks for the solving of problems, practical difficulties etc., by using learned material in new situations, e.g. How would you apply the principles of media selection to choosing a-v equipment for a lesson? On what basis would you classify these faults?
> **Analysis:** asks for the breaking down of a topic or skill into component parts and relationships, e.g. What are the relationships between the parts of a design system? What faults are there in the electrical system of this car? Which of these statements on good customer management are consistent with the handout which I gave you?
> **Synthesis:** asks for the building up of new patterns or wholes, e.g. What actions could the firm take to improve sales? Using current financial restrictions as a guide, how would you make a plan to increase productivity?
> **Evaluation:** asks for the making of judgements and valuing, using definite criteria rather than personal opinions, e.g. How would you judge the firm's new products using the principles of customer safety as a guide? How efficient do you consider this tool to be, using the firm's criteria on expense and adaptability? Which software programme is most useful to us, remembering the range of our products?

FIGURE 113

LEVELS OF ACTIVITY

FIGURE 114

What do the four activities shown in Figure 114 illustrate?

Illustration One is analysis, probably the analysis of an engine fault.
Illustration Two is application, with the trainee applying his knowledge to the interpretation of a graph.
Illustration Three is evaluation, with the trainee judging the relative merits of three plans.
Illustration Four is synthesis, the trainee having built up a plan.

Depending on what you are teaching, you should try to include as many higher order questions in your lesson as possible, because the higher the level of question then the more the trainee is likely to learn consequently.

Frequently, you will find that you can ask questions requiring recall of knowledge or skills only at the beginning of a lesson, or at the start of a series of questions, then moving on to the more demanding ones later.

* Effective Questioning Techniques

"Good" questions, that is those which are both effective and efficient in promoting learning, have two aspects.

What do you consider these two aspects to be?

First, *they should help the trainee to* **respond.**
Second, *they can be used as a basis for developing trainees'* **participation.**

1. * Trainees Responding

There are several elements to encouraging trainees to make a full clear, accurate and thoughtful response. These elements are:

Pausing
Prompting
Classifying
Refocusing

Let's deal with each of these in turn.
Pausing. Have a look back at Figure 108 in this Component which shows the proper form for a good question. These are your steps when asking an effective question.
1. Ask the question.
2. Pause before requiring a trainee to give an answer.
3. Receive the answer.

What do you think the pause is for?

This signals to the trainees that you are giving them time to **think** *about their replies. They will realise that their answers have to be thoughtful and clear and will make an effort to achieve this. Another advantage of the pause is that* **all** *of the trainees have to think about the question, because they don't know who is going to be asked to reply.*

Don't ask a question like this:
"What's the first thing you do when you have opened your till every morning, Mary?"
The question should be phrased like this:
"What's the first thing you do when you have opened your till every morning?"
PAUSE of about 3—6 seconds.
"Mary?"

More difficult questions should allow a thinking time in the pause of over five seconds; easy questions, say three or four seconds, but **never** less than three.

You may have to train your learners in not shouting out answers at first, without being asked. If they are permitted to do that, the fastest thinkers will always answer first and the slower ones never have sufficient time to consider their answers. So your pause "gags" some of the class, in a way.

FIGURE 115

Whether or not you ask your trainees to hold up their hands to show they know the answer is up to you and depends on the type of group you are dealing with. Certainly, don't use this technique with mature trainees as it's far too much like being in school again, and most trainees, of whatever age, resent being treated like schoolchildren.

Occasionally, when you have a "tough" question, you may phrase it like this:
"What are the ascending order of categories in the psychomotor domain?"
PAUSE (long pause).
"Anyone?"

You are throwing the questions open to the group to avoid the embarrassment of asking a person who doesn't know the answer.

Develop a sensitivity to who might and might not know the answer: there are always lots of signs showing who is confident and who is not. Usually, you know someone whom you think can give a good shot at replying accurately.

However, make sure that by the end of the lesson you have asked a roughly equal number of questions around the class so that no-one feels left out. Give the easier questions to the weaker trainees; save the more difficult ones for the more able. You are trying to help each trainee to be successful in answering your questions.

Tell your trainees at the start of your course how you are going to formulate your questions and let them know the sort of standards you require for an answer to be adequate.

What do you consider the standards for a "good answer" to be?

111

We believe that a good answer should:

Be spoken clearly.
Contain the essential facts.
Be relevant to the question.
Contain supporting reasons and examples, if necessary.
Give an idea of how the trainee arrived at the answer.
Be concise.
Not contain any jargon.
Not be a sort of "shorthand", but constructed of proper sentences.

By the last, we mean that the reply should be sensible to an observer sitting in the class. Too often the trainees, even experienced ones, will give a jargon word, or a "catchword" which they consider is adequate, e.g. "What is one characteristic of the design system?"
PAUSE
"John?"
ANSWER: "Cyclical or loop."

John should tell you and the class what he means by cyclical, or loop, not just leave the couple of words to do all of the work.

Why did we place Figure 108 at the beginning of this Component?
PAUSE

Because it emphasises the importance of the PAUSE in the structure of an effective question. The pause gives the trainee time in which to think of a good answer.

Prompting. When you have received a **"good" answer**, i.e. one which achieves the standards which we mentioned in the last Checkpoint, reward it positively with recognition and praise, e.g. "Correct" or "That's a good answer", or both.

When the answer is **partially correct**, or is an "I don't know" response, then give credit for the correct part and do some **prompting** on that wrong bit.

▰▰▰

What do you think prompting is?

Prompting is developing a series of questions with hints which prompt the trainee to develop the correct answer. Ask intermediate questions, give clues and hints and perhaps information which points the way to answering the question properly.

An example of Prompting
Q. "What does it mean when we describe the design system as being cyclical, or loop?"
A. **"Don't know."**
Q1. "Well, does the design system begin at one point and end at another?"
A. **"It has a series of stages, or steps, succeeding each other."**
Q2. "What's the last step then?"
A. **"I think it's improvement of the training."**

Q3. "Yes, good. But what happens after you've completed the last step?"
A. **Oh! Yes! You go back to the beginning of the system, having revised it in time for the next course. That's where the cycle must come in."**
Q4. "That's fine. But what about the use of the word loop?"
A. **"Well, a cycle is a loop structure, if you think about it."**
"OK. I think we've got that clear now."

In that series of questions, the original question (Q) was succeeded by four questions (Q1 to Q4) which probed the trainee's answer and pointed him along the correct path.

PROMPTING TECHNIQUE

FIGURE 116

If the trainee's reply is **incorrect** you must prompt but don't make a critical observation on the answer. No "Rubbish" or "That's wrong. Try again". Try to soften your comment, say "That's a good try, but what about ....", or "Perhaps, but is that the main point, do you think?"

Accept all honest answers even if they are incorrect. Turn the wrong answers to advantage.

Clarifying. When clarifying you are trying to persuade the trainee to improve on an answer which is basically correct, but is organised badly, not detailed enough, or incomplete, i.e. you haven't got the reply you want, but the answer isn't wrong.

Ask prompting questions like, "Can you say that another way", or "I'm not sure I know what you mean. Can you restate that?"

Refocusing. Here you have received a good answer, but you'd like the trainee to focus on another topic, by transferring his or her response to an item which is related to the one under discussion. Here's an example:
Q. "What part do objectives play in the design system?

112

A.. **"Well. They are fundamental to it, because they give specific direction to a course and provide detail on the behaviour, or performance which the trainee is expected to achieve. They help the trainees to know what they are expected to do."**

Q2. "That's a clear answer. Now can you tell me how objectives relate to assessment?"

A. **"You can gauge how far the trainees have progressed by linking assessment items directly to each objective. Success in a particular piece of assessment shows that the trainees have mastered that objective."**

"Good, that's correct."

Q2 is a refocusing question asking for other links to be made.

Remember that when encouraging good trainee answers it is often useful for you to think out some key questions **before** your lesson, including them and the main points you expect in the answers in your lesson notes.

2. * Trainees Participating

Naturally, you want as many of the trainees to participate in Q and A sessions as possible. An effective way of doing this is by **redirection** of the question. Redirection means that having asked the original question, you then ask several others to make a reply to the same question, without restating it.

Such questions need to be open-ended and be capable of producing several different answers.

Give an example of redirection.

Here is ours:

Q. *"What are the advantages of careful course evaluation? Pat?"*

A1. **"You can build up strong parts of a course for the next time round."**
(You then ask another trainee)

Q. *"That's correct. Julie, can you suggest anything else?"*

A2. **"Well, I suppose the other side is that you can pick out any weaknesses and revise them for future training."**

Q. *"Good, Nick?"*

A3. **"Evaluation flies "danger signals" which tell you that the course isn't going too well. In the end that keeps you out of trouble."**

Q. *"Yes. Simon, can you add anything?"*

A4. **"Well, I think that you get a good idea of your own performance if you ask the trainees directly what they think."**

Q. *"I agree. Now, Saffron, have we missed any points?"*

A. **"I think evaluation gives the cyclic quality to training. It means that your courses are dynamic, never get in a rut and improve constantly as you go along."**
"Very good. I think that covers the main points to the question. Well done everybody."

In the series above you helped the trainees to participate by redirecting the original question from one to another.

If you ask higher-order questions you will find that they increase trainee involvement. Ask questions which involve summarising, synthesising evaluating, comparing and analysing. Usually, such questions are capable of extensive answers, or more than one answer and each trainee has a chance to chip in with a contribution.

Prepare such a question and indicate the likely facts which responses should bring out.

Our example is

Q. *"You have just evaluated the series of lessons which we've had on course design and we've discussed your replies to the questionnaires. Now, analyse the main points which were brought out. John, will you begin, please?"*

The analysis could possibly include the facts that the lessons were:

Informative. Well-structured. Interesting. Some were too long. Not enough activity by trainees. Didn't have enough visual material — and so on.

You have asked a higher-order question involving analysis and can expect full trainee participation because of the variety of replies which are possible.

So don't forget to improve the quality and amount of trainee participation by:
— planning higher-order questions.
— knowing what you expect to find in answers (especially to key questions).
— making sure the trainees have enough information to take part in Q and A sessions.

Remember, sarcasm and negative observations or responses inhibit trainee participation.

* Dealing with Trainees' Questions

Just a few important pointers here to help you handle the questions posed by the trainees.

— Do remember that questions from the trainees should be encouraged as they signify a lively learning environment.
— Give time for their questions in your lesson planning.
— Use other trainees to answer another trainee's question, e.g. "Fred, what do you think of Bob's question?" (You can also use this technique to have a trainee observe on the obviously wrong answer given by a peer).
— If the questions are off-topic or skill being considered, talk about it to the trainee after class.
— Ask anyone who tries to trip you up with a trick or difficult question to provide the answer themselves during the next lesson.
— Put incorrect grammar right by repeating the question in correct English.
— If the question is confused, restate it clearly.

— If you don't know the answer to a trainee question, don't try to blind your way through with bullshine. Admit it and say you'll find out. Better still, ask them to find out, too, then you can compare answers, later. Don't hide if you don't know.

Well, have you had enough material on questions? (And why is this not a good question?)

We hope that you answered that it only produces a "yes" or "no" reply and we know that's no good.

Instead of summarising this Component in the usual fashion, we are going to make our Summarising by designing a Checklist on "questions". Write your own Checklist before you read ours.

CHECKLIST FOR ORAL QUESTIONS

DID I ASK QUESTIONS WHICH WERE
Clear?
Brief?
Precise?
Not obvious?
Relevant?
Covering key points?
Not capable of being answered by a "yes" or "no"?
Adapted to individual differences in the trainees?

DID I
Pause?
Pitch my questions at a suitable level?
Use enough higher-order questions?
Prompt effectively?
Clarify effectively?
Refocus effectively?
Give my questions an orderly sequence?
Ensure good trainee participation?
Encourage good trainee responses?
Deal with trainees' questions efficiently?
Cover each objective with a planned question?
Avoid sarcasm and negative observations?
Use trainees' previous experiences?
Distribute the questions around the class?

FIGURE 117

If you use your Checklist on the questions which you asked in your last, or recent lesson, then you will have summarised this Component effectively, for yourself.

Did you draw any blanks with some of your questions? If you did, why was this?

Remember, you shouldn't be using blanks now when asking questions. Use real live "ammunition".

FIGURE 118

114

One last point: in the skills lessons, the "answer" to a question may well involve the trainee carrying out a technique or part of a skilled procedure, rather than making an oral answer. Nevertheless, the questions preceding the practice must be just as good as those requiring verbal replies.

Ask a colleague if you can sit in on his or her lesson. Using one of our Checklists, or one which you have prepared yourself, evaluate the quality of the trainer's questioning techniques. Send your evaluation, with suggestions for improvement, to your Programme Tutor for observation, if you would like to.

or

Evaluate your own questioning technique, stating to your Programme Tutor how you propose to make it more effective.

Component 5:

Methods of delivering the learning to Larger Groups: The Skills Lesson

Key Words

Skill definitions; learner activity; demonstration; practice; principles of planning and execution; basic procedures in teaching a skill; steps and points of demonstration; explaining and practising a skill by the trainer; motor skills lesson plan; skills lesson checklist.

Introduction

In the M.S.C.'s glossary of terms, we find a skill defined as an **"organised and co-ordinated pattern of mental/or physical activity"**.

In this Component, we are going to have a closer look at skills training and give you an example of lessons for a psychomotor skill, or motor skill as we prefer to call it.

However, we feel we must begin by giving you another one of our Golden Rules; this is;

> "Skills are best learned by repeated practice"

We would like you to bear this in mind throughout this Component.

▨▨▨ Checkpoint

Modify that Golden Rule to produce another, appropriate to learning in general.

Our modification would be:
"Learning is best achieved through Learner Activity."

When you consider what we have to say in this Package, so far, especially the emphasis we have laid on the vital importance of your planning and the trainees carrying out learning activities, we think you will place a high value on the truth of these two Golden Rules.

Returning to the preparation and implementation of motor skills lessons, there appear to be two basic elements to this type of lesson.

▨▨▨

What do you consider these two elements to be?

Our answer can be shown by a diagram:—

BASIC ELEMENTS OF SKILLS LESSONS

THE SKILLS LESSON

| DEMONSTRATION BY TRAINER | PRACTICE BY TRAINEES |

FIGURE 119

Obviously, there is much more to a skills lesson than these two basics, but getting them right will go a long way towards making your lessons successful.

In this Component we shall consider:
Principles of Planning a Skills Lesson.
Demonstration and Practice.
A Motor Skills Lesson.
Skills Lesson: Checklist.

* Principles of Planning a Skills Lesson

Most of you will have given many skills lesson before. We would like you to think back over these lessons and consider what were the most significant things you did when planning and implementing the lesson. These are the principles which we are after.

PRINCIPLES SHOW!

Now what are these principles? We show them in the next Figure.

SKILLS LESSONS: PRINCIPLES OF PLANNING AND EXECUTION

Principle One: Demonstrate the skill in full.
The skill, whether motor or mental must be demonstrated in entirety by either the trainer, by a master performer, or a highly competent performer. This may not be you, as few possess all the skills of a factory or firm at their fingertips.

The trainer must have someone who can demonstrate all the skilled procedure as a fully integrated operation, if he cannot do this. The correct skilled movements and manipulations must be shown right at the beginning of the lesson. You should add a clear commentary as to what is going on, preferably using a non-technical vocabulary. Often what comes as second nature to the master performer, things like holding and guiding tools accurately and standing correctly, have to be learned by the trainees and a skilled demonstration might be a little baffling just because of the speed and expertise of the competent performer.

So, first, reassure the trainees that they can all learn the skill if they practice hard and then help them understand the procedure for observing the next principle.

Principle Two: Break the skill down into its parts.
We'll look at this in detail later, but in the general terms of observing this principle, you will wish to break down the skill into its components, so that it is more easily understandable to the trainees.

Principle Three: Give the trainee plenty of practice.
Each trainee will only become competent at the skill if adequate practice is allowed.

Principle Four: Ensure Feedback.
As with all training, providing adequate feedback is vital. Remind the trainees of the criteria for ensuring a skilled performance; give feedback about discrepancies between the skilled performance and the trainee's performance; show how differences between the two can be closed; tell the trainee when he is reaching the standard desired.

Principle Five: Teach the skill in realistic conditions.
Unfortunately there is sometimes a big difference between training conditions and the noise, dirt and activity of the assembly line or the workshop floor. The training rarely reproduces the stress of being faced by an irate customer or a queue of clients who are all in a hurry!

However, try to reduce these differences as far as possible, or at least warn the trainees, especially new ones, of what may lie in store when they are on the job.

FROM THE SUBLIME TO . . . . . . REALITY

But what's in store in reality?

Principle Six. Use your design system information.
Your design system provides a great deal of valuable information which will help you to plan your skills lesson. Apart from a thoroughgoing knowledge of **Resources and Constraints**, your **Entering Behaviour Analysis** should have helped you to identify the skills which the trainees possessed before coming to you. Obviously, they will need to have certain pre-requisite skills, before they can begin to learn the new skill, unless they really are starting from scratch.

Task analysis will have shown you elements of the skill itself and your **Objectives** should all have been identified together with the initial learning outcomes which they are to produce.

Criterion Tests are important in skills lessons, as they will show you and the trainees just how well they are learning the skill. Do remind the trainees, as they are progressing, that even when they have acquired competence in the skill, this may not be an end in itself and that this skill could lead on to others, e.g. a competent word-processor has many other skills to learn before becoming an efficient secretary.

FIGURE 120

There are the principles of training in a skill. Let's have a look now at those two vital parts of the skills lesson, the **Demonstration** and **Practice.**

* Demonstration and Practice

The first principle of planning and execution which we considered dealt with the demonstration, in outline. Write down the major points which we made then.

If you feel you have missed anything check back to our explanation of the principles.

From what we have said and from your own experience you will know that the demonstration, which we believe to be one of the two major elements of a skills lesson, is also accepted widely as a well-tried and effective tactic in teaching a manipulative skill, whether it is tiling a wall, welding a frame, making a dovetail joint, just wiring a plug, or one of the million other industrial skills.

Mental skills are frequently best taught by demonstration and are effective in showing how to balance an account, deal with a customer, solve a problem, interpret a graph, or whatever.

To teach a skill effectively, you will usually follow four basic procedures or steps. From your own experience, what do you consider those to be?

BASIC PROCEDURES IN TEACHING A SKILL

Procedure One.	**Preparation.**
Procedure Two.	**Showing.**
Procedure Three.	**Practice.**
Procedure Four.	**Follow-up.**

FIGURE 121

Let's deal with each of these in turn.

* Procedure One. Preparation
Here you prepare the trainees to receive the skill and you motivate them to attend. Here are the points which you must ensure are covered when you prepare for the demonstration:

Objectives. Check with your specific objective(s) for the lesson and make sure that a demonstration is the most effective way of helping the trainees to achieve them.

Clarity. Be clear in your own mind **what** you are going to demonstrate.

Decision. You have to decide if one lesson is sufficient. If not, prepare your plan for the others.

Information. All skills lessons are a mixture of teaching the skill itself and of the trainees acquiring knowledge, e.g. of technical terms. Make sure that the trainees have the necessary information to be able to follow your explanations and directions during the demonstration.
You may have to begin by giving this information, often by exposition, or have arranged a previous session where this was done.

Length. Demonstrations require a lot of concentration and attention from the trainees. Usually, the maximal time for which you can expect such effort is about twenty minutes.
If you cannot demonstrate the whole skill in twenty to thirty minutes then you will have to break the skill into twenty or thirty minute **segments**, following each by practice.
Should you have only one forty or sixty minute lesson, then you'll have to teach the next segment(s) of the skill in later lessons. This is important.

DON'T OVERSHOOT YOUR TIME.

FIGURE 122

On the other hand, if you have, say, a full morning in which to teach the skill, then you can cover all or several segments by interspersing them with practice by the trainees thus:—

TIME	ACTIVITY
20 minutes 45 minutes	Demonstration — Segment One Trainee practice — Segment One
20 minutes 50 minutes	Demonstration — Segment Two Trainee Practice — Segment Two
10 minutes 30 minutes	Demonstration — Segment Three Trainee Practice — Segment Three
15 minutes 40 minutes	Demonstration — Segment Four Trainee Practice — Segment Four
60 minutes	Trainee Practice — Segments One, Two, Three, Four.

In the trainee practice for each segment, they will probably run through the skill of the **previous** segment once or twice before trying out the new one.

Lesson Plan. You prepare a lesson plan. You must identify each step in performing the skill and place them in the correct sequence for carrying out the skill.

Cues. You'll recollect that these are key points, where one part of the skill sequence ends and/or another begins. These key points are essential elements in each part of the skill, i.e. actions which have to be done.

Job Card. The section of the lesson plan which shows the parts of the skilled sequence and the associated cues, or key points, may be reproduced separately as a job card and issued to each trainee, so that he can check his own performance when practising.

Resources. Check all of your resources before use. Most of us will have had the experience when training of switching on an OHP or projector and the bulb blows almost immediately! It's much worse if your tools are broken, or not working properly, or you have to hunt for the tool which you thought that you had brought along and which turns out to be missing.

If you need technicians's help, make sure that's available, too.

Some items may need to be **pre**-prepared. If you are doing a cookery demonstration for example, you may wish to have a finished gateaux prepared already and at hand, should the cooking take an hour or two, otherwise the trainees might not get to see the finished product.

Environment. Make sure that the physical conditions in which the trainees work are suitable and that they can see and hear everything. Obviously light, ventilation, and comfortable seating are important.

Don't pass specimens of the product around during the demonstration: if you do, some of the trainees will miss part of what you're doing. Leave it until the demonstration is finished, or show them at the beginning.

Safety. Not only do you and the trainees need to be safe during the demonstration, but you'll have to point out the safety requirements of the skilled procedure as you demonstrate. Certainly, you must observe all of the safety requirements yourself.

Practice. You should practice the skill yourself before you demonstrate. It's easy to forget something which you thought you knew well and it is embarrassing when you make a mess of the demonstration!

FORGOTTEN SKILLS, FORGOTTEN SAFETY

FIGURE 123

Interest. You must capture the interest of the trainees, straightaway. That way you'll develop their motivation.

Tell them how, enthusiastically, the demonstration and skill fit in with the job. Show them the finished product. Make sure they know what the demonstration is about. Let them ask questions. Motivate them.

* Procedure Two. Showing

Write down the procedures of the last demonstration which you made. Check them with ours, shown in Figure 124.

It depends on the skill which you are demonstrating as to the exact steps which you take, but there are certain procedures which you follow and points which you make when actually showing the trainees how the skill is performed.

SHOWING THEM HOW: STEPS AND POINTS OF A DEMONSTRATION

1. Show a complete run-through of the whole procedure.
2. Show the process step-by-step, slowly.
3. Explain each step.
4. Emphasise cues and key points.
5. Show the best technique for each step.
6. Explain technical terms as you go along.
7. Ask questions which check that trainees know what's going on.
8. Let the trainees ask questions.
9. Emphasise important points by keeping silent when you are showing them.
10. Select the best procedure for the skill. Don't confuse trainees by presenting a variety of techniques first time round.
11. Be sensitive to trainees' responses. Make sure you maintain interest.
12. Recapitulate steps when necessary.
13. Turn out a good product. Give the trainees something to aim at by setting a standard.
14. Summarise the key points and cues.
15. Ask definite, pre-planned, summarising questions, which give you feedback on trainees' difficulties and understanding.
16. Repeat the demonstration, or parts of it, as necessary.
17. Ask one of the trainees to repeat the demonstration,
    or, parts of it,
    or, involve several trainees in doing the whole procedure again,
    or, parts of it.
18. Ask the trainees what is going on as they repeat the procedure,
    or, ask them to explain what they are doing as they
    perform repeats.
    Be careful only to ask the stronger trainees to perform, or, if you select a weaker trainee make sure that you pick easy parts of the skill which you are sure they can manage.
19. Don't criticise: be positive and helpful.
20. Finally, ask if the trainees want to have the whole procedure repeated, or points of it, before they begin their own practice.

FIGURE 124

Why are demonstrations such a useful tactic in skills training?

The demonstration involves all of the trainees' senses of seeing and especially of hearing and touching and their personal thinking skills. Frequently, there are simultaneously recalling information and skills, following and performing a logical skills sequence and being aware of hazards.

All of these are excellent learning activities and are rewarding when mastered.

* Procedure Three. Practice.

This is just as important a part of a demonstration as the actions which the trainer performs. As we said at the beginning of this Component, **"skills are best learned by repeated practice"** on the part of the trainees. There are several **important points to remember when practice is taking place**, and they are these:

1. Supervise carefully to note, analyse and eliminate errors.

CLOSE SUPERVISION

FIGURE 125

2. Distribute the practice so that you do not have one long unbroken period of practice in the early stages of training. Three, twenty minute periods will be better, at first, rather than a "solid" hour. Give the breaks in between practices, so that the trainees have time to consolidate. Save the longer periods until they have become reasonably competent and are reaching towards making the skill automatic.
3. Try to help the trainees carry out the operation with an efficient rhythm, characteristic of the skilled operative.
   Developing such a rhythm is helped by the trainee thinking about what comes next and so developing a "smooth", flowing skill.
4. Don't overload by inputting too much information. Don't underload by communicating too little and boring the trainees. The trainees' responses will help you gauge the optimal speed. So watch closely for strain or boredom and keep your foot on the "accelerator" with sensitivity.
5. Feedback, yet again, is what you're after. This is feedback about stress, lack of interest, mistakes, parts of the skill well-learned and the patterns of movement which the trainees are developing.
6. We know it is banal to say that "practice makes perfect" but it is so true. "Perfection", competency, is reached by the trainees through practice, and remember that is so in your training. However, make sure that the practice is efficient and effective.
7. Check throughout the practice that the trainees have a positive attitude and that they understand the whole skilled process.

Procedure Four. Follow-up

You seek feedback not only during the training, but after it is finished as well. Go and see how they are getting on in the workshop, on the floor, in the laboratory, in the office, at the reception desk.

Talk to their supervisors; chat to the trainees. Find out if the training has "stuck". See if faults have developed that training could have avoided.

Then go back to your office and think about the training and the trainees. Evaluate what has gone on and make it better next time.

HERE'S TO THE NEXT TIME.

FIGURE 126

Three camels in the Ark? Looks as if Noah's evaluation wasn't perfect either!

We hope to have demonstrated the crucial significance of "practice" and of the "demonstration" in the skills lesson. Let's have a look now, briefly, at an actual motor skills lesson, but before we do so, answer the following checkpoint.

Why is it important for the trainer to practise a skill before a lesson and why should he write a lesson plan?

Giving a demonstration is not just giving a performance of the skill, but it includes making an **explanation** *of the procedure. In a way, therefore, demonstrating requires* **two** *skills: the* **doing** *and the* **explaining**.

Remember that your **explanation** *should include:—*
1. *a logical succession of steps in the skill which the trainees can follow.*
2. *all the steps in their proper logical order.*
3. *the techniques, cues and key points of each step.*
4. *a description of the safety procedures.*
5. *a list of the tools, supplies and equipment required.*

122

You need to practice your skill i.e. the **doing**, *before the demonstration to ensure that:*

1. *You can explain and demonstrate the skill at the same time.*
2. *You are confident in dealing with this double requirement.*
3. *You keep a smooth, polished performance and you locate any difficulties before you start.*
4. *You teach them* **one** *way of doing the skill, only.*
5. *You have made adequate arrangements for obtaining feedback.*
6. *You know how you are going to summarise, whether at the end of the demonstration, or at the end of each phase of the skill.*
7. *Everything works.*

PRACTICE MAKES PERFECT.

FIGURE 127

It is especially necessary to prepare a lesson plan to help with your explanation of the demonstration.

* A Motor Skills Lesson

Can you recollect where you made an outline of a skills lesson previously?

Well, it's a long time ago, way back in Component Eight, Study Unit Two, Package One, where we showed you an example of the instructional events of a skills lesson in Figure 289. Have a look at that now and at Figure 85, Component Two, Study Unit Two, Package Two, where we showed a similar layout in Lesson Plan Six.

Incidentally, in Figure 85, we did not divide the lesson plan into a Beginning, a Middle, and an End. Naturally you will will break the plan up like this, if you feel that it will help you and for some subjects such a division is essential. If you want to subdivide, the plan would look something like the version shown next:–

Methods of Training: Groupwork

LESSON PLAN SIX, SUBDIVIDED

GENERAL INFORMATION OBJECTIVES	TITLE OF LESSON	
TRAINER ACTIVITY.	LEARNING ACTIVITY.	RESOURCES EVALUATION.
BEGINNING Gaining attention Informing trainees of the objectives Stimulating recall of pre-requisites **MIDDLE** Presenting the stimulus material Providing learner guidance Eliciting the performance Providing Feedback (1) **END** Providing Feedback (2) Assessing Performance Retention Transfer		

FIGURE 128

Your Transfer (Generalisation) phase might well have to until another lesson, after the trainees have had more practice (eliciting the performance).

As another example let's use Lesson Plan Eight, from Component Two of this Study Unit as the basis for our motor skills lesson. We think that we shall have to use a fairly simple example of a motor skill so that everyone is familiar with it. We pick **changing the wheel of a car as the skill.**

USING MODIFIED LESSON PLANS, FIGURE 89, COMPONENT TWO: MOTOR SKILLS LESSON

GENERAL INFORMATION

COURSE TITLE: Introductory Car Mechanics.

TRAINING STAFF: Bob Wilson

LENGTH OF COURSE: Two months.   DATES: 23 March to 20 May.

DURATION OF SESSIONS: 90 minutes.

DAY AND TIME: 4 April. 0930 to 1100 hours.

VENUE: Workshop.

TARGET AUDIENCE: Trainee mechanics, Phase One.

JOB/OPERATION: Changing a car wheel.

TOOLS: Wheel brace; Jack.

RESOURCES: Spare wheel. Car owner's manual. Two cars.

OBJECTIVES: At the end of the lesson the trainee will be able to change a car wheel in 10 minutes, in the workshop or on the road, without error and in complete safety.

DEMONSTRATION (25 minutes)	TRAINEES OBSERVING. Q AND A
STAGES OF OPERATION	CUES/KEY POINTS
1. **Introduction**	
a) Show location of spare wheel, jack and wheel-brace	a) Note securing of spare wheel by retaining bolt.
b) Show appropriate pages in car owner's manual.	b) Mention use of warning triangle and safety at night.
c) Remove spare wheel, jack and wheelbrace.	c) Check pressure of spare.
2. **Jacking the vehicle**	
a) Apply handbrake	a) Check gradient. If necessary use wheel chocks on opposite side of vehicle.
b) Turn jack-handle until jack can be slid under vehicle	b) Check if ground is sufficiently firm to support jack.
c) Remove wheel trim.	
d) Loosen wheel bolts with wheel brace; half-turn anticlockwise.	d) Do not overloosen.
e) Locate channel in head of jack in flange under rocker panel.	e) Location shown by indentations on rocker panels at rear and front jacking points. Do not use in any other locations.

f) Position jack correctly.

g) Turn jack handle to lower jack base to ground.

h) Turn jack handle to raise vehicle so that wheel to be changed is well clear of ground.

3. **Removing Wheel**

a) Loosen off bolts and remove.

b) Remove wheel and place in boot.

c) Place spare wheel over locating pins.

d) Replace wheel bolts and tighten loosely.

e) Lower vehicle to ground by turning jack handle.

f) Remove jack and place in boot.

g) Tighten wheel bolts with wheelbrace.

4. **Checking**

a) Check pressure of spare again with vehicle standing on all four wheels.

b) Check wheel taken off is bolted securely in boot.

c) Check to find out if you have left anything lying around.

---

d) Locate jack positively.

e) Lower slowly and firmly.

f) Give adequate clearance: stop when clearance is adequate for inflated wheel. Do not get under vehicle when jacked up.

a) Put them where you'll find them easily.

d) Do not overtighten at this stage.

g) Tight, but not overtight.

a) Inflate, or deflate, to correct pressure, as soon as possible.

PRACTICE (55 minutes) Allow trainees to practice changing a wheel. Divide into two groups, one group to work on each car.	TRAINEES PRACTISING Q AND A
SUMMARY (10 minutes) Question and Answer Check these points carefully: a) all safety points b) correct positioning of jack c) tightness of wheel bolts Ask if trainees have any questions.	TRAINEES ANSWERING

EVALUATION

FOLLOW-UP EVALUATION

FIGURE 129

* Skills Lesson Checklist

We intend to summarise this Component by presenting you with a checklist for a skills lesson.

Write out your own list before you examine ours.

SKILLS LESSON CHECKLIST

1. Was the lesson given in a reasonably comfortable environment?
2. Were all the tools available and working?
3. Were all resources provided?
4. Did the trainees know the objectives of the lesson?
5. Did they know how the lesson related to past and future experiences?
6. Did the trainees have an adequate technical vocabulary?
7. Did they have appropriate pre-requisite skills?
8. Were they interested and motivated?
9. Did I demonstrate all of the necessary procedures of the skilled operation?
10. Were my explanations clear?
11. Were the skilled procedures ordered correctly and logically?
12. Did I emphasise all my cues and key points?
13. Was the procedure I showed the trainees the best for performing the operation?
14. Did I pace the demonstration correctly?
15. Could all the trainees see and hear the demonstration?
16. Did I practice before I started?
17. Did I demonstrate good practice and workmanship?
18. Did I summarise the lesson effectively?
19. Was there enough time for the lesson and were the lesson timings correct?
20. Did I follow the principles of planning and execution by
    a) demonstrating the skill in full?
    b) breaking the skill down into its parts?
    c) giving the trainees plenty of practice?
    d) ensuring feedback?
    e) teach in realistic conditions?
21. Did I emphasise all of the dangers?
22. Did I observe, practise and emphasise all of the safety rules?
23. Did I evaluate the lesson immediately, especially the efficiency and effectiveness of
    a) the demonstration by me?
    b) the practice by the trainees?
24. Have I carried out follow-up evaluation?

FIGURE 130

domain shown there to a skills lesson plan which you have written recently.

Send your work to your Programme Tutor for comment, if you wish.

This is the last of our Components on lessons, although we shall cover more points about effective teaching in subsequent Study Units. We now continue our consideration of delivering the learning to larger groups by examining the lecture method.

Although we have described the lesson as a method suitable for larger groups it has, of course, a wide range of uses and of group number which it can accommodate. Very large audiences and quite small numbers can be trained by lessons, but small groups of less than seven or eight trainees are usually often best taught by small group methods.

However, a lot depends on what you are training for and your subject.

Before you move on to the next Component, have a look at a skills lesson which you have taught recently and apply our Checklist to it. Write down what you find. Next, select a Lesson Plan which we have described in Component Two of this Study Unit and modify the lesson which we showed at Figure 129 to fit the different plan. Finally look at Figures 187 and 188 of Component Three, Study Unit Two, Package One and relate the categories of the psychomotor

Component 6:

Methods of delivering the learning to Larger Groups: The Lecture (1)

Key Words

Lecture method; "one-way" lectures ("Owl") and "two-way" lectures ("2WL"); introducing Plodworth, claims and counter-claims for Owl; advantages and disadvantages of Owl; the importance of trainee activity in lectures.

Introduction

The lecture method is still very widely used in training and in education, especially higher education. It is probably the oldest method of delivering the learning, **especially to larger groups**.

There are several types of lectures, which differ from each other in the way they are given, but basically there are only two main types.

▨▨▨ Checkpoint

What do you think these are?

Our answer is shown in the next diagram.

THE TWO BASIC METHODS OF LECTURING

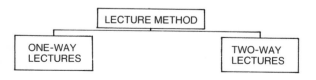

FIGURE 131

As part of our answer to this Checkpoint, we should define what we mean by these two types of lecture.

LECTURES: DEFINITIONS

A "one-way lecture" is a method of delivering the learning where one trainer teaches a group often numbering 20 or more, exclusively by **one-way communication,** usually by talking **at** the group.

A "two-way lecture" is a method of delivering the learning where one trainer teaches a group often numbering 20 or more, by **two-way communication,** usually by talking **at** and **with** the group and by **involving the trainees in learning activities.**

FIGURE 132

In this Component, we are going to consider:
Claims for the one-way method of lecturing.
Strengths and weaknesses of one-way lecturing.

* Claims for the One-Way Method of Lecturing

We are now going to introduce a colleague of ours, Mr. Plodworth, who is a middle-aged trainer in our department. Plodworth has been training for many years and a great deal of his teaching is carried out by one-way lecturing, which we call "OWL". He is a firm believer in this method and one day, after we had both been marking test papers, we took a break and I became involved with Plodworth in the following discussion in a scene which looked something like this.

INTRODUCING PLODWORTH

FIGURE 133

"You're looking a bit glum Plodworth!"

PLODWORTH: **"Not surprising. This last lot of results aren't too good."**

"Poor group, eh?"

PLODWORTH: **"Seems so. Don't seem to have picked up much of what I told them in the lectures."**

"Lectures? You mainly lecture to them, do you?"

PLODWORTH: **"Of course. Lecturing is a very good way of training. Always used it, always will. Best way to get the facts across to them, you know."**

"I see. When you use the term "lecturing" what do you mean exactly?"

PLODWORTH: **"Well telling them what they need to know. Nothing like a good talking to."**

"Using questions and all of that?"

PLODWORTH: **"Questions! (Plodworth snorts). Certainly not. No time for that. If they kept on asking questions, they'd interrupt my train of thought, wouldn't they? Sometimes, I pop in a few at the end, or ask them if they have any, but they never say much."**

"I call lecturing without questions, 'Owl'."

PLODWORTH: (Looking blank) **"Owl?"**

"Yes, 'Owl' stands for 'one-way lecturing and communication'. You're talking at them, one way, with nothing coming back from the trainees."

PLODWORTH: **"Really?"**

"There's no evidence from research to suggest that Owl is the best way of getting the facts across, you know."

PLODWORTH: **"No I didn't know!"**

"In fact, the trainees would probably learn just as much if they read a couple of books for themselves."

PLODWORTH: **"What're you saying? That I should just give them a book and tell them to get on**

with it? They won't work on their own you know. Not these days, anyway, not like we used to do!"

"I'm not so sure. We set our trainees some projects to do last month and I think they worked harder at them, than they do if we're watching them."

PLODWORTH: **"Well I'll admit that they do work hard at their projects. And produce some good material. But there's nothing like a good full timetable to keep them at it."**

"On the other hand, if they're doing nothing but attending lectures all of the time, then they have less time for their own work and for projects. That must be true."

PLODWORTH: **"Yes, but when they attend my lectures they have to think about what I'm saying. (Plodworth smiles smugly). I certainly believe I tax their grey matter."**

"Sorry Plodworth, but the evidence is all against what you're saying. One-way lecturing, 'Owl', as I said we call it, hasn't produced a single piece of evidence that lectures are more effective in producing thought than any other training method. Not one! Not effective thinking, that is. Somebody found that trainees do think about the subject passively and then forget it. And a lot of the time they are daydreaming about something else anyway!"

PLODWORTH: **"They take notes. They've got to think about that. (Plodworth smiles again). I'd like to believe that my trainees have a really good set of notes after coming to my lectures."**

"Well, no offence, Plodworth, but we've been checking on some notes written by trainees who've just had a dose of Owl and we found that they manage to note about one-fifth of the information that's put across. One-fifth, Plodworth!"

PLODWORTH: **"I find that hard to believe."**

"Then try it for yourself. Ask to see some of their notes after your lectures. Tell them you're checking on how well you have put the stuff across, not how well they write notes. You'll be surprised."

PLODWORTH: **"What at?"**

"Before you do your check, put down what you think are the main points of your lecture. I'll bet you (hesitates) a pound that they've only got about one in five of your main points."

PLODWORTH: **"You're on! You must be confident."**

"Certainly am. We've tried it out already, you see. You know what they say about lectures: a period when information passes from lecturers to students without going through the heads of either!"

PLODWORTH: **"Oh! Come on! Surely that's for bad lecturers. A good lecturer like me can certainly get it across."**

"You may be partly right. You might be so good that you can lecture reasonably effectively. But everybody thinks that they lecture well. Few of us are trained to lecture. However, the average lecturer and certainly the poor lecturer, cannot be efficient using Owl."

PLODWORTH: (Thinks for a while). **"I can see that point. (He glances around). We certainly have our whack of average lecturers around here."**

"Must have. By definition. Most of us have to rate only average, otherwise how would we have an average?"

PLODWORTH: (Thinks again). **"You're worrying me a bit, but there is one thing. When I've completed my lectures, I'm absolutely sure that I've covered all of the ground they need to know."**

"Mmmh! (shakes head). Not sure about that. You cover the ground in the sense that you go through your syllabus covering each topic, but you're not sure that your trainees are learning it as well."

PLODWORTH: **"Oh! Yes I am! I watch them for the old non-verbal cues, you know, facial expressions, how they are sitting. All of that."**

"Well, that's certainly good. It's important that all lecturers watch their audience closely. However, my point is that every member of your audience is different and they're all probably translating what you're saying, the ground you are covering, in different ways."

PLODWORTH: **"Well that's normal. That's life. That's what happens whatever activity you're engaged in with trainees."**

"Yes. But in Owl you don't get any feedback from the trainees, do you? After all, it's one-way communication. They don't ask you any questions and you usually don't ask them many. That's why it's called one-way, isn't it?"

PLODWORTH: **"OK. I must say, I've been a bit unhappy about that myself. Felt I could have got a bit closer to them at times."**
(Plodworth looks pensive).
Pause.
(Plodworth continues to look thoughtful, then asks a question).
"Have you ever felt that the trainees are dropping off to sleep, a bit, in your lectures?
(He looks a little embarrassed).

"Let me ask you a question first. Do you lecture straight — by that I mean talk most of the time — for an hour?"

PLODWORTH: **"Yes. Usually. What's wrong with that?"**

"That's it then. There's no doubt about it that your audience's attention drifts off badly after about twenty minutes. From that point on, you're almost wasting your time. Even when you're on form with some fascinating subject, half-an-hour is the maximum they can reasonably attend to what you're saying."

PLODWORTH: (sighing). **"More research evidence, I suppose?"**

"No doubt about it, friend! It's been proved by lots of research and it's widely accepted that concentration has declined radically half way through an hour's lecture."

PLODWORTH: **"Well, they do seem to drop off a bit. Mind you, they always come back towards the end."**

"True. Last five or ten minutes they do perk up a bit. They think it's all going to be over soon!"

PLODWORTH: **"I'm beginning to believe that it's a pity my lecture periods last an hour!"**

"It's funny, isn't it, how many times we are scheduled for an hour at a time."

PLODWORTH: **"Traditional, I suppose. Don't know why."**
(Plodworth brightens up). **"A lot of my trainees have said that they enjoy my lectures. What have you got to say to that?"**

"I'm sure they do. You can get some interesting stuff across in one-way communication. But that's not the question you should ask yourself."

PLODWORTH: **"What?"**

"Not the right question. You've got to be asking if other ways of training aren't more efficient. If they are, use them. And there's another question."

PLODWORTH (groans). **"I'm sure there is."**

"Have you asked yourself if there's a better way of lecturing than through one-way communication lectures?"

PLODWORTH: **"No. But there's one question I want to ask you. (He gives a little snort of triumph). And it's this. Why is it that there's so much lecturing going on in training? If it's so bad, I mean."**

"That's a 64,000 dollar question. (Pause). Tell you what, Plodworth, I'll give you a little lecture on that, right now. One-way, of course!" (Plodworth settles himself more comfortably into his chair, looking resigned).

PLODWORTH: **"OK. I'm ready."**

"Well, lecturing is still popular, Owl included, because many trainers — and teachers — are ignorant of any other ways of presenting their material. Even you, Plodworth, didn't know all that much about the evidence of the effectiveness of Owl. (Plodworth shifted uneasily). And everybody has a lot of work to do already. They think that different methods of training will take more time to prepare and the effects will take a long time to work through the system. There's a shortage of resources and Owl lecturing doesn't make great demands on resources. You know, a couple of slides and an OHP transparency, perhaps an A4 handout and that's it.
(Looking hard at Plodworth). "And there's always a great resistance to change amongst trainers. Some of us fear to lose our authority, perhaps even our status and the ego-boost we get from giving what we think is a good lecture.
(Plodworth looked uncomfortable).
Remember, we think it's a good lecture, but the trainees don't. A recent survey in the North showed that two-thirds of students thought that lectures 'were rarely or never stimulating'.

That's a terrible thought, Plodworth.
(Plodworth looks even more unhappy and uncomfortable).
Probably, we sense their feelings ourselves anyway. That's one reason why some of us don't trust the

trainees. We don't trust them to do any work on their own either. They probably feel that from us, too. Sometimes, trainers believe that opening up a lecture into a discussion, say, may take us past the point where we feel competent enough to cope. And that knocks out self-importance, as well.

Then there's the firm to think about. Some of the managers expect to see a list of lectures when they read our training schedules. Agreed, Plodworth?

(Plodworth nods).

So do some external validating bodies. They like to see hour-long lecture slots all neatly labelled with one topic from the syllabus each. Try telling the Support Staff Training Council that you are lecturing for, say 5% of your course only and they'll want to know why! You know something, Plodworth, if we didn't have lectures we'd have to think a hell of a lot more about how we design our courses, wouldn't we?

(Plodworth shrugs).

And half the time, there's only one trainer who knows what some of the lecture topics are about. No objectives are mentioned, for example. Anyway, part of our tests only ask for recall of information. Owl can usually manage to get across lumps of information, sometimes remembered in bits, but not understood. Like those tests you're marking now are showing, Plodworth. Plodworth! Are you asleep? (Slumbering Plodworth). Ah! You're coming around again. Our attention lapsed, did it? Just like in a one-way lecture?"

PLODWORTH: **"Yes. Sorry. Dropped off."**

(Plodworth yawns).

"Proof of the pudding, Plodworth. Proof of the pudding".

PLODWORTH: **"There's another question I'd like to ask. You've gone on and on about one-way lectures. What other sorts are there?"**

"Ah! Two-way lectures, of course".

PLODWORTH: **"Two-way?"**

Yes. Two-way communication in lectures. Where there's some interaction between you and the trainees."

PLODWORTH: **"Like questions?"**

"More than that. Questions, yes. But also where the trainees are active in lectures. You give them something to do, rather than their just sitting and listening, passively."

(Plodworth thinks deeply).

PLODWORTH: **"And where do I get information about two-way lecturing?"**

"Well, you've heard of the Training Technology Programme, I believe?"

PLODWORTH: **"Have indeed. That's what you've been writing about for ages, isn't it?"**

"Seems like years. Anyway, if you look at Package Two in the Programme you'll find a Study Unit Two in there and several Components which will tell what you want to know about two-way lectures."

PLODWORTH: **"OK. Where can I get a copy?"**

"I'll lend you one. Or you can buy one. Here's the adress to write to."

(Plodworth turns to his marking).

"Just one thing, Plodworth."

PLODWORTH: **"What now?"**

"You reckon that Owl has some advantages and the method can be useful at times. In short bursts, and keeping the talking down to twenty or thirty minutes a shot, I don't entirely disagree. What about you writing down the advantages of one-way lecturing and I'll list the disadvantages and we'll compare notes?"

PLODWORTH: **"Oh, OK. Might be worth a try."**

"See you tomorrow, then."

From what we have said so far in this Component and from your own experience, write down what might appear on the two lists.

---

* Strengths and Weaknesses of One-Way Lecturing

Here is what we imagine the two lists might look like: Plodworth's list (strengths) and mine (weaknesses).

STRENGTHS AND WEAKNESSES OF OWL

PLODWORTH'S LIST	MY LIST
*Lectures are cost-effective. You can train 50 trainees as easily as five.	*Lectures are cost-effective. But they do not provide for effective learning.
*Lectures convey information efficiently.	*They convey lower-level information e.g. knowledge, as well as most methods, but are poor at developing the mental skills of analysis, synthesis and evaluation. They offer little opportunity for application.
*Many trainees are familiar with and therefore comfortable in using lecture techniques.	*True. But we can all fall into a rut.
*An efficiently delivered lecture can stimulate learning.	*Only the very best trainers can deliver the learning goods by using lectures and even then they might produce better results by trying other ways.
*Lectures are popular with the trainees.	*Experience and research shows that lectures are unpopular with trainees: about 2/3 do not like them, especially the younger ones.
*Lectures are easy to mount.	*Agreed.
*Lectures cover more ground in a given time than active methods like group discussions.	*Whilst lectures are good at covering ground there is little evidence that the ground covered is understood well.
*The information given is covered consistently and uniformly.	*Lectures are bland and the information is pitched at "middle" level, which might be too fast for the weaker trainees and too slow for the best. So individual differences in trainees' abilities, interests and experience are taken little account of.
*Lectures are well-organised because they are produced by an expert.	*Really good lectures are systematically organised, but trainers aren't expert in everything and we all have off-days. There's no place to hide if you're not at your best when lecturing.
*The trainer can adapt the lecture to the time and equipment available.	*Adaptability in lectures is restricted by having to aim at satisfying "Mr Average Trainee".
*Content in lectures is adaptable.	* Content in lectures is adaptable within limits of providing for the average.
*A lecture can become spontaneous and the trainer can develop themes which interest him.	*The lecture can become side-tracked away from the main theme, unless the lecturer is careful to avoid digressions.
*A lecturer can always pick up non-verbal cues from the audience which show how far the audience are with him or her.	*One-way lectures don't allow trainee participation. It is difficult for the trainer to know where the audience are at. Often the trainees can look interested when they are not.
*The audience can always take notes and have a good record of the lecture. Follow-up can be made by personal tutorials of trainees with the trainer, on a one-to-one basis.	*Lecturers put a great stress on the audience having efficient skills in note-taking and often trainees don't have these skills. If the notes of trainees are read by the lecturer after the event it's amazing what they have missed. Tutorials are effective, if there is time for them.
	*Recall of information after a lecture is poor, dropping from about 30% the day after, to 10% the week after and to 5% later.
*Trainees can always read their lecture notes later.	*Research and experiences show that trainees usually do not refer to their notes more than once or twice after a lecture. They prefer their own notes made up from reading.
*Lectures give the opportunity for giving out handouts pointing up the main message of the lecture.	*Handouts in lectures are useful, but do the trainees need to attend the lecture to be given them, in the first place?
*Audio-visual presentations help lectures to be stimulating.	*Audio-visual presentation helps provide stimulus in lectures, but demand quite high levels of visual and aural concentration to be sustained.
	*Owl does not permit active trainee participation and precludes most effective learning activities.

*Lecturing is a method of delivering the learning to larger groups which has been used since the time of Socrates. It's well proven by time and will be used for ever.

*Although lecturing has a long history, newer methods are available which provide more efficient delivery of the learning message and therefore of learning. Excessive dependence on lectures prevents a lecturer from keeping up with the times and innovating.

FIGURE 134

Which of the strengths and weaknesses mentioned do you believe to be the most telling?

We think that the last two are. Lecturing by one-way communication, Owl, is really well-established and it is difficult to reduce the amount of lecturing which is done, or modify that type of delivery.

However, the greatest criticism of Owl, is its non-participative and non-active nature, from the learners' point of view. The lecturer actually does most of the work and paradoxically, therefore, of the learning. This can't be right.

HE'S BEEN LECTURING LIKE THAT A LONG TIME.

FIGURE 135

You can see how Plodworth and I tried to avoid repeating most of the points made in the discussion which we had with each other, previously. No point in going over old ground and maybe the dialogue had taught Plodworth something!

Clearly, a well-delivered, efficient lecture can cause learning, even if it is a one-way lecture. This is especially so where lower level cognitive objectives are to be attained, e.g. passing across knowledge. Many of Plodworth's points have a grain of truth in them and the occasional well-done lecture has a part in most training systems.

However, the key to all of this seems to be that Owl fails to generate trainee participation in effective learning activities.

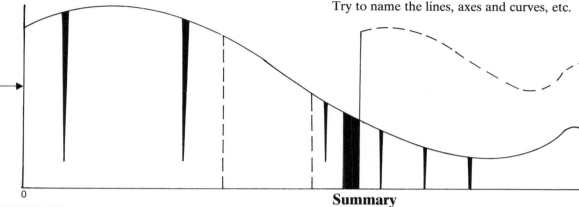

FIGURE 136

Can this situation be improved?

It certainly can be improved by using two-way communication in lectures. We call such lectures **"two-way lectures"** *or* **"2WL"** *and we are going to examine how 2WL can be used and organised in the next Component.*

Before you go on to that Component have a look at the next Figure and try to figure out what it is telling you. Try to name the lines, axes and curves, etc.

Summary

There are two basic methods of lecturing, which we have called "one-way" lectures "Owl" and "two-way" lectures (2WL).

Both may be delivered to large groups. In the one-way lecture the communication is only, or mainly, from the lecturers to the audience.

Whilst Owl has some advantages, such as "covering the ground", being cost-effective, traditional and therefore familiar to trainers, comparatively easy to prepare and organise, consistent and successful in imparting lower levels of knowledge, most of these "advantages" are rather mixed blessings. Even they have drawbacks inbuilt into the benefits which they seem to confer.

The list of disadvantages of Owl is long and weighty and includes the inability of one-way lectures to take account of differences between trainees, lack of feedback from the audience, incapacity to help the trainees analyse, synthesise and evaluate.

There is no way that a skill can be taught effectively by the lecture method and change of attitudes and values is unlikely without discussion, which Owl prevents.

The biggest single drawback of Owl is the inactivity of the audience and the fact that the lecturer is doing most of the work. Participation in learning activities is difficult with Owl and the time used in Owl lecturing could usually be better spent in other forms of learning.

However, used judiciously and sparingly, Owl can form **part** of a learning system, provided that it is well performed.

Active learning can be achieved by lectures, but mainly through two-way communication between the lecturers and the audience. Such two-way lectures, 2WL and the tactics which may be used to develop audience participation, are to be considered next.

Component 7:

Methods of delivering the learning to Larger Groups: The Lecture (2)

Key Words

 General Factors which affect learning in lectures; memory, including forgetting and remembering, attention, motivation; "trace decay"; retro and proactive interference; reinforcement; testing, ordering, questioning, sequencing; types of stimulation; declining attention; "microsleeps"; breaks; lecture "shapes"; buzz groups; types of lectures; general outline, tape-slide; video and film, epidiascope; Learnermass reappears.

Introduction

In this and the next Component we are focusing closely on the **two-way lecture** and how the lecturer may generate interaction with the audience.

In this Component we shall consider those factors which can affect lecturing and the lecturer, in fairly broad terms. Remember that much of what we say is applicable to other methods of training.

We will also look at various types of lecture, some of which are really only giving talks. So the structure of this Component is:—
   General Factors which affect learning in lectures.
   Types of lectures.
We shall begin with a Task Analysis of

* General Factors which Affect Learning in Lectures.

By considering these factors, we are setting the scene for developing the audience participation which is characteristic of 2WL.

▨▨▨ Checkpoint

Give some thought to what these factors might be and draw a flow diagram of them.

Our diagram is shown in the next figure

GENERAL LEARNING FACTORS IN LECTURES

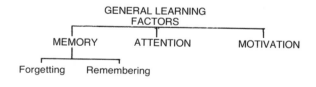

FIGURE 137

Let's have a look at each of these in turn.

* Memory.
There are two broad areas here:
a) "Why do trainees forget?" and b) "How does the trainer help remembering?" Let's examine both of these areas.

a) **Why do trainees forget?** These general factors could apply to anybody, not just trainees who form a lecture audience. So we all forget because of

— **"Trace decay."** Everybody forgets much of what they have been told in the first five or six seconds after the telling. The "trace" of the memory is lost very rapidly.

Trainers can help by writing their most important points on an OHP or blackboard; this helps delay trace decay.

— **Retroactive interference.** What we are told **first** becomes camouflaged by what we are told later or what happens later. The second telling, or event confuses and partly obliterates the memory of the first, especially if the subjects are similar.

RETRO OR PROACTIVE?

FIGURE 138

We consider that there is retroactive interference here. The trainer formulated the intention of putting on his pants, then something interfered and he forgot!

— **Proactive interference.** This is the other way round and this type of forgetting is not as powerful as retroactive. In this case what is learned **second** is interfered with by what has been learned first.

— **The middle piece** of a lecture often suffers from both retroactive and proactive interference.
   If you leave a few seconds for what you have said to "sink in", then these types of interference are minimised.

— **Learning overmuch.** Obviously if you try to remember too much, you forget.
   Equally obviously, you'll need to restrict the information which you give in lectures and structure it well. Clear structures aid memory.

b) **How does the trainer help remembering?**

Well, we're sure you know lots of ways of helping the trainees remember, so write a few down before you look at ours.

GETTING THE TRAINEES KNOTTED

FIGURE 139

We really don't think that tying the trainees in knots helps a great deal, even if tying a knot in your handkerchief is supposed to help you remember.

Some more orthodox ways of **assisting memory** are to:

— **Reinforce** what you say by repeating it.

— **Rehearse** what the trainees have heard by applying it to a problem or a practical situation, or

— **Test** what they have learned, immediately.

— **Make what you give meaningful** to the trainees by showing how it links with what they know already and how it fits in, or applies to their job directly.

— **Order** your lecture content logically; this will avoid confusion and clearly organised material is easier to remember.

— **Question** the audience to provide feedback about where you all are.

— **Sequencing:** do you remember the rules of sequencing from Component Five, Study Unit One, Package One?
Of course you do, but just in case . . .
   Proceed from the
   Known to the Unknown
   Concrete to the Abstract
   Observation to Reasoning
   Simple to the Complex
   What happens First to what happens Next
   (chronological order)
   The Whole view to the Part view, back to the Whole view.

All of these are general aids to memory; we will give more examples of a specific nature later in this Component and in the next Component, provided we don't forget through_____?_____interference!
                                      (retroactive interference)

Now what about attention, the second major factor in our Task Analysis shown in Figure 137?

* Attention

If the trainees don't concentrate on what you are saying and doing in the lecture, or anywhere else, they are not going to learn much.

▰▰▰

How do you engage the trainee's attention and ensure concentration? Mention general points, only.

There are many ways. We give a few below.

— **Vary the types of stimulation** which you give the trainees.

In **auditory** stimulation, use the full range of your voice, whisper occasionally, making them strain to hear for short periods, alternate your normal tone with an occasional bellow, let them hear each other's voices discussion and answering questions, play audio tapes.

Use **visuals:** OHP's photographs, charts and in discussion and answering questions, play audio tapes.
— **Move** around yourself so that they have to follow your movement, but don't overdo this, otherwise you will interrupt their concentration. Move **them** to, "Come and look at this", "Stretch yourselves for a minute" etc.
— **Change your pace:** talk quickly, with "quickfire" questions, say, through an easy section, appear to go very slowly then pick up the pace again by speaking at normal speed. Vary the intensity of delivery by

relaxing your attitude, then becoming more intense and projecting strongly.
— **Try** something **different;** be novel. Show them unusual realia, like a skull, or a paste jewel, or flash some lights (a favourite method in discos of providing stimulation).

TRY SOMETHING NOVEL

FIGURE 140

— **Humour** helps to change pace and relax the audience.
— **Make signals** like, "Listen! this is important", or, "Now! What have I just said?" or, "Right, summarise the lesson so far", or, "I want you to . . . . . .", or, "Everybody! Will you all . . . . . .".
— **Give them a break.** Have another look at Figure 136 at the end of the last Component. What did you make of it?

What it shows is the decline in the attention of an audience over an hour's lecture. Here is the full Figure.

DECLINING ATTENTION

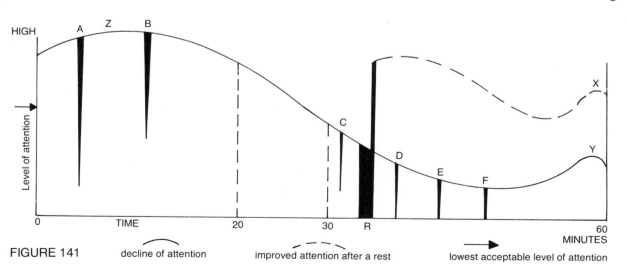

FIGURE 141

▰▰▰

Now you have seen the full Figure, say what you think it means.

The Figure shows how the attention of a trainee declines in a lecture. The lecture begins at "0" and ends after sixty minutes. After twenty minutes you are definitely beginning to lose the audience and after 30 minutes attention has dropped to a level which is unacceptably low. An "Acceptable level" is where the audience is attending well enough to learn something.

At about 35 minutes you gave a break of about two or three minutes and that improved attention as shown by the pecked line. The solid black shading shows *complete loss of attention, as would happen in the short rest period, R, and at A, B, C, D, E and F.*

A to F are "microsleeps", where the attention of the trainee has been lost, because he has wandered away completely and is "daydreaming". There can be a dozen or more microsleeps in any lecture for a single individual, depending on the powers of concentration of the trainee, how interested the trainee is and on how well the lecturer is performing. At A and B and C concentration went below an acceptable level and at D, E and F (where the lecturer did not give a break) you lost the trainee completely and he saw, heard and learned nothing. X and Y show the slight "perking up" of attention at the end of a lecture, when the audience thinks they are going to be freed soon. Z is the period of maximum concentration.

SWEET DREAMS!

FIGURE 142

So, if you want to buck up attention give them a break!

Incidentally during a lecture, your own level of performance also shows a decrement, roughly parallel to that of a trainee, but with you as a lecturer operating at a more active level throughout.

Acting on the axiom that "a change is as good as a rest", breaking your lecture up into other activities which the audience performs, like discussions, has the same beneficial effect on concentration as a rest. Buzz groups, considered later, also provide good changes.

Draw a diagram, on the lines of Figure 141, to show how dividing up a lecture into active periods and talk periods can sustain attention.

Our diagram is shown next.

A TYPICAL 2WL

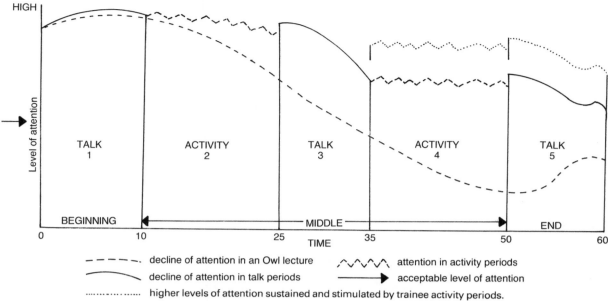

FIGURE 143

Figure 143 shows how it is possible to maintain trainee attention by interspersing periods of talking by the lecturer (1, 3 and 5) with periods where the trainees carry out an activity themselves (2 and 4). The talk periods last for ten minutes each and the activity for fifteen minutes each.

In practice, concentration during activity periods tends to vary up and down as shown by the pecked line, but it is generally high. Such activity periods could take the form of small trainee discussion groups which discuss a problem or point which you have suggested. Each then report their views back to the whole group towards the end of the activity period, answering further questions which you pose about their discussion and findings.

Attention tends to remain high in the shorter talk periods, 1, 3 and 5, because the trainees are keen to hear what you have to say about their findings, to answer questions on their discussion or activity and to prepare for what they have to do next.

This, then, is one "shape" for one type of two-way communication lecture, 2WL. The decline in attention for an Owl is shown by the dotted line in Figure 139 and makes an interesting comparison with 2WL.

2WL can take various forms, depending on the proportions of trainer talk and trainee activity. The next diagram shows another shape, where a great deal of discussion takes place in the lecture.

In 143 and the following Figures the Activity periods themselves (2, 4, 6) could have been shown at a level of attention **above,** or partly above, the level of the previous talk periods (1, 3, 5, 7). This is an alternative way of drawing these graphs, showing how trainee activity actually **raises** attention. These higher levels of attention, sustained and stimulated by trainee activity, are shown by dotted lines in the Figures.

WHERE 2WL RUNS INTO A DISCUSSION GROUP
SHAPE

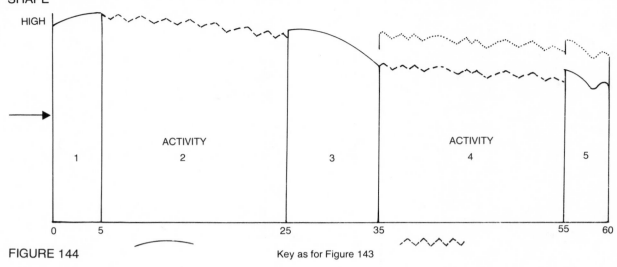

FIGURE 144   Key as for Figure 143

In Figure 144, the activity periods 2 and 4, are much longer and the talk periods, 1 and 3 really only set the scene for them as well as providing a summary at 5. A 2WL shape like this is bordering on the shape for a discussion group.

A BUZZ-GROUP 2WL

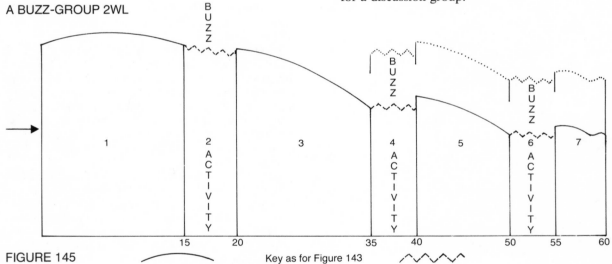

FIGURE 145   Key as for Figure 143

Figure 145 is a characteristic shape for a "buzz" group lecture. Here the trainees are asked to discuss a question or problem, which the lecturer has set them, for about five minutes. The talk periods are then used to discuss their conclusions and to introduce new material. We shall discuss this in detail in the next Component.

As you can see, there are three buzz groups in this 2WL. They arrest decrement in attention, sustaining it at an acceptable level throughout the lecture.

As a comparison with these 2WL shapes, draw what you believe should be a typical shape for a skills lesson.

We show this in the next Figure.

SHAPE FOR A SKILLS LESSON

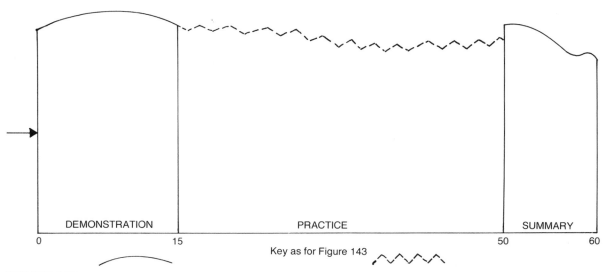

DEMONSTRATION   PRACTICE   SUMMARY

0   15   50   60

Key as for Figure 143

FIGURE 146

The comparison is an interesting one, isn't it?

Generally, it shows that it is possible to sustain a higher level of concentration in a skills lesson and proves the significance of active participation by trainees in successful learning.

The pecked line can vary considerably, depending on what the trainees are doing and on their skilled capability.

You should now relate the shapes which we have shown in Figures 141, 143, 144, and 145 to other training methods, perhaps drawing some more diagrams, in rough, for yourself.

There are other types of lecture, in addition to Owl and 2WL and we shall look at these briefly now.

* Types of Lectures

* General Outline Lectures.

Here the trainees are given a guide to the lecture which shows all of the headings which the lecturer is to follow. The trainees then write notes into the appropriate spaces, adding further notes and references later.

Write down the headings which you would use for one of your lectures. Make a decision as to whether you will also name sub-headings (this will depend on the nature of your subject and the time you have available).

Here is an example. Note that this outline would be on two sides of A4 paper, in practice. We have squashed it up to save space.

OUTLINE HEADINGS FOR A LECTURE

OUTLINE SHEET

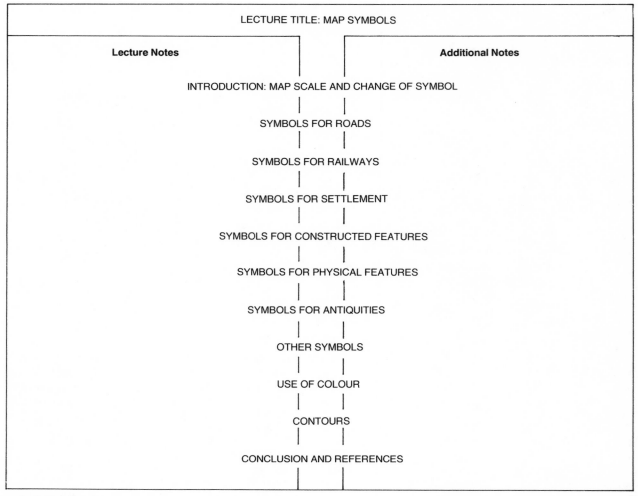

LECTURE TITLE: MAP SYMBOLS	
Lecture Notes	**Additional Notes**

INTRODUCTION: MAP SCALE AND CHANGE OF SYMBOL

SYMBOLS FOR ROADS

SYMBOLS FOR RAILWAYS

SYMBOLS FOR SETTLEMENT

SYMBOLS FOR CONSTRUCTED FEATURES

SYMBOLS FOR PHYSICAL FEATURES

SYMBOLS FOR ANTIQUITIES

OTHER SYMBOLS

USE OF COLOUR

CONTOURS

CONCLUSION AND REFERENCES

FIGURE 147

A LIGHTED ARROWHEAD

From time to time, you should check the completed outline sheets after a couple of weeks to see who has done any extra reading.

* Tape-slide lecture.
Lectures are always brightened with an audio tape or a tape-slide programme, or just slides themselves, with you adding commentary. Be careful to make definite points with each slide, or during the audio tape, otherwise the trainees will drop off to sleep in the dark!

If you wish to avoid this situation a useful ploy is to use an illuminated arrowhead. This device is battery driven and throws a lighted arrowhead onto the screen, like this, actual size.

The moving arrowhead helps the lecturer to keep trainees' attention.

We also use the arrowhead to "spotlight" trainees for questioning: ask a question and then spotlight the trainee who is to answer with the arrowhead. Good for concentration, this!

"ARROWHEADING"

FIGURE 148

* Realia Lecture

Bringing a piece of real-life, or realia into the lecture room is a type of lecture which provokes interest. Show the trainees the actual piece of equipment, experiment or machine, or produce a model if the real thing is not available or is too large.

REALIA IN THE LECTURE ROOM

FIGURE 148A

* **Video lecture.** Much like the tape-slide lecture, but more difficult to control and to emphasise the significant points which you wish to make.

Why is this and how can you avoid it?

The video is a continuous offering of information and can take a bit of "digesting" by the trainees. Unless it is specially made up for the job a lot of information is missed.

So avoid this by using the **pause button** *on the video cassette recorder, either before and after the main events.*

During the pause, you can say, "Now what is the significance of what we've just seen?" or "The next bit is important. Watch carefully. I'll ask you what's going on when we've seen it".

Of course, you'll need to know your video backwards so that you pause at exactly the right time.

Film lectures compound the difficulties of the videotape lecture and can't be paused.

So be careful to outline the main points before and after the film is shown.

* **Epidiascope lectures.**
These were very commonly used before video and film became so popular. They can be very useful in projecting complicated diagrams and lightweight epidiascopes are now available.

The heavy, brass-bound epidiascopes of yesteryear were difficult to manage and this technique became unpopular, consequently. OHP's can also reproduce diagrams faithfully and are more easily handled, but the epidiascope is particularly good for showing actual photographs and illustrations.

An Epidiascope is worth occasional use because of the different stimulus which it provides to the audience and it is better for pacing the lecture than video and film. It also encourages the trainees to use the books which they see projected and there are no copyright problems.

Most of the types of lectures which we just described have a lot more variety in them than the typical Owl. However, they are not truly interactive in the manner of 2WL, which we shall discuss in the next Component.

Summary
There are three learning factors of a general nature which affect the lecture and the performance of the trainer as lecturer.

These factors are concerned with memory, including forgetting and remembering, with attention and with motivation.

Attention declines in a one-way lecture, where the lecturer is concerned with talking mainly **at** the trainees rather than **with** them. The decrement in attention in Owl is very marked after twenty minutes and falls below an acceptable level after half-an-hour.

During microsleeps the trainee in the audience daydreams and loses concentration entirely.

Attention can be improved by giving the audience a rest break after thirty minutes, or by including activities for the trainees during the lecture. Attention is sustained during these participatory periods and this transforms the shape of the lecture by keeping interest and concentration at higher levels.

Such sessions of activity can vary from the buzz group, which occupies four or five minutes of interaction between the members of the audience, to longer periods of up to fifteen minutes at one "go". Eventually, lengthening the periods of activity, which usually involve discussion between the trainees, changes the shape from that of a lecture towards that of a discussion group.

By contrast a skills lesson, which includes a large proportion of practice by the trainees, usually sustains a high level of interest and concentration throughout.

There are various other types of lectures, in addition to Owl and 2WL, often involving the projection of still or moving images and these do increase the degree and frequency of stimulation in a lecture. All are suitable for delivering the learning to larger groups, but they are still largely trainer-centred.

Consequently, non-interactive lectures of the Owl type especially, do cause loss of attention by the trainees in the audience because they engender only limited participation and they do not succeed in distinguishing between members of the audience.

As a consequence, Learnermass still survives in the form of one-way lecture audiences, yet to be banished in the next Component by 2WL.

THE SURVIVAL OF LEARNERMASS

FIGURE 149

Before reading the next part of the Study Unit, develop ways in which you would encourage trainee activity in lectures, building upon the material which we have considered in this Component and drawing upon your own experience. Ask your Programme Tutor to comment on your proposals.

Component 8:

Methods of delivering the learning to Larger Groups: The Lecture (3)

Key Words

 Owl; 2WL; 2WL with multi-way communication; communication and interaction in 2WL; telling the trainees where they are going in a lecture; keeping the trainees active; questions, "buzz" groups, "pyramiding" duos, jury voting, trial by jury, notes and diagrams, handouts, testing, asking opinion; planning lectures; preparing for the lecture; the lecture plan; learning activities.

Introduction

We said at the end of the last Component that lecturing is a trainer-centered method of training. Some forms of lecturing, like Owl, emphasise this orientation; others move away from it by using learner activities.

We know already that learning activities play an essential part in effective learning, so we should now consider how we can develop trainee participation in lectures. Basically, we can begin by making the lecture a two-way communication between the lecturer and the audience. We can support this by developing interaction between the trainees themselves. Here we have a **multi-way communication** system.

For the sake of simplicity we shall use the term **"two-way lectures"**, 2WL, for those lectures which involve

— audience activity, communication and interaction between the lecturer and the trainees, and,
— audience activity, communication and interaction between the trainees themselves.

The best and most effective of 2WL's are those which develop multi-way communication and interaction.

▨▨▨ Checkpoint

Draw simple diagrams to illustrate communication and interaction in:—
a) Owl lectures
b) 2WL's
c) 2WL's with multi-way communication.

Our diagrams are shown in the next three figures.

COMMUNICATION IN OWL

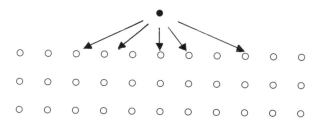

● Lecturer

○ Audience

→ Communication

FIGURE 150

COMMUNICATION AND INTERACTION IN 2WL

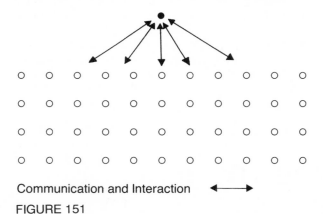

Communication and Interaction ⟷

FIGURE 151

MULTI-WAY COMMUNICATION AND
INTERACTION IN 2WL

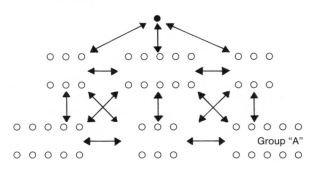

Group "A"

Group "A" Interaction

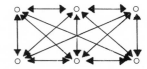

Multi-way
Communication
and
Interaction

FIGURE 152

Obviously, we can't draw all of the possible interactions and our last three Figures are simplistic. However, we hope that they show what we mean by 2WL interaction and communication, in broad terms.

In this Component we are going to examine this **communication** and **interaction** in 2WL more closely. As the goal of communication and interaction is to make the lecture audience **active**, we are also dealing here with **learning activities**, which we have discussed previously in Study Unit One.

Before the trainees begin their learning activities, they need to know where they are going, so we'll look at this aspect of lectures first.

Naturally, an effective lecture depends on **organisation**, so we shall examine the **planning** and **preparation** of lectures, as well.

Thus the structure of this Component is to be:
Telling the trainees where they are going in a lecture.
Keeping the trainees active.
Planning lectures.

* Telling the Trainees Where They Are Going in a Lecture.

In some ways the beginning of a lecture is like the beginning of a lesson. So glance back at Component Three of Study Unit 2 and then sort out some ways of **putting the trainees in the picture** about the lecture which you are about to give.

Our suggestions follow:

1. *State the **objectives** for the lecture, clearly. Use on OHP if necessary. If you have adopted the technique of using key words at the beginning (like this Programme) and keep the objectives until the end, then list your **key words** on an OHP or handout.

2. *Use an **advance organiser** for the lecture topics.

3. *Specify relevant **reference** material, e.g. textbooks, manuals, articles and handouts.

4. *Give the trainees an idea of the general **shape** of the lecture and how it will include various **activities, visuals,** and **breaks**, etc.

5. *Emphasise that they are welcome to ask you **questions** (and look pleased when they do!)

6. **Show** them the **structure** of the lecture by using an OHP or a (Chalk, white, magnetic, felt) board. **Talk** about it. Make sure they know which **topics/ contents/skills/concepts/issues** that you are going to consider. Above all give them a strong visual stimulus which fixes the order, the **logicality and organisation** of your structure.

   Many of the **flow diagrams** which we use are suitable for showing the structure of lectures. **Spray diagrams** can be used, but you'll have to pick out the most important parts in different colours, otherwise the mass of information may be confusing.

   Content and method maps are helpful, but once again you'll have to distinguish the important pieces from the rest of the detail.

   If you are centering your lecture on a **problem**, or problems, then give them an idea of the problem early in the lecture, writing it down or showing it on an OHP.

   It is often useful to have two OHP's in a lecture. One is for display of structure showing topics, problems or objectives (or all of those on two or three transparencies) and the other for use as you develop your lecture. You refer back to the structure by switching the first OHP on from time to time.

   35 mm Slide Projectors can be used effectively in the same manner.

7. *Make a **connection** between what you and the trainees did in your last **lecture(s)** and how today's job links in with the **next lecture**.

MAKING A CONNECTION

FIGURE 153

Our trainer in the last Figure is making his connections so that trainees know how this lecture **fits** into the system.

8. *Pursuing the railway analogy, give the trainees a **"timetable"** showing how your lecture is part of a series. This timetable may include **lecture titles**, a **commentary** on each, **book references, coursework** expected from the lecture material, **assessment criteria.** Your trainees will come to regard your timetable as a **course guide,** detailing your **lecture programme.**

9. *If you have an **overall theme** in your lecture series, hark back to it constantly. If, for example, you are discussing course design (see Package One) constantly show how the current lecture (say on Task Analysis) fits into the whole design system by displaying that **whole system** on, say, an OHP.

Now the audience knows where it is going, you want to make sure that the trainees stay with you during the journey. That leads us to

* Keeping the Trainees Active

We have seen the importance of developing activities if we are to deliver successful learning in our lectures. **So let's examine now what these learning activities are and how we can make our lectures effective by using them.** There are twelve of these **Activities.**

We'll start with that fundamental of effective teaching, Questions.

Activity 1. *Questions. As we learned in Component Four of this Study Unit, well-organised and timed questions are invaluable agents in stimulating the trainees and in keeping their concentration at high levels.

This is probably the best and simplest way of changing Owl into 2WL, by engendering that vital exchange between the trainer who is lecturing and his audience.

Be sure to pre-plan questions on the key points of the lecture. Although you may not have quite as much time to develop questions as in a lesson, nevertheless, effective questioning is always found in active lecturing.

Activity 2. *"Buzz" groups are used to set the lecture buzzing and are so-called because of the noise which is created when they are working! Accept this; it's part of the nature of this activity.

The steps in **operating a buzz group** are:—

> — **Pair** the audience off; in very large groups you may have to divide into threes or fours.
> — Set a **task** for each buzz group to consider. Such a task could be to solve a small problem, or review the lecture so far, apply the material which has been given, or prepare for the next part of the lecture.
> — Let the buzz groups operate for two to five minutes of **discussion**.
> — Ask one group only to **comment** on their findings to the whole audience.
> — Finally, give **your own views** on the material which the buzz groups have been considering.
>
> After a buzz group, you'll find that attention is restored for another fifteen minutes or so, when you can all buzz again. If you wish, the last stage, reporting back, can be omitted.

BUZZ GROUP TECHNIQUE

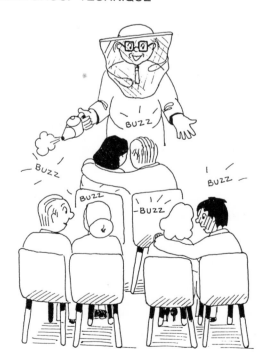

FIGURE 154

Activity 3. *Extended Buzz Groups. The buzz group may be extended into groups of five or six trainees, who consider the solution to a problem or apply new ideas. These topics are more penetrating and demanding than those used in a normal buzz group.

Extended Buzz Groups are allowed ten or fifteen minutes to grapple with the problem and then each group, number permitting, present their solution or application to the whole audience, taking a few minutes to do so.

This reporting back is an **essential** function of the extended buzz group, but not of the ordinary buzz group. If the lecture audience is very large, only three or four groups may be able to report back.

However, it is very important that the findings, solutions and observations are reported and are commented on by the audience and the lecturer.

Consequently, whilst you can manage four or five ordinary buzzes in a lecture, you will only have time for a couple of extended buzz groups. Or, try a mixture of a couple of ordinary buzz groups and one extended.

Activity 4. *Reading Buzz Groups. Give the trainees a short photocopied reference, or a handout and ask them to discuss it in groups of six to ten, either in the lecture room or elsewhere. Allow about fifteen minutes for this exercise then have each group report on their observations of the readings, giving them five minutes to do so. Frequently, they will pick on one or two spokespersons to do this.

You will find you have to be strict about the time allowed for discussion and presentation, as the trainees almost always want longer than you have told them is available.

Activity 5. *"Pyramiding". This is a very popular way of producing activity amongst the audience. Here is how it works:—

YOU SAY: "Right, I've described how urban rent theory works. Now I want you to think about how it operates in Sunderland. You have five minutes to list the main points of application. Work alone."

AFTER FIVE MINUTES. "Now divide in pairs and check the main points on each other's lists. Try to make sure that you agree on the main factors. Five minutes should do."

AFTER ANOTHER FIVE MINUTES. "OK, please make up fours by combining two pairs. Agree on the main stages of your application and then list the variables which apply to each stage. Give some local examples to support your statements.

I'm going to ask a couple of groups to tell us all what they decided.

Fifteen minutes will be enough for that."

AFTER FIFTEEN MINUTES. "Time's up now. Could that group over there tell us about their findings, please?"

AFTER THE FIRST GROUP STATEMENT (three or four minutes). "Right. Can another group now describe their application to us?"

AFTER SECOND GROUP STATEMENT. "Does the third group over there see this differently?"

FINALLY. "Any more comments on what's been said?" After these comments, "I'll try to sum up now" or, "Would the fourth group sum it up for us?"

Using the pyramid technique does take time, but is very useful in helping the trainees sort out their thoughts and can be used for very large groups.

It is helpful if the groups of four pick someone to report their findings at the beginning of their discussion. Ask the groups a few questions on their findings to keep them on their toes. Pick people who haven't contributed much, so far.

You may have to help groups organise themselves when you pyramid for the first time, but they soon get the hang of it and become confident in this tactic and in speaking to the group.

The pairing technique can be used widely in different lecture situations, especially to help the trainees through difficult parts of a lecture by discussing problems which have arisen, with each other.

A DISTANT VIEW OF A LEARNING ACTIVITY

FIGURE 155

Activity 6. *Duos and Debates. Lecturers can give a lecture as a twosome, each offering part of the lecture by alternating their presentation or by giving opposing viewpoints.

This method can be extended by dividing the whole audience into halves and **debating** an issue, for and against.

Activity 7. *Jury Voting. Having asked the audience to prepare a topic a couple of weeks previously you select two teams of, say, three or four trainees each and ask them to support opposing viewpoints on some controversial or two-sided issue.

Each team presents their case for four or five minutes per person, making their own points and trying to refute the claims of the other team.

The remainder of the audience acts as a "jury" and votes on which side made the best presentation.

Whilst this method appears to be similar to a debate, there are differences:

— The audience, or "jury" is given fifteen minutes before the teams make their presentations to decide which main points they consider the teams should bring out.

— The jury can ask questions of the teams when they are presenting their cases.

The lecturer sums up after the vote.

Activity 8. *Trial by Jury. Having been warned previously (three or four weeks are necessary) one member of the group is accused of some alleged crime, e.g. being accused of "persistently using Owl", or of "transgressing the organisation's staff relations policy", or of "disregarding safety regulations" etc.

The "accused" must be a knowledgeable individual and pretty stable in being able to withstand questioning and not taking it personally. At the same time, i.e. three or four weeks before the event, the accused is given three defence "lawyers". On the other side you select and warn three "prosecutors" and you pick three "judges". Alternatively, the trainees can choose their own representatives.

At the beginning of the trial you give the defence and the prosecutors a final twenty minutes to put their case together. This short period is only for last minute organisation. Usually defence and prosecution teams meet several times during the previous weeks to sort out their positions.

The "jury", that is the remainder of the audience, discuss amongst themselves the points which they believe both prosecution and defence ought to bring out, i.e. the strengths and weaknesses of the topic under consideration and of the accused's position. The twenty minute period immediately before the trial is used for this discussion.

The accused then takes the stand, usually a centrally situated chair and the judges take their places.

The "trial" now begins, prosecution leading. Apart from presenting their case initially, both prosecuting and defending teams have to refute the points of the other team, as well as making their own.

The judges run the trial, ensuring that each individual presentation by prosecution or defence lasts exactly five minutes. Whilst prosecutors and defence present points, they are mainly concerned with questioning the accused to prove their own case and to refute that of the other side. The judges, who can ask questions of the accused also, must ensure that prosecutors and defenders spend most of their time questioning and not addressing the jury in long monologues.

After half-an-hour (six periods of five minutes allotted to each member of each team), the judges sum up the evidence. Each judge is allowed three minutes to do this.

The jury then votes on whether the accused is "guilty" or not. Judges must strive for impartiality.

If guilty, the chief judge pronounces some humorous sentence, such as, "Sentenced to one extra assignment", or "Sit through two additional Owls."

After sentence, the jury is allowed ten minutes in which comment on cases presented by defence and prosecution, highlighting strengths and weaknesses of each.

Finally, the lecturer may wish to sum up for a few minutes.

Considerable interest and excitement is generated in a trial by jury, but a lot does depend on the abilities of the defence and prosecution teams to make their points succinctly and tellingly and to question with penetration and relevance. So pick teams which are balanced in their abilities.

However, it is a fact that you can never tell how well they will perform on the day nor how able they are at using questioning techniques of this type.

Feelings can sometimes run high in this unusual type of role play.

TAKING A WIGGING

FIGURE 156

Activity 9. *Notes and diagrams. Another way of promoting attention is to have the trainees exchange their notes a couple of times during the lecture.

Reading through each other's notes encourages the trainees to concentrate on what you are saying and to write something neat and intelligible. Frequently, they find they have missed important points which the other has remarked.

Note-taking can be improved further if you do not allow the audience to write anything when you are actually talking in the lecture. Trainees then have to attend your points closely, so that they can remember what to write down later and they have to think actively to sort out your main points. Give them a few minutes now and then to write up short notes.

Alternatively, you can restrict note-taking to the writing down of key points only, to be filled out later by recommended reading. Give the trainees examples of this key-point note-taking.

NOW HERE'S AN EXAMPLE OF GOOD NOTE-TAKING

FIGURE 157

Yet another technique is to warn the trainees at the beginning of the lecture that they will be required to identify individually the three or four most significant points at the end. Discussion can be allowed around the differences in what individuals have believed to be important.

Diagrams are an effective way of summarising material and provide yet another technique which causes the trainees to be active.

For example, the lecturer can say, "For the past 25 minutes I've talked about and demonstrated the correct stages in tiling a wall. I want you to draw a flow diagram showing these steps. You have five minutes."

(You'll have used flow diagrams before, so the trainees will know how these are drawn).

"Now I want a volunteer to draw his diagram on the board for us."

Finally, you can show your own flow-diagram on the OHP.

A similar exercise is to show a flow-chart of your own on an OHP and ask the trainees to fill in the gaps which you have left deliberately.

Another example of this technique for encouraging trainee activity in lectures is to complete a diagram as we did in Figure 136, complete in itself, but with names omitted. You then add the legends and the key, with the trainee's advice, on an OHP in the lecture room.

Alternatively, you may prefer to give out the unlabelled diagram and have the trainees complete it in pairs, or individually.

Sometimes a complete diagram can be shown on the OHP, or board, which illustrates material not yet explained, but which the trainees already know something about, e.g. by having pre-requisite knowledge. They then describe what they think the diagram shows.

Activity 10. *Handouts. Whilst full handouts are useful to trainees, they frequently "Switch off" completely in lectures if they believe the information is to be given to them in this way.

So leave **gaps** in your handouts which the trainees have to fill in for themselves. You can

> — List points, 1 .... 2 .... 3 ....
> — Write headings with no notes beneath them.
> — Half finish calculations.
> — Include direct questions.
> — List six major points in the conclusion and ask for the trainees to fill in the detail about the points.
> — Give detail, asking for suitable headings.
> — Give a couple of multiple choice questions.
> — Dictate a few explanatory lines and ask the trainees to select suitable sentences or phrases from a handout to complete the dictated lines.
> This exercise has its humorous aspects when mis-matches occur.

Activity 11. *Testing. Not a popular technique, this, but very effective.

Either tell the trainees that they are going to be tested at the end, or,

Spring a "spot" test either during or at the end of the lecture. If you spot test frequently, they'll come to expect it from you and that will keep them on the edge of their seats.

SPOT ON!

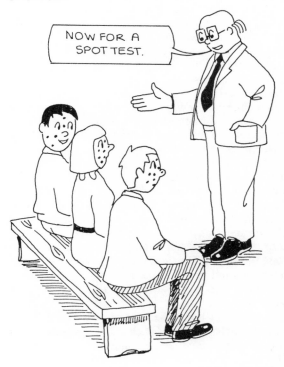

FIGURE 158

A milder form of testing is to ask the trainees to write down what they believe to be the specific objectives of the lecture. Don't be disappointed with the results! This exercise may be used frequently if you have adopted the technique of giving out key words at the start of a lecture, rather than objectives.

Alternatively, say "Now, I'm going to let you ask me some test questions. Make up one tough question on this lecture with your neighbour and then I'll ask four pairs to test me to see if I really know my stuff! You can include suitable material in your questions which you've read or learned elsewhere but it must be relevant to this lecture. You have three minutes to make up your questions."

The trainees love turning the tables!

Finally, you can say, "OK. That's the end of the lecture. Next week I'm going to ask each of you (or some of you) for one good reading reference. I'll want the name of the textbook, article or journal, date of publication and a brief summary in about twenty or thirty words of what the author has to say."

Activity 12. *Asking opinion. If you've been presenting a controversial issue, have prepared rating scales for handing out, to the lecture audience.

Ask the trainees to fill in the scales (see Component Three, Study Unit One, Package One) indicating their opinion in the appropriate box. Their responses are returned to you.

Now give the audience another topic to discuss whilst you work through the rating scales quickly to find out what they indicate about the trainees' opinions and feelings on the controversy.

Announce the result and comment upon it.

Finally, take one or two of their findings on the topic which you issued, for discussion.

No doubt you can add learning activities to those which we have described here and perhaps those explained will set you off with other ideas which you can develop.

Whilst lecturing is very much of a larger group activity, let's now turn to a solitary one: getting ready for your lecture.

* Planning Lectures

There are two areas which we would like to consider here: preparing for the lecture; the Lecture Plan.

* Preparing for the Lecture

As subjects for lectures vary enormously, the ways in which you may set about preparing the lecture also vary considerably. Here are some pointers which we have found useful:—

Timing. Usually, we do not begin preparation until the week before the lecture is due to be given. This allows time to modify the lecture in view of what may have happened recently in the rest of the Programme. Also with such a short "run in", it is unlikely that you will forget what you have read and written.

Design System. You must certainly take note of the information which your design system has provided. Needs, resources and constraints must be considered and Entering Behaviour Analysis will help to pitch your lecture at an appropriate level.

You will wish to select one or more specific objectives which you are to deal with and should have a good idea of the material to be considered from your Synthesis of Content.

Method. It is likely that you'll want to elaborate on the material indicated by the Synthesis of Content and we have found these techniques useful:

Content Mapping. This technique is described in Component Six, Study Unit Two, Package One and is a very useful tool when you are expanding on the content of the lecture.

Method Mapping. Described in the same Component, this method is quite invaluable in giving you a picture of your lecture content. It has the big advantage of making the material easy to scan as it is usually written on a single side of A4 paper. Method mapping is helpful in providing references which you can look up again should you be repeating the lecture in the future and which can be used as a source for your trainees. You can let them see your method maps or duplicate them for distribution as a handout.

This is the technique which we use most when preparing lectures.

Spray Diagrams are like Method Maps and are explained in the same Component. They are more of a "shorthand" form and consequently can be prepared quicker, but they are less useful for future use.

OHP Visuals. These should be prepared carefully. Don't make too many, as that is confusing and do not put more than three or four major points on each, otherwise clarity will be lost, detail will dominate and the trainees will be confused. Flip chart and black/white boards should be used to elaborate material.

Prepared Questions. Always think out and write down if necessary, your half-dozen questions which emphasise the key points of your lecture.

Learning Activities. These have to be very carefully prepared, timed and fitted around the major issues and topics which you want to emphasise. Leave plenty of time for the typing out of the instructions and materials for the learning activities. Be sure you know what learning is generated by each activity and how the activities will help the trainees fulfil the objectives of the lecture.

Task Analysis. Apart from information gained from your original task analysis, you may well want to carry out other analyses using material gleaned from reference books, manuals and articles.

The last stage of preparation is that of making up

* The Lecture Plan.

You can use as a basic plan any of the lesson plans which we described in Component Two of this Study Unit, modified suitably. Your course Scheme of Work will also provide information and a framework for your lecture.

Our suggested plan for a lecture is shown in the next Figure.

THE LECTURE PLAN   GENERAL INFORMATION
(See Component Two of this Study Unit).

TITLE OF LECTURE

TIMING	OBJECTIVES	TOPICS	LEARNING ACTIVITIES
BEGINNING	14	MAIN 1 a b	
MIDDLE	14	MAIN 2 a b c d	
	14	MAIN 3	
	15	MAIN 4 a b c	
END			

PREPARED QUESTIONS

REFERENCES

RESOURCES

EVALUATION

FIGURE 159

Summary

To make a lecture a worthwhile learning experience and an effective method of delivering the learning to larger groups it must generate audience activity.

There are five basic ways of developing such activity:

a) two-way and multi-way communication between the lecturer and the trainees.

b) interaction between the lecturer and the trainees.

c) multi-way communication between the trainees.

d) interaction between the trainees.

e) trainees participating in learning activities.

A two-way communication lecture, or 2WL as we have called it, usually involves all five types of activity to varying degrees and therefore develops two-way communication into multi-way communication.

It is important to tell the trainees where they are going in a lecture and to keep them active by participation in buzz groups, pyramiding, duos, jury voting and trials, debates, using handouts, testing and other learning activities.

Active questioning and answering questions is a vital ingredient of any 2WL and helps hold and increase trainee attention.

Lectures have to be prepared and planned carefully. Using information derived from the design system and method mapping of content are invaluable in ensuring efficient preparation.

This Component completes our survey of methods and techniques of delivering the learning to larger groups. We have shown a variety of lessons and lectures and the techniques which you can use in them. In both lessons and lectures we have stressed the importance of learning activities and of making the trainees active.

Effective lessons and lectures ensure successful learning by doing as well as by listening and seeing and learning.

Before you begin the next Study Unit you might like to develop a series of learning activities which you can use in a lecture or lesson which you are to give. Consider how important it is to break down your lesson or lecture audience into smaller groups so that active trainee participation is encouraged.

This exercise will prepare the way for the next Study Unit, where we consider the delivery of learning to smaller groups.

Finally, undertake the exercise of writing down the Objectives for this Study Unit yourself. Send your work to your Programme tutor for comment, if you wish.

Study Unit 3:

Methods of Training: Groupwork

Component 1:

Delivering the learning to Smaller Groups

Key Words

 Number in groups; arbitrary limits; continuum of delivery strategies; organisation of learning activities; definitions of group, group discussion, group structure, group dynamics; task analysis of learning groups; types of smaller group delivery; aims of learning groups; division of time and activities in groupwork; effective discussion.

The Study Unit examines methods of delivering the learning to smaller groups

---

Introduction

In this Study Unit we are concerning ourselves with methods of delivering the learning to smaller groups.

If you look back at Component Four of Study Unit One, you will find a section which deals with group size and delivery. Figure 53 is particularly important in that section and we reproduce it here.

METHODS OF DELIVERING THE LEARNING TO SMALLER GROUPS

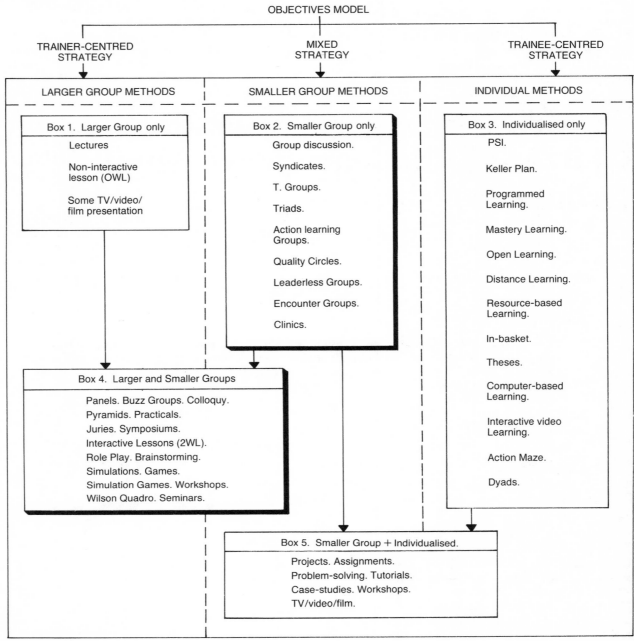

OBJECTIVES MODEL

TRAINER-CENTRED STRATEGY

MIXED STRATEGY

TRAINEE-CENTRED STRATEGY

LARGER GROUP METHODS

SMALLER GROUP METHODS

INDIVIDUAL METHODS

Box 1. Larger Group only

Lectures

Non-interactive lesson (OWL)

Some TV/video/ film presentation

Box 2. Smaller Group only

Group discussion.

Syndicates.

T. Groups.

Triads.

Action learning Groups.

Quality Circles.

Leaderless Groups.

Encounter Groups.

Clinics.

Box 3. Individualised only

PSI.

Keller Plan.

Programmed Learning.

Mastery Learning.

Open Learning.

Distance Learning.

Resource-based Learning.

In-basket.

Theses.

Computer-based Learning.

Interactive video Learning.

Action Maze.

Dyads.

Box 4. Larger and Smaller Groups

Panels. Buzz Groups. Colloquy.
Pyramids. Practicals.
Juries. Symposiums.
Interactive Lessons (2WL).
Role Play. Brainstorming.
Simulations. Games.
Simulation Games. Workshops.
Wilson Quadro. Seminars.

Box 5. Smaller Group + Individualised.

Projects. Assignments.
Problem-solving. Tutorials.
Case-studies. Workshops.
TV/video/film.

FIGURE 160

We shall concentrate on boxes 2 and 4 of Figure 160. These boxes show methods which are suitable for delivering the learning to smaller groups. Generally, those methods shown in box 2 are **particularly** suitable for smaller groups, whilst those in box 4 may be equally used for larger groups, as well.

▰▰▰ Checkpoint

Can you recollect from Component Four, Study Unit One, what numbers are involved in describing "smaller" as distinct from "larger" groups?

We suggested that smaller groups numbered from two trainees to eleven and that larger groups consisted of twelve, or more, trainees.

However, we also made the point that those numerical divisions are very **arbitrary***. It is far more significant that you select a method which is suitable for delivering your learning effectively. And that's a matter of common sense and what you're teaching, rather than numbers.*

It is also a matter of knowing what the capabilities of each method are and when to apply them. That's what we are going to find out in this Study Unit.

▰▰▰

What other points strike you as significant about Figure 160?

There seem to us to be two major aspects which are noteworthy.

The first is concerned with **delivery strategies.** *In considering the delivery of learning to smaller groups we have moved from the mainly trainer-centred strategy used with larger groups, to a mixed strategy, where the learning is much more directed towards individuals. Generally, this means that the trainees are much more active in smaller groups and although the learning is often still directed by the trainer, the trainees have much greater opportunities to participate and to engage themselves in learning activities. Usually, this leads to more efficient and effective learning.*

The second major aspect of Figure 160 which we believe to be noteworthy is shown in Box 5 where we see some of the methods suitable for both smaller group and individual learning.

Second, it is important to remember that methods of delivering the learning, like delivery strategies, are part of a continuum which we showed first in Figure 257, Component Eight, Study Unit Two, Package One. We give an adaption of that diagram in our next Figure.

THE CONTINUUM

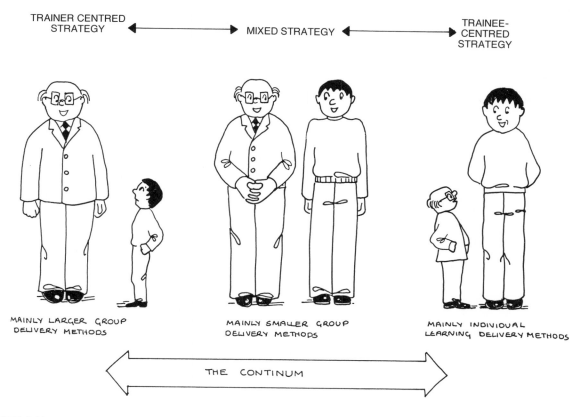

FIGURE 161

Figure 161 shows how the role of the trainer in the learning process changes along the continuum from left to right.

Don't forget how the trainer can increase active learning by the trainees even in larger group methods, mainly by increasing interaction and improving communication, for example by using 2WL, including multi-way communication and interaction, rather than Owl, and by using interactive lessons.

So let's have a closer look at those methods of delivering the learning suitable for smaller groups.

The structure of this Component is

A conversation.
Some Definitions.
Types of smaller group delivery.
Objectives of learning groups.
Division of time and activities in group work.
Effective discussion in smaller groups.

* A Conversation

I was having a cup of coffee in the staff canteen the other day when Plodworth appeared with his friend Maxmin. They made their way to our table. Now Maxmin is an interesting character. We believe that he founded the maxim that life is about getting the maximum reward for the minimum effort. Except in Maxmin's case the effort always tends to be minimal!

Plodworth, by the way, was a bit gloomy. He had just read what we had written about larger group learning. Still, he managed a smile when he sat down.

OUR TRAINER TALKS TO PLODWORTH AND MAXMIN

FIGURE 162

"Well, Plodworth, how are you doing?"

Plodworth: **"According to you, it's how are they doing, not me."**

Maxmin: "The trainees, you mean?"

Plodworth: **"That's right. Seems like it's got to be activities, activities and participation, all the way!"** (He surveyed the table gloomily). **"Anyway, who's getting the coffees in?"**

"OK. I will. I owe you that."

Safely supplied with coffee, Plodworth asked, **"What are you doing now?"** He looked at Maxmin. **"Always thinking up something new, our active trainer here."**

Maxmin: "Saves us bothering, eh!"

Plodworth: **"Yes, so what's new?"**

"Groupwork. Working together in groups."

Plodworth: **"Groups?"**

"Yes, Plodworth. Having cleared off lessons and lectures we're on to learning in groups, now."

Plodworth grinned. **"All that stuff about a camel being a horse designed by a committee?"**

Maxmin laughed. "Not likely. Meetings can't decide anything except when the next meeting is going to be!"

"Well, I don't disagree with that completely. Anyway, I'm talking about groups, not committees and —"

Plodworth interrupted. **"You mean a group of the unfit, designated by the unwilling to do something unnecessary for the ungrateful trainees?"**

"Not quite. I mean —"

Maxmin broke in this time. "I know. A meeting of trainers who can't do anything by themselves and they get together to decide that nothing can be done."

"You've missed one, haven't you?"

Plodworth: **"Missed one?"**

"That's right. The one about a meeting being a group of people who save minutes and waste hours."

Plodworth: **"Minutes, minutes!"** He smiled. **"Hey, that's a good one. Must remember that."**

Maxmin: "Making you feel better, is he?"

Plodworth nodded.

"Well I ought to be. Anyway, we're not supposed to be talking about committees. The groups we're talking about are trainee groups."

Plodworth: **"Groups of trainees?"**

"Yes. Brought together in groups so that they can learn something. And can you stop repeating everything I say, please?"

"Maxmin: "Wrong again Plodworth."

Plodworth: **"Oh I see! Groups eh! Use 'em all the time myself. Always having debates. That kind of thing."**

"Only debates? What about seminars, panels and brainstorming?"

Maxmin laughed. "Brainstorming, eh! That's you alright."

Plodworth was looking a bit uncomfortable. **"Well, I do a lot of demonstrations. That's a good way of working in groups."**

Maxmin: "Not one of my favourites. You've often got

to practice for ages to get it right. Lot of work entailed."

"True. But demonstrations are the best way of teaching skills. Anyway, it's the other methods I'm talking about really."

Plodworth: **"So it's more than demonstrations and debates?"**

"A lot more!"

Plodworth: **"There's an inevitability about this. You're going to tell me all about different types of learning in groups, aren't you?"**

"Well, I'm not, actually. I've got to get back to my group, funnily enough."

Plodworth and Maxmin looked relieved.

Maxmin: "Wouldn't mind giving a list, or something, if you've got one."

"OK. I'll let you have a list. With definitions and types of groups all laid out."

Plodworth grimaced. **"What a boon!"**

"Indeed. See you."

What main points have you picked up from the conversation with Plodworth and Maxmin?

We think the points are that there is too much confusion of the poor experiences which people have had on committees, with learning groups; of course the two have completely different purposes. A big "hangover" is the belief that committees and therefore groups waste time, decide (or learn) little or nothing and are full of unwilling members. We shall see how true these views are in this Study Unit.

The key to successful groups is the efficient organisation of learning activities. In running a committee meeting there are certain techniques which lead to efficient work; in the learning groups there are many tactics which lead to successful use of the various methods of delivery.

So we must now organise ourselves to examine these methods and tactics. Let's begin this organisation by using a familiar technique, that of Task Analysis.

Make a Task (topic) Analysis of the topic "Learning Groups". One level of analysis will do to begin with.

Our analysis is shown in the next Figure.

TASK (topic) ANALYSIS OF THE TOPIC, "LEARNING GROUPS"

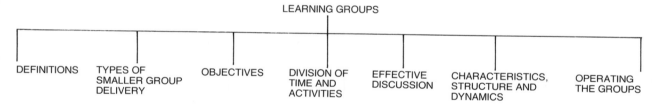

FIGURE 163

Right; we've made our first level of analysis, so we had better get down to examining some of level one Units of Analysis more closely.

* Some Definitions

It would be boring if we attempted to make all of our definitions at once, so we shall begin with a couple of basic ones, only.

Define a "group" and a "group discussion".

Our definitions are shown in the next Figures.

DEFINITION OF A "GROUP"

> A Group is three or more persons whose interaction causes and assists learning.

FIGURE 164

This definition clearly refers to **learning** groups. Obviously, other groups meet for different purposes and their purposes might be to assist making music, for pleasure and social interaction, etc.

OTHER GROUPS

Now for that other basic definition: group discussion.

DEFINITION OF "GROUP DISCUSSION"

> A group discussion is an activity where group members learn through communicating and interacting with each other

FIGURE 166

The group discussion is the basic method of learning in groups and we shall look at this closely in Component Three.

You will have heard or read of the other two terms which are used widely when group learning is being considered. These are "group structure" and "group dynamics".

▨▨

Can you suggest what these terms mean?

The definition of group structure is not too difficult:

DEFINITION OF "GROUP STRUCTURE"

> Group structure is the number composition and organisation of the people who form the group.

FIGURE 167

DEFINITION OF "GROUP DYNAMICS"

> Group dynamics are the forces, processes and relationships which interact within a group.

FIGURE 168

Incidentally, "group dynamics" is a dodgy term to use, because different authors use the term in varying ways. Sometimes all groupwork is wrongly referred to as group dynamics.

The forces and relationships which we mean are those which arise from the differing patterns of activity caused by group member's characteristics, like their personalities, experiences, abilities and attitudes, the purposes of the group and the physical and social environment in which the group works.

We now have enough fundamental definitions, so let's move on to

* Types of Smaller Group Delivery

▨▨

Write down a list of the different methods in which learning can be delivered to and by groups.

Well, we have already done this for you in Figure 160.
Remember that we are especially concerned with boxes 2 and 4 in that Figure.

Perhaps we ought to distinguish between the most commonly found group activities. These are group discussion, seminars, panels, buzz groups, symposia and brainstorming.

Don't forget the two-way and multi-way communication lectures. These are "lectures" in name only, because the tactics used in them break down the audience into groups so that the lecture is not delivered to a large passive group of trainees, but to a collection of smaller active groups.

Now here are the

* Objectives of Learning Groups

As each type of smaller group has different purposes and therefore different objectives, we are talking about the objectives of groupwork in general.

Have a go at writing out these objectives yourself.

Our suggestions are shown in the next Figure.

OBJECTIVES OF LEARNING GROUPS

- To promote learning by communication and interaction between the group numbers and between the group members and the trainer.
- To promote learning by utilising the different knowledge, skills, abilities and experience of the group members.
- To stimulate critical thinking.
- To promote learning by increasing the motivation of group members.
- To give group members the opportunity of expressing and clarifying their own ideas.
- To offer group members the chance to formulate and examine their own attitudes and to compare them with the attitudes of others.
- To give group members a situation in which they can practise and improve their social skills.
- To provide group members with situations in which they can make decisions and solve problems.
- To help group members study the processes of decision-making and problem-solving.
- To allow group members to pool and pass on information.
- To give group members the experience of applying and studying group processes, norms and dynamics.
- To develop a learning situation in which group members can achieve objectives and, in particular, the objective of the group.
- To enhance oral communication skills.
- To develop a critical approach to new material.
- To help the group members, as learners, be less dependent on the trainer in managing their own learning.
- To improve collaboration between group members and consequently to increase independent thinking by the group and members of it, which becomes independent of the trainer.
- To establish the group as a resource which can be drawn upon by its members.
- To cause the group members to take more responsibility for their own learning and consequently to improve their preparation for it.
- To place group members in an active learning situation.

FIGURE 169

No doubt you can add others to your list. We hope that your group objectives are at least as worthwhile as that shown in the next illustration.

A WORTHWHILE GROUP OBJECTIVE

FIGURE 170

What strikes you about the differences in these objectives when you compare them with the objectives characteristic of many larger group methods of delivering the learning?

The differences seem to us to be encapsulated in the last objective: the placing of group members, the trainees, in a situation where they can learn **actively**.

That is the fundamental objective. Most of the other qualities expressed in the objectives, shown in Figure 169, stem from that one.

* Division of Time and Activities in Groupwork

At this stage, we do not propose to examine the layout of lesson plans for groupwork, in detail. Nevertheless, this activity is considerably different from the time allocations and from the distribution of activities shown in the lesson plans of Study Unit Two. Our next diagram shows the organisation of a typical session organised for smaller groups.

SMALLER GROUP LEARNING: TIMINGS AND ACTIVITIES WITH SUB-GROUPS

TIMING	TRAINER ACTIVITY	LEARNER ACTIVITY
BEGINNING 0 - 6 minutes	Trainer sets scene by describing subject (issues, problems, objectives topics, etc.) for discussion.	Trainees listen, make notes.
MIDDLE 7 - 40 minutes	Trainer issues handout describing subject for discussion.	Trainees read handout, divide into sub-groups and discuss.
END 41 - 51 minutes		Trainee sub-groups briefly present findings to whole group.
52 - 60 minutes	Trainer de-briefs group. Trainer summarises.	

FIGURE 171

In Figure 171 when are the trainees passive?

You can see that the trainees are only passive for perhaps 13 or 14 minutes, that is during the Beginning and at the End of a session. This is when the trainer is setting the scene and when he is summarising and de-briefing the group.

It may well be that the trainees do not sub-divide, but that the subject is discussed by the whole group. In this case, Figure 171 might be modified as shown in the next diagram (draw your own diagram first).

SMALLER GROUP LEARNING: TIMINGS AND
ACTIVITIES WITH WHOLE GROUPS.

TIMINGS	TRAINER ACTIVITY	TRAINEE ACTIVITY
BEGINNING 0 - 6 minutes	As in Figure 171	Figure 171
MIDDLE 7 - 45 minutes	Trainer writes subject on board	Trainees begin and carry out discussion.
END 45 - 60 minutes	Trainer summarises and de-briefs	Trainees summarise.

FIGURE 172

We shall now consider, briefly, what elements make for

* Effective Discussion in Smaller Groups

In general terms, there are several characteristics which can be observed in an effective group discussion. Consider what these may be, before you look at our suggestions, which follow.

Effective group discussions have these characteristics:—

— Group members who accept and recognise the **objectives** of the group and work towards realising them.
— The group possesses **adequate information** in the shape of knowledge, facts, skills and evidence to be able to deal with the subject for discussion.
— The group recognises that certain members have **greater expertise and experience** and must accord the opinions of these members with great credibility.

WEIGHT BEHIND THE OPINION

FIGURE 173

So groups must accept that degree and validity of contributions to discussion from members will vary in quality and credibility.

> — The group must approach the discussion **systematically** and not beat around the bush. There are certain procedures for problem solving and decision making and we will consider these later.
> — Effective groups usually have an understanding, sometimes intuitive, of **group dynamics.**
> — The group should talk the **same language** and have commonly understood vocabularies for the subject being discussed, especially where it is a technical one.
> — Effective groups have effective **leadership**. Consequently, they are managed efficiently.
> — Effective groups learn by **talking** and **interacting**.

These are general statements but it will help if you bear them in mind during this Study Unit.

Before reading the summary of this Component, consider a group which you have attended, or given, recently and decide how far it was effective in terms of the characteristics which we have just described. Send your conclusions to your Programme Tutor for examination, if you wish.

Summary

In this Study Unit, we are examining the methods of delivering the learning to Smaller Groups.

The delivery strategy is a mixed one, that is one which contains elements of both trainer-centred and trainee-centred strategies. However, most of the methods of delivering the learning to smaller groups, numbering between, say, three and twelve trainees, lean towards trainee-centred learning.

There are many methods for developing groupwork and the subject of "groups" is quite a complex one. A task (topic) analysis of "learning groups" shows the main topics (level one units of analysis) to be: definitions of learning groups; types of smaller group delivery; objectives, division of time and activities; group characteristics, structure and dynamics; operation of the groups.

An important definition is that of the learning "group" which is "three or more persons whose interaction causes and assists learning".

Learning groups have many objectives; perhaps the most important of these is that of placing the group members in an active learning situation.

The division of time in groupwork emphasises the importance of activity and participation by group members.

Effective groups, which are those promoting effective learning, having several well-defined characteristics including group members recognising objectives; having adequate information; recognising expertise and experience; discussing subjects systematically; understanding group dynamics; talking the same language; having effective leadership and talking and interacting.

The next Component will examine leadership and people working in a group, more closely, by making a discussion of the "Characteristics, structure and dynamics" of groups. This is the penultimate first level unit of analysis, Figure 163. "Operating the Groups" will be considered in Component Four.

Component 2:

People in the Group

Key Words

Processes; content; forces; group dynamics; group characteristics; personality, cohesion, laws, size, commitment, risky shift; group structure, individual variables, type of group, physical environment; group interaction, communication patterns, behavioural patterns, positive behaviours, negative behaviours and group barriers.

Introduction

In this Component we are making a survey of **how people work and of interaction in smaller groups.** So we are looking at the first level unit of analysis, "Characteristics, structure and dynamics", shown in Figure 163, Component One.

When a group meets, the interactions within the group are concerned mainly with two major elements: content and process.

"**Content**" is what the group are working upon: a topic, a skill, or a task like solving a problem or making a decision.

"**Process**" is concerned with the atmosphere in which the group works, participation by and interaction between group members, conflict, co-operation and leadership.

In addition to those processes which make the group work, there are those which hinder its efficiency and which form barriers to effective functioning of the members.

The processes which we have described can be grouped under several broad headings and these will form the structure of this Component:
Group characteristics
Group structure
Group interaction
In looking at group processes, we are considering the **forces** which operate within a group. If you turn back to Figure 168 in Component One, you will see that these forces and processes are the **dynamics** which drive a group. So in examining the forces, processes,

interactions, patterns, barriers and relationships which operate within a group we are making a study of **group dynamics**.

Of course, we are not forgetting the other major element of groupwork: the content. However, as later Components in this Study Unit are to examine different types of group in detail, it will be more efficient if we consider content in direct relation to each type of group. Being more specific in this way will allow us to give relevant examples at the proper time.

GROUP CONTENT AND GROUP DYNAMICS

FIGURE 173

KEY
➡ GROUP DYNAMICS
⇨ GROUP CONTENT

169

So let's begin our examination of group dynamics, the processes and forces at work within a group, by looking at

* Group Characteristics

There are a variety of interesting group characteristics which we can consider. Remember that we are not viewing the characteristics of the individual members of the group, at this stage, but at the characteristics of the group as a whole.

▨▨▨ Checkpoint

Try to show what we have said in the last paragraph by a simple diagram.

Here are a couple of suggestions from us:—

GROUP AND INDIVIDUAL MEMBERS: CHARACTERISTICS

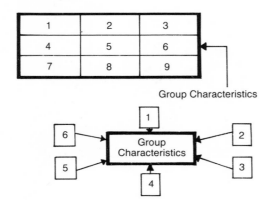

Key: Heavy black rectangle = group characteristics.
Numbered boxes = characteristics of individual group members.

FIGURE 174

We have tried, in our diagrams, to show how the individual members' characteristics add up to make the group characteristics, something quite different.

So what are these group characteristics? First, we shall deal with

* Group Personality

The presence of others releases latent energy. Think of how much more effort sports players put into a game held before a large crowd than a small one. They have what almost amounts to a temporary change of personality.

Similarly, the group develops its own personality, which differs from that of the individuals within it.

Workshy individuals can become productive when placed in a group which criticises lazy behaviour; quite passive people can become "balls of fire" when they have a group "stage" on which to act.

GREAT BALLS OF FIRE!

FIGURE 175

* Group cohesion

The longer groups are together, then the more closely they combine and the more co-operative they become.

Friendliness and identity within the group increase with time, unless the group is unsuccessful, or is dominated by awkward personalities.

THE NEW GROUP

FIGURE 176A

THE LONG-STANDING GROUP

FIGURE 176B

Members of cohesive groups have greater attraction to the group and become increasingly loyal to it. As the group cohesiveness leads to satisfactory outcomes, like successful learning, cohesiveness increases, almost in a circular fashion. Our next diagram shows this.

COHESIVENESS IS CIRCULAR

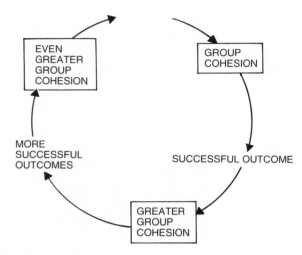

FIGURE 177

* Group Laws

Members of a group increasingly conform to what they see as the laws, or **rules** or **norms** of a group. They come to believe and act in accordance with the ways the group thinks is proper.

This conformity strengthens the group.

* Group Size

Groups tend to work more effectively up to a certain point, because the members are able to provide an increasingly large pool of expertise and experience.

However, past that certain point, both group and potential and productivity fall off as quieter members become more passive and more aggressive individuals come to dominate increasingly. As you know, "too many cook's spoil the broth".

Where do you think the "certain point" is?

*Difficult to know: we'd place it between six and ten members depending on what they are doing. It is worth noting that the productivity and participation of each **individual** begins to fall off at around seven or eight people and declines very rapidly over that number. Other factors affect the location of the "certain point", such as group members' personalities, pressures from outside the group, even climate and working conditions.*

In a way, there is a conflict between **optimal group size for participation**, when everyone gets a reasonable chance to speak and **optimal size for breadth of expertise and experience**, where greater numbers

mean greater available knowledge and skills.

Size and cohesiveness are related: cohesiveness declines over six or seven members because of reduced participation and interaction; the requirement for dividing up the work; the development of cliques and a need for more authoritarian leadership to prevent confusion occurring.

* The Sum Effect

If six individuals, working independently, can produce "W" amount of work each, then they may produce 7W (not 6W) when working in a group, i.e. the sum of the efforts is greater than their individual contributions added together.

This greater sum of efforts is effected by the group members inspiring each other to new thoughts; their co-ordination of effort; availability of wider expertise and experience to draw upon; less psychological tension than working alone; more assurance from the security offered by the group. This is a sort of "effect of the sum", where togetherness oils the group's productive mechanisms.

We've all used sun oil. Now we're advocating that group members should try a little "sum oil"!

*Group Committment

Most individuals are committed to the success of the group. If they're not, then they are either thrown out or censured by the other persons.

Normally, group members subscribe to the success of the group, but a high level of committment is usually necessary to ensure that success. Committment is high when the aims of the individual are the same as those of the group and are relevant to the job of both. Increasing committment is usually characterised by increasing interdependence between group participants.

GROUP INTERDEPENDENCE

FIGURE 177A

* The Risky Shift

When faced with a choice of decisions, the group not uncommonly selects the riskiest. Often the group will switch from the predisposition of members to a cautious approach to one which is much more chancy. This shift is probably due to the belief of persons in the group that responsibility for the decision, or solution, is that of the whole group and that they will not be blamed personally if things go wrong, subsequently. So they become more daring as a group than each would be individually.

THE RISKY SHIFT

FIGURE 178

Having looked at those processes which affect the group as a whole, we will now continue our examination of the dynamics of a group by looking at the structure within which these forces interact.

* Group Structure

Obviously, the group characteristics which we have just looked at will affect the inputs into a group and therefore the structure of the group itself. Another set of variables is connected with the individuals who make up the group.

* Individual variables

Just as we accept that we must not regard any body of trainees as a Learnermass, so we must acknowledge that a group is composed of individuals who are all different from each other. The characteristics which members bring to a group can vary around different:

— **attitudes**

— **values, beliefs and attitudes**, which give rise to different ways of acting and of evaluating other people, things and events.

— **personality**, where the dogmatic can clash with the flexible people, the aggressive with the passive.

— **intelligence** and **ability**, which partly determine status in the group.

— **oral** and **verbal facility**, where sometimes the person who has the most to say is least able to say it.

— **experience** which teaches different things and reinforces attitudes.

— **expertise**.

— **previous education** and **training**.

— **social class**, which handicaps some group members from full participation, particularly if they lack assurance.

— **interests** and **general knowledge**.

— **family** and **social patterns** which help decide how socially adept the individual is in the group.

— **status**, both natural presence and status in the firm are important variables, as we know that senior group members with a high status are accorded more time and credibility, at least in the formative stages of the group.

— **role**, where members see themselves as being there to perform certain roles, e.g. that of the rational thinker, the systems expert, the conciliator, the activator, etc.

— **friendships** have often been formed years before a group meets. Sometimes these external links cause the formation of cliques within the group, so markedly affecting group structure.

Another set of variables which affect smaller group structure are those which relate to the

* Type of Group

Mostly we are concerned with learning groups, but the dynamics of those groups which meet for social purposes, or get together voluntarily, or for management reasons, are similar to processes which operate in learning groups.

Even within learning groups there are great variations in group structure caused by the differing inputs from varying goals. Write down as many different types of learning group as you can think of.

Ours are groups which meet to
— *discuss a training issue*
— *solve a problem*
— *make a decision*
— *consider a topic*
— *view a skill*
— *carry out role-play*
— *develop a project*
— *play a simulation game*
— *carry out an assignment*
— *listen and talk to a panel*
— *hold a tutorial or seminar*
— *share information*
— *recommend action (persuasive)*
— *create, generate ideas*
— *develop a new training course*

There are many others, but this variety is reflective of the many different structures which arise to suit the group to the learning job which it has to do. The structure of each of these groups varies therefore, to accommodate the **task** *with which the group is faced and the reason it has come together.*

Further differences are caused by variation in

* The Physical Environment
Variation in lighting, seating, temperature, position of audio-visual aids, noise, window space, room decor and the general comfortableness of the location in which the groups work, will obviously affect efficiency.

Which of these factors do you believe to be the most important and why?

Well, they're all important, but we think that the seating is very significant. We don't just mean whether it is comfortable or not, but also how it is **arranged.** *How you place people in a room affects the structure and functioning of the group, emphatically.*

However, we are really talking in general terms here, so we propose to examine seating arrangements more closely when we look at the different types of groupwork, relating each type of group to the organisation most suitable for it.

When we do this, do remember that we are considering yet another significant variable in group structure. The situation shown in the next illustration will have an impact on the functioning of any group, wouldn't it?

"NOW I WANT YOU TO THINK OF US ALL AS EQUALS!"

FIGURE 179

Well, we have now viewed group characteristics and group structure. Both affect our next topic, which is

* Group Interaction
Interaction within a group follows various patterns which reflect the group characteristics, structure and the task in hand. Let's do a brief task (topic) analysis of "group interaction" to find out what these patterns might be.

Try making your own analysis before you look at ours, which is shown in the next diagram.

TASK ANALYSIS OF TOPIC: "GROUP INTERACTION"

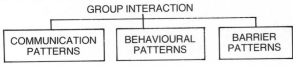

FIGURE 180

We will now examine these patterns in turn.

* Communication Patterns
We have already made a study of communication patterns. These patterns reflect interaction in the group.

Can you remember where we considered this before?

Have a look at Component Two, Study Unit One, where we show a variety of **communication networks** *in Figure 26. These networks show the patterns which we are considering now. Of the basic patterns shown in Figure 26, which do you think apply to smaller group learning?*

We believe these patterns in Figure 26 are relevant: FAN 2; "Y"; Large Loop; Daisy; Wheel; Circle; Wheel 2; Star.

Some of these patterns show a **centralised structure**, *where the trainer is central to the discussion. Which are they?*

Centralised patterns are shown in Fan 2; "Y"; Daisy; Wheel 2. Some of the patterns represent communication in other methods of delivering the learning, e.g. Fan 2, can also represent an interactive lecture and "Y" a distance-learning situation.

Perhaps the best pattern for effective groupwork is shown in the Star, where there is free communication and therefore interaction between all group members.

FIGURE 181

When we examine different group structures and the way they work in later Components, we shall look at these more closely.

However, we should stress now that if group discussion topics and issues are to be discussed fully and in depth and if the collective expertise and experience of the group is to be used most efficiently, then interaction must take place between all the members, e.g. as in Star. Consequently, centralised patterns are more restricting and often less fruitful, although they are suitable for certain tasks and types of groupwork.

* Behavioural Patterns

These are the patterns of behaviour of the persons in the group. At the beginning of groupwork each member is asking himself three questions, either consciously or unconsciously.

From your experience of working in groups, whether learning groups or committees, what do you think these questions are?

We believe them to be

1. **What am I supposed to be doing in this group?**
   This question asks about my role; how much I participate; what am I representing; who is watching my performance?

2. **What am I after?** *This question is about my needs and objectives, how far they are compatible with the groups and what I do if they aren't.*

3. **Do I like the way the group works?** *This asks if I feel popular and liked (and if I care!) and who seems to be influential in the running of the group and if I like the way he is doing it?*

These questions are answered by the way in which each member of the group behaves and what roles they adopt. This is a central issue in the study of group dynamics.

The behaviours shown in a group fall into two main categories, according to the functions which they fulfil. These are **positive** and **negative** behaviours.

Let's have a look at positive behaviour more closely, now. We'll look at negative behaviours when we view Barriers Patterns later.

Positive Behaviours. These can be further subdivided into three main groups:
Behaviours which help to get the group job or task done.
Behaviours which support and maintain the group.
Behaviours which get both the job done and support the group.

No doubt, you have your own ideas of the behaviours and interactions of the group **members** which fall into each of these three categories. Write your ideas down before you scan ours.

Here are our suggestions, shown in the next Figures.

POSITIVE BEHAVIOURS WHICH GET THE GROUP JOB AND TASK DONE.

— **Initiates**: suggests new ideas, solutions, definitions, perspectives and approaches.
— **Gives information**: offers knowledge, skill, expertise and draws on own experience.
— **Gives one's own views**: states opinion, values and beliefs; elaborates suggestions and gives examples.
— **Clarifies**: asks for classification of material; requests more information.
— **Asks for other views**: tries to find out what the others think and feel.
— **Organises**: tries to co-ordinate ideas and activities; shows relationship between suggestions.
— **Gives direction**: orientates the group; gives direction to information and ideas; confirms progress.
— **Concludes**: summarises where the group is at.

FIGURE 182

BEHAVIOURS WHICH SUPPORT AND MAINTAIN THE GROUP

— **Shows Solidarity**: gives help and rewards; may even raise the status of other group members, especially the weaker ones.

SOLIDARITY

— **Conciliates**: harmonises opposing viewpoints, compromises.
— **Releases tension**: by jokes, laughter, shows pleasure and satisfaction.
— **Encourages**: by maintaining a warm, friendly atmosphere.
— **Agrees**: shows understanding, complies, concurs.
— **Sets norms**: describes acceptable standards for group procedures and decision making.
— **Listens**: hears the contributions of others with thought and respect.
— **Expresses group response**: says what the feeling of the group appears to be; summarises reactions.

FIGURE 183

POSITIVE BEHAVIOURS WHICH GET BOTH JOB DONE AND SUPPORT THE GROUP

— **Analyses**: checks handicaps to learning and progress and breaks down difficulties and problems; analyses likely courses of action; analyses learning.
— **Synthesises**: builds up what has been agreed into possible solutions; synthesises what has been learned into a meaningful structure.
— **Evaluates**: checks progress, suggestions and solutions against objectives, task and group norms; measures progress; evaluates validity, workability and feasibility of group decisions; evaluates the learning which has taken place; evaluates the context of what has been learned with other learning; evaluates how far the learning, skills, knowledge and capabilities have been accepted and valued.

FIGURE 184

As you can see, the behaviours which group members can exhibit are very complex; this in turn makes the study of learning in smaller groups complex, as well. You should read through Figures 182, 183 and 184 from time to time so that you will be able to identify the behaviours of group members and know how to cope with them.

As we suggested, other areas of behaviours in a group are those which are **negative** and these, along with other considerations, form

* Barrier Patterns

We have already considered some of the barriers which handicap effective groupwork. Where was this?

If you look back to Component Two, Study Unit One, you will see that we looked at "barriers to effective communication". Revise that Component now. All of those barriers hinder communication in the group and therefore handicap effective interaction.

Negative Behaviours. There are other barrier patterns of group interaction and these centre around the negative behaviour of the types shown in the next Figure.

NEGATIVE BEHAVIOURS WHICH HINDER THE GROUP

— **The Aggressors**: who belittle and criticise different opinions, are hostile to the group and deflate others. Rudeness and direct attacks create
— **The Defenders**: who are so fed-up with the aggressors that they defend their own views to the death, rather than give in yet again. Logic is lost and the group begins to operate on feelings and emotions rather than commonsense.
— **The Blockers**: who talk all the time, or not at all and are constantly negative. Blockers are often anecdotal, irrelevant, over-argumentative and either long-winded or inarticulate.
— **The Ulteriorists**: who hide their ulterior motive in attending the group and often have a "hidden agenda" of their own.
    Identify what this "hidden-agenda" might be. What has been yours in the past?

The items on the hidden agenda could be: joining the group to meet other people socially rather than getting on with the job; impressing a senior member; always having a crack at someone who is disliked; showing own superiority; joining an influential clique; pushing interests which are not declared; covering the tracks of a past mistake; "fixing" a favourable decision by soliciting support before the meeting.

Not a very nice collection; ulteriorists can be dangerous people!

— **The Idealists**: who use the group to reach an ideal, but unpractical decision, rather than face the reality, sometimes harsh and complex, of a difficult yet realistic solution.
— **The Conformers**: who like to go along with the group decision whether they really agree with it or not. Homogeneous groups often fall into this trap; heterogeneous groups do not, but they spend and waste much time in arguing.

"ARE WE ALL AGREED?"

FIGURE 185

— **The Groupthinkers**: a severe form of conforming seen in long-established groups who believe the stereotypes which they develop are true reflections of reality; exert great pressure against anyone who challenges their way of thinking; believe they are invulnerable and unanimous.
— **The Mindguards**: who protect the Groupthinkers from information and facts adverse to their complacency and which might question their decisions.
— **The Confessors**: who use the group for catharsis, i.e. confessing to get a load off their minds.
— **The Clowns**: who usually horse around.
— **The Little Pleaders**: who push "pet" ideas.
— **The Competitors**: who try to "top" everybody elses' ideas and suggestions. Sometimes their ideas become extreme, or behaviour loud and unusual in an attempt to gain recognition.
— **The Sympathy Seekers**: who gain support by describing their own problems, often unrelated to the group's, or who disparage their own suggestions, so seeking assistance.
— **The Withdrawers**: who think the group's a waste of time so don't participate, becoming a nuisance. Some withdrawers are just daydreamers, or they cannot keep up because of lack of ability or knowledge, or are passive by nature. Other withdrawers are inexperienced in groups and don't understand the conventions and the way groups work.

— **The Frightened**: who fear that they don't know enough to contribute, or that they may be assessed adversely, or they don't know the technical vocabulary necessary, or are not easy talkers. The Frightened do not wish to display their shortcomings in public.
— **The Hoarders**: who find it difficult to get in on a discussion, not knowing when to intervene, how to seize a silence or anticipate the end of another member's contribution. When Hoarders do get in they bring out a whole hoard of points, many of which are irrelevant and which lead the group into irrelevant paths. In doing so they add to the number of
— **The Wrongthinkers**: who are always leading the group up the wrong "garden-path" and away from their objectives.

FIGURE 186

What a collection! No-one ever said that holding fruitful discussions was easy. Groups can be a minefield of people problems.

Have a look next at the next illustration and identify as many of the examples of negative behaviours as you can.

NEGATIVE TYPES

FIGURE 187

The answers are at the end of the Component.

In addition to the positive and negative behaviours shown by the members of a group, another very important group dynamic, which can embody both positive and negative aspects, is **Group Leadership**. We shall look at this in the next Component, when we home in on a group discussion.

Summary

This Component has been concerned with how people work in groups and the forces and processes which operate as group dynamics.

Group characteristics involve a consideration of the personality of the group; group cohesion; group laws; group size; the sum effects; group commitment; the risky shift.

Another aspect of group dynamics is concerned with group structure which depends upon factors such as individual variables; the type of group; the physical environment. Structures vary to accommodate the task in hand.

Group interaction evolves through communication, by the communication patterns which result and through the behavioural patterns of members, which may be positive or negative. Negative patterns form barriers which hinder effective groupwork.

Whilst there are numerous positive behaviours, which help to get the group job or task done and which support and maintain the group, there are also many negative behaviours reducing the effectiveness of the group.

Accordingly, delivering the learning to smaller groups can be a very complicated business, requiring good leadership. A thorough understanding of the ways in which people in a group react and interact is necessary if trainers are to ensure that groupwork is effective and fruitful.

Before beginning the next Component think of a dozen of your trainees and categorise them according to their behaviour in groups. Consider how you may improve those who show negative behaviour. Send your suggestions to your Programme Tutor for comment, if you wish.

KEY TO FIGURE 187

1. *The Aggressors*
2. *The Blockers*
3. *The Sympathy Seekers*
4. *The Frightened*

Component 3:

The Group Discussion

Key Words

Group discussion, definition; "great person" and "situational" theories; leadership style, autocratic, democratic, laissez-faire, diplomatic, bureaucratic; styles and effects of leadership; functions of leader; physical environment of groups; learning spaces, acoustics, lighting, temperature, furnishings, a-v, seating; checklists; seating arrangements.

Introduction

The **Group Discussion** is one of the **basic** methods of delivering the learning to smaller groups. All of the other types of discussion spring from this format; they are variations on the group discussion "theme".

VARIATIONS ON A THEME

FIGURE 188

In Figure 166, Component One of this Study Unit, we defined a group discussion. That was a basic definition. We are going to add detail in this and the next Component.

However, before we do so, answer the following Checkpoint.

▰▰▰▰ Checkpoint

Using the definition shown in Figure 166, add a short explanatory text to define more closely what you understand by the term "group discussion".

It seems important to us that your explanation should show a **"group discussion" to be communication and interaction in a group around a topic, skill, issue or problem, presented to the group by the trainer for discussion.**

So, a group discussion is a method of delivering the learning to smaller groups, usually of four or five to eleven or twelve trainees, where the members talk about a given subject, under the guidance of the trainer.

Now we know we're all talking about the same thing.

As a link with the last Component, we are going to consider **leadership** in the group, here. We shall then go on to answer **some questions about people in groups**. Finally, we shall have a look at the **Physical Environment** of the group discussion. In the next Component we can then get on to the methods of running a group discussion.

So the structure of this unit is:—
Leadership in group discussion.
Some questions about people in groups.
The Physical Environment of groups.

* Leadership in Group Discussion

A great deal of the effectiveness of a group is a reflection of the effectiveness and type of leadership which the group has. So it is well worth our examining what makes leaders tick. This will be a fairly general discussion of leadership; we shall focus in on what leaders are supposed to be doing in various sorts of group activity as we deal with each type.

Another reason why we wish to examine leadership is because there is usually a struggle for leadership and status in most groups. As a trainer running a group discussion for trainees, you'll need to understand this struggle so that you can control it. This is particularly so if you organise groups in which you fancy yourself as leader most of the time!

NOW, WHO'S LEADING TODAY?

FIGURE 188A

Whether or not you are justified in seeing yourself as the "Big Chief" most of the time is something which we shall have to sort out in this Component.

Many of the general approaches to leadership have followed two lines: the "great person theory" and the "situational theory".

The **great person theory** suggests that leaders have certain specific attributes. Some of the work on the physical characteristics of leaders is quite amusing: bishops are taller than clergy; insurance men are taller than policy buyers; sales managers taller than sales persons; generals are taller than lower ranks.

Have a look around your organisation.
Is the great person theory about physique true?

Well, we're not sure and we are certainly not sure that it matters! We don't recollect some famous and in-famous leaders like Churchill, Stalin, Hitler, Freud,

John Kennedy, Napoleon, Lenin, most male and (one) female Prime Ministers, Rommel, Wellington, Mao Tse Tung, Ho Chi Minh, Einstein et al. being of above average height; often they are less.

The work on great person personality is not too convincing either. Great leaders may be more intelligent than average, but this doesn't hold in small group situations, necessarily.

Often leaders are more self-confident, more controlled, less anxious and more dominant, but there are lots of other qualities which a leader may or may not have.

However, if you look again at the list of great leaders which we mentioned above, you'll notice that many were called to lead in a certain **situation.** Often this was in extreme situations like conflict.

So perhaps we can go along more readily with the thesis that situations can throw up leaders. This probably holds good for most groups, where changing situations also tend to throw up different leaders who have the greatest expertise to deal with a particular set of circumstances facing the group at any one time.

Looking more closely at the group discussion, can we identify any particular types of

* Leadership Style

Think back to recent discussions in which you have been involved. What different styles of leadership did you see being demonstrated? If you were a leader, what style do you reckon you adopt?

There are considered to be five major styles of leadership in a group. These are
    The Autocratic Leader
    The Democratic Leader
    The Laissez-faire Leader
    The Diplomatic Leader
    The Bureaucratic Leader.
Whilst we don't know about your leadership style, we can now look at the five which we have mentioned in more detail.

The Autocratic Leader: adopts a self-centred approach and controls the group rigidly, determines and monitors group progress and work, policy, controls information, lays down rules to be followed, seeks power and prestige, requires members' compliance, praises and criticises people in the group, does not require feedback.

Group usually productive, but negative behaviour develops and the members become dissatisified in the short term.

The Democratic Leader: shares responsibility, encourages participation and feedback, tries to improve interaction through good interpersonal contacts, reduces group tensions, wants feedback from people in group, avoids hierarchies. Uses leadership to serve; the group shares decisions and control.

Group works happily, produces creative and original work, uses each person's abilities to the full, although is less organised and efficient than an autocratically led group.

The Laissez-faire Leader: gives freedom to make decisions, communicate, manage the group, participates and tries to be "one of the group". Supplies materials, information and advice if asked, but plays a small part in discussions.

Groups tend to disorganisation, leadership functions fail, apathy develops as members feel lack of a group purpose. Group discussion and productivity low.

The Diplomatic Leader: manipulates the group, often in a Machiavellian way, subtly seeks power, may use either authoritarian or democratic methods, often has a "hidden agenda" and allows discussion so that the group meets the needs of this agenda, often without knowing it, appears to accept feedback, looks for recognition and personal gain.

Groups tend to work well with this type of leadership, but may become antagonistic when the leader's true style and motives are rumbled.

The Bureaucratic Leader: believes in the firm's rules, implements them to maintain personal security, acts impersonally and relates to group members in an "official" way.

This type of leader is not often found in training groups, but when he is the groups tend to apathy, minimal effort and low productivity.

Let's apply what we have learned to training group discussion more closely. Fill in the following table, showing whether the qualities which we name are achieved by various types of leadership, or not. Use H (high) M (medium) or L (low) to indicate the degree of achievement for each quality.

STYLES AND EFFECTS OF LEADERSHIP

STYLE OF LEADERSHIP	GROUP QUALITIES					
	Organisation Efficiency	Interaction/ Communication	Control	Feedback	Content-ment	Productivity/ Effectiveness
Autocratic						
Democratic						
Laissez-faire						
Diplomatic						
Bureaucratic						

STYLE OF LEADERSHIP	GROUP QUALITIES					
	Organisation/ Efficiency	Interaction/ Communication	Control	Feedback	Content-ment	Productivity/ Effectiveness
Autocratic	H	L	H	L	L	M
Democratic	M	H	L	H	H	H
Laissez-faire	L	M	L	M/L	M/L	L
Diplomatic	M	H	M	H	H/M	H/M
Bureaucratic	H	L	H	L	L	M/L

FIGURE 189

It is important that you as a trainer who has to lead group discussions know about styles of leadership and their effects on the productivity and effectiveness of the group. In this sense, the right hand column of Figure 189 is the most important one.

Clearly, the Democratic and Diplomatic styles are the most productive and effective and should be used in delivering the learning to smaller groups, wherever feasible.

Is this last statement entirely true?

Not quite; most group leaders change their style according to the circumstances which the group faces. So a leader faced with an initially apathetic group may have to become authoritarian; an antagonistic group may require diplomacy; a task which is complex, or must be done quickly may require an autocratic, "let's-push-on" approach.

Nevertheless, you need to understand and recognise your own basic and natural style of leadership to realise the effects it will have on groups. Wherever reasonable, try to be democratic, or at least diplomatic and **mix the styles** when you have to.

Obviously, trainers do not function just in training groups. You'll attend and lead many other meetings in your organisation to decide policy, management, budgeting and training matters. Knowing how leaders operate will give you an edge in improving the effectiveness and efficiency of your meetings.

Identify the styles of leadership shown in the next illustration.

LEADERS AT WORK

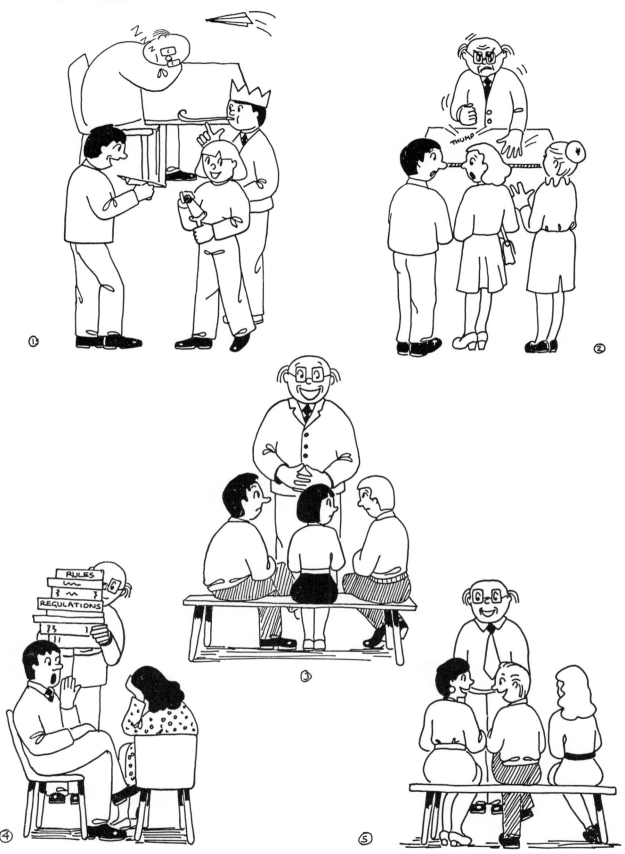

FIGURE 190

Now, what is the group leader supposed to be actually doing?

What are his or her general functions?

Write down your list of functions before looking at ours. Keep to generalities as we are looking at broad leadership roles, rather than specific functions.

Our suggestions are shown in the next Figure.

GENERAL FUNCTIONS OF THE LEADER IN GROUP DISCUSSION

He:—
- **Works** for the benefit of the group.
- **Presents** material for discussion.
- **Encourages** internal communication and interaction between the members.
- **Initiates** new approaches, ideas and practices.
- **Orientates** the group activity, especially when he feels that it is moving in the wrong direction.
- **Retains** group membership.
- **Organises** external relationships with other groups and bodies, defending the group if necessary.
- **Filters** the information entering and leaving the group. This is the sort of "gatekeeping" function.
- **Structures** his work and that of the group.
- **Creates** a friendly atmosphere conducive to work and the security of group members.
- **Takes** major responsibility for achieving group goals.
- **Rewards** where appropriate with praise and recognition.
- **Disapproves** where necessary.
- **Evaluates** the work and progress of the group.
- **Encourages** decision making by the group.

FIGURE 191

As we said, these are **general** functions and can be applied to most groups. The detailed mechanics of group leadership will be considered in the next Component. Using Figure 191 as a basis, you may like to consider what these specific functions might be, meanwhile.

* Some Questions About People in Groups

Now, by way of a revision of what we have said about groups, so far, consider the following statements, deciding whether they are **true, false,** or **maybe true.**

1. A group produces better solutions than individuals working alone.
2. Groups produce answers quicker than individuals working alone.
3. Individuals learn quicker than groups.
4. Working in a group increases motivation.
5. Groups make more cautious decisions than individuals.

These questions concern the individual group member and the group and the answers are:

1. True: the group has a large "combined" intelligence and knowledge.
2. False: groups work more slowly. This presumes that the individual can actually answer the questions when working alone.
3. False.
4. True: the presence of others increases motivation and productivity.
5. Maybe: thinking in groups is often polarised. So some decisions are more cautious than individuals would make, others more venturesome (the "risky shift").

Now for some general questions about group work.

A. The bigger the group the greater the individual participation.
B. The bigger the group the more likely it is to see a leader established.
C. Members would rather work in groups of 15 or 16 than 5 or 6 people.
D. The brighter you are the more you'll contribute in a group.
E. The more intelligent you are the more popular you'll be.
F. Anxiety inhibits the work of the group.
G. The member with special expertise and experience is more active in the group.
H. Members who are sensitive socially improve the efficiency of the group.
I. The older the group members, the more they socialise.
J. Women conform more to the majority group opinion than do men.

Answers

A. False. You have less chance to participate in a larger group than a small one.
B. True.
C. False. Smaller groups are more popular than larger.
D. True.
E. Maybe. Other personality factors matter more.
F. Maybe, if the group becomes over-anxious then work is inhibited. However, a little anxiety, especially initially, acts as a stimulus.
G. Maybe. The group has to believe in the expert; if they do they'll accept his contribution.
H. True.
I. True.
J. True. Well, that's what the research shows. However, we don't know why they conform more.

Ready for some more? Let's finish off the alphabet.

K. Cohesive groups communicate more than those which are not cohesive.

L. People like working in cohesive groups best.

M. Groups which have members possessing diverse skills, knowledge, expertise and experience are the most effective.

N. Senior members (more experienced, older, of higher status) interact more than more junior members; they also receive more communications.

O. Conformity in the group increases group order and organisation.

P. Groups often punish deviation by members from the group norms.

Q. Active, high-powered people are better liked and more influential in a group.

R. The more powerful a group member is, then the greater the likelihood that the power will be used.

S. Smaller group delivery methods, like discussions, are more trainee-centred than larger group methods.

T. An important aim of groupwork is to place the group members in an active learning situation.

U. In an effective group the group members know what the objectives of the group are.

V. Effective groups can speak a common language and understand each other's vocabulary.

W. Group characteristics involve a consideration of the size and personality of the group and of the group laws, cohesion and commitment.

X. "Group dynamics" is particularly concerned with group structure, individual variables, type of group and the physical environment.

Y. Group structures vary according to the task in hand.

Z. Behavioural patterns of group members may be either positive, which facilitates group interaction, or negative, which inhibits groupwork.

Answers: all these last statements are true.

Well, that must be one of the longest self-assessment questions ever! So relax now; sit back in your chairs, because that's what we are going to talk about next: seating and things concerning

* The Physical Environment of Groups

Part of the **learning environment** is the physical conditions in which the group works. Bear in mind these four points when thinking about the physical environment.

— The physical environment must provide a **learning space** where the processes of training and learning can go on efficiently and effectively.

— Therefore, this learning space should facilitate the methods of delivering the learning and the ways in which knowledge, information and skills are presented to the trainees.

— The learning space should allow effective communication and interaction between the group members, that is the trainer and the trainees.

— The learning space should be furnished to allow the effective use of equipment, materials and learning resources to support and facilitate effective learning.

Obviously, it's time for another Golden Rule. This is:

> "The physical environment, or learning space, must allow effective implementation of learning."

Let's make a content map of the topic "learning spaces for groups". Try your own, first.

CONTENT MAP OF TOPIC "LEARNING SPACES FOR GROUPS".

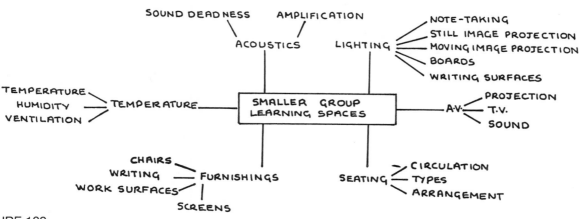

FIGURE 192

There are six main areas we can look at, then, when considering learning spaces.

▰▰▰

Which of these factors in Figure 192 do you think is the most important from the point of view of delivering the learning to smaller groups?

Well, they're all important, but in talking about smaller group learning we would like to concentrate on seating arrangements. You may be surprised at this; after all, if, say, the lighting's wrong you can't teach in the dark! But mostly getting acoustics and furnishings right is a matter of commonsense. Putting the seating in arrangements which facilitate group discussion has more latitude for being right, or wrong, so we need to look at that more closely.

First, a few checklists concerning the other aspects of the physical environment.

ACOUSTICS CHECKLIST

1. Is sound distributed around the learning space equally and adequately?
2. Does background noise interfere?
3. Has the learning space adequate sound deadening like curtains, pinboarding and acoustic boarding on walls?
4. Does the learning space need sound amplification?

FIGURE 193

ACOUSTICS

FIGURE 194

FURNISHINGS CHECKLIST

1. Are the chairs comfortable?
2. Are there adequate writing surfaces?
3. Is there adequate storage space?
4. Are the wall, window and floor coverings suitable?
5. Are portable screens available for sub-dividing the room so that groups may be broken down into 3s and 4s?
6. Are display surfaces adequate?

FIGURE 195

FURNISHING

FIGURE 196

AUDIO-VISUAL FACILITIES CHECKLIST

1. Are writing board surfaces, like black, white and felt-boards available together with pens, wipers etc?
2. Is all of the needed projection equipment available and working and are there spares available for still and moving image projection?
3. Is technician's help available?
4. Is all a-v equipment placed so that it does not block trainees' views?
5. Are the projection screens/surfaces well placed?

FIGURE 197

AUDIO-VISUAL

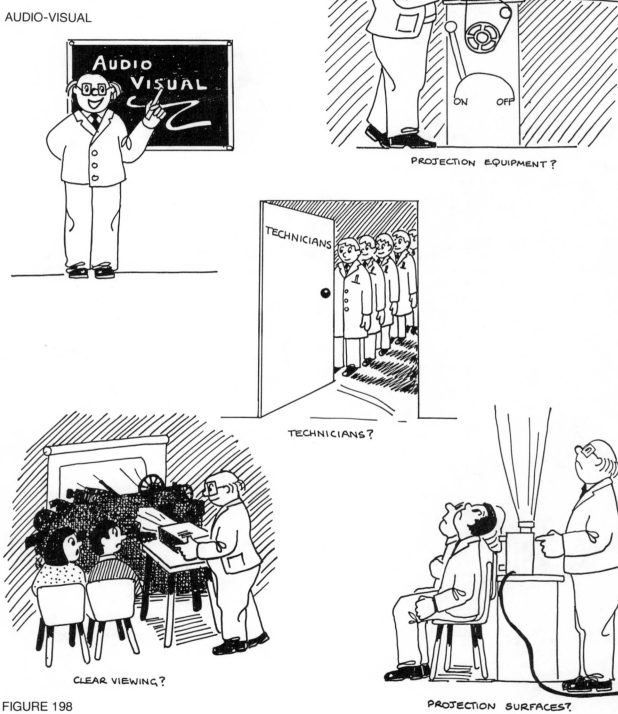

PROJECTION EQUIPMENT?

TECHNICIANS?

CLEAR VIEWING?

PROJECTION SURFACES?

FIGURE 198

TEMPERATURE CHECKLIST

1. Is there an efficient means of maintaining a suitable working temperature between, say, 60°F to 70°F (15°C to 20°C)?
2. Can humidity be controlled?
3. Is ventilation adequate?
4. Are room thermometers available?
5. Are there suitable arrangements to heat rooms before the first groups meet early in the morning?

FIGURE 199

TEMPERATURE etc.

VENTILATION?

WORKING TEMPERATURE?

THERMOMETERS?

HUMIDITY?

EARLY HEATING?

FIGURE 200

Now for

Seating

There are two situations concerning seating: first, if you're lucky; second if you're not lucky.

If you are not lucky, you'll have a load of heavy tables in your classroom which are difficult to move and which provide "anchor points" around which your discussion has to take place. It then becomes a question of moving the persons in the group around the tables, should you wish to break the main group down into smaller units to facilitate discussions.

USING TRAPEZOIDAL TABLES

If you're lucky, you'll have special tables which can be moved easily to make for flexible seating and discussion arrangements. The most usefully shaped table for flexible seating patterns is the trapezoidal, shaped like this in plan view:

Here are some arrangements for group discussion made with two or three trapezoidal tables, which are well worth buying, if you haven't got them already.

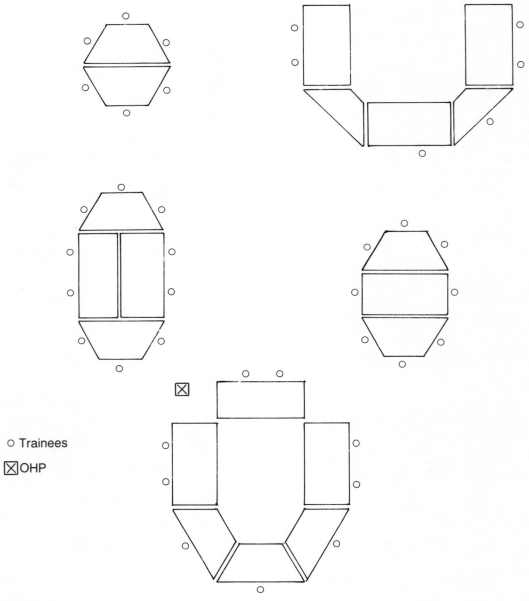

○ Trainees

☒ OHP

FIGURE 201

Ordinary, rectangular or square tables can be moved to make efficient arrangements for smaller group discussion and we show some patterns here.

ARRANGEMENT OF TABLES AND CHAIRS FOR SMALLER GROUP DISCUSSION

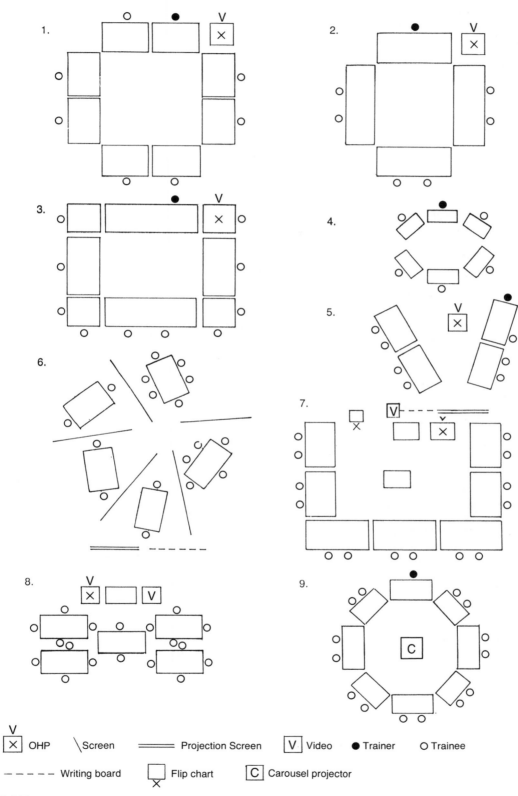

Symbol	Meaning	Symbol	Meaning
$\boxed{\times}$ with V	OHP	\ Screen	
═══	Projection Screen	$\boxed{V}$ Video	
●	Trainer	○	Trainee
‒ ‒ ‒ ‒	Writing board	Flip chart	$\boxed{C}$ Carousel projector

FIGURE 202

Depending on the size of the group, we use numbers 2, 5, 7 and 8 the most as they need less space and re-arrangement than most of the others.

Each of these four have advantages and disadvantages. Suggest what they are.

Advantages	Disadvantages
No 2. *Easily arranged.* *Good viewing.*	*Trainer has to walk around group.*
No 5. *Good visibility.* *Good trainer-trainee contact.* *Informal.*	*Needs a lot of space to accommodate a small group.*
No 7. *Requires little re-arranging.* *May be used as a basic pattern.* *Becomes familiar.* *Business-like.* *Visibility mostly OK.* *Trainer can enter "horse shoe".*	*Formal.* *Rear trainees well removed from screens/board.* *Front trainees have to turn to screens/board.* *Some viewers masked from screens/board.* *If group sub-divided further, trainees have to move.*
No. 8. *Very informal.* *Encourages maximal small group interaction.* *Ideal for team use, buzz groups.* *Trainer can circulate easily and unobtrusively.*	*Some visibility obscured.* *Difficult for trainer to know what's going on.* *Encourages cliques and splinter groups.*

Try the different patterns and see how they work for you and your trainees. We use Number 7, the "Horseshoe" as our basic arrangement. It can be left in place and used for other training methods. If you have more than 16 trainees, then place a few tablet-arm chairs (with a flip-over small writing surface attached to the chair arm) in the central area. You can accommodate numbers in excess of 20 quite easily, this way.

Summary

The group discussion is one of the basic methods of delivering the learning to smaller groups. Other types of discussion are variations of it.

Group discussion is communication and interaction in a group around a topic, skill, issue or problem, presented to the group for discussion.

Leadership in group discussion is concerned with leadership style, of which there are five main types; autocratic, democratic laissez-faire, diplomatic and bureaucratic. The democratic leadership style is generally the most effective, with diplomatic second, but most trainers mix their leadership methods to suit the group and the task in hand.

The leader has many functions in a group and a well-led group usually works effectively.

The physical environment of a group should ensure that the members have a suitable learning space, properly organised for efficient acoustics, lighting, temperature, furnishings and seating.

Seating is particularly important and there are several arrangements of tables and chairs which provide for different patterns of communication and interaction between the trainees who form the group. Of these, the "horseshoe" is widely used, is quite flexible in operation and gives good access.

Consider your own group seating arrangements and how they may be improved with the resources which you have.

In our next Component we look at how the trainer runs an actual group discussion.

Observe leadership tactics in a group of which you are a member. Analyse carefully what is going on, the success and effectiveness of the techniques. Send your analysis to your Programme Tutor for comment.

Component 4:

Holding a Group Discussion

Key Words

The three types of discussion; leadership orientation; stages in group formation; communication patterns; trainer's role in group discussion; preparing and planning, beginning, during and ending discussions; members' roles; advantages and disadvantages of the group discussion method; checklist.

Introduction

Smaller group discussion allows the trainer to introduce issues, ideas, tasks and problems into training and to give this material a thorough examination through active trainee participation.

We should point out that **group discussion is not an effective method of teaching a motor skill**: obviously, the trainees need to practice a skill and group discussion largely precludes this.

However, even when training in a skill, the trainer can introduce some of the advantages of group discussion into the **demonstration** part of the skills lesson. Active discussion of the skill which is being shown can be encouraged by the trainer before and after the demonstration. This ensures that the trainees are taking on active interest in what is going on.

Similarly, during the end of a skills lesson, the trainer can encourage discussion of the practice which the trainees have undertaken. Such talk is helpful in clearing up difficulties and ensuring that the trainees have understood the procedures and stages of the skilled process which they are being taught.

Several other aspects of group discussion are worth looking at before we move on to examine how a discussion is organised and run.

The three types.

Group discussion can take three basic forms:

Planned: where the trainer knows the conclusions and objectives which he wishes the trainees to reach. He has an array of opening statements which arrange the key factors which he wants to be talked about in an appropriate sequence, e.g. a chronological order, a logical sequence, or a linear succession, first-things-first. Discussion is guided by the trainer along these lines.

Partly-planned: concluding and opening statements are known, but the discussion in between is not directed or only very loosely guided.

Unplanned: where the trainer presents the matter for discussion, with no other opening statements and the talking which follows is entirely spontaneous with little or no guidance from the trainer. Such discussion can be very rewarding, but the great degree of freedom can result in irrelevancies, interesting though they might be.

As the next illustration shows, unplanned discussions can take off in completely unexpected directions and can wax anecdotal rather than relevant. "Accountability" and "Budgeting" have been translated in very different and personal ways by the persons in the next Figure.

INTERESTING IRRELEVANCIES

FIGURE 203

When organising your group discussion make sure that you know what sort of interaction you are planning. The type you choose will depend on the structure and the composition of your group and the task which you are undertaking. Another factor in group work is the leadership style and the group orientation which it produces.

Leadership Style and Group Orientation
▨▨▨ Checkpoint

We identified five major types of leadership. Write them down, with a short explanation of each.

Check back through the last Component to find out how accurate your descriptions are.

Each type of leadership tends to give the group a certain orientation. Before we suggest what these are, have a try at deciding what they might be for yourself.

We believe that **leadership gives these orientations** to the group:— **Democratic:** group-oriented, concerned with achieving the group objectives and achieving satisfaction for the members.

Diplomatic: partly group-oriented and partly group-manipulative, concerned with achieving objectives with some superficial member satisfaction. Also partly self-oriented, designed at fulfilling the personal purposes of the leader.

Autocratic: oriented towards achieving the group job or task with self-orientation and little membership satisfaction.

Laissez-faire: showing self-oriented behaviour for both leader and group members.

Bureaucratic: rules-oriented and task-oriented with little care for members' wishes.

Be aware that any orientations which you introduce through the leadership style which you use, either naturally or by design, will affect the interaction of the group and therefore the productivity, effectiveness, behaviour and attitudes of the persons involved in the discussion.

Let's have a closer look at these interactions and the stages which the trainees follow when groups form and meet on several subsequent occasions.

Stages in group formation

When groups meet, their **interaction** usually follows four stages:—

Stage One: Forming. Here the group members are getting to know each other, focusing in on each other's wavelength and testing out reactions. Most persons in the group are a little anxious or uncertain, especially about their ability to deal with the task. This leads to the next phase, which is

Stage Two: Rebelling. When the group meets again, the testing out process continues, conflict arises between those struggling for leadership and between sub-groups, or cliques. The norms, or rules, of the group are questioned and the task itself may even be rebelled against. Of course, rebelling may be a valid activity if the task is ill-conceived, or if there is a struggle for leadership.

CONFLICT AND REBELLION

FIGURE 204

Stage Three: Norming. Gradually, the group now becomes stable, the members know each other, accept their roles and most of the conflicts are resolved. Acceptable norms of behaviour are recognised.

Stage Four: Co-operating. This is the most fruitful stage for the group. There is little conflict, the group becomes cohesive and the whole energy of the group turns to profitable discussion of issues, solving problems and getting on with the task.

This stage continues as long as the persons in the group are satisfied with their roles and no-one feels left out of the group decisions and the working of the group.

The members are cohesive, threats from outside the group are resisted, interaction and communication are good and an acceptable leader is recognised. As long as the job of the group continues to be achieved and objectives fulfilled, the group will carry on effectively.

The stages in group formation which we have described are General Guidelines and they vary according to the task in hand and the duration of the life of the group.

Nevertheless, as a trainer who will often be a group leader, you should be able to recognise the stages as they arise, whether telescoped into a few meetings or appearing over a longer period. Consequently, you have a perspective on how your group is developing and be able to place progress in a context which should allow you to deal with problems as they arise.

Another aspect of understanding and encouraging interaction in a group is a knowledge of channels of communication, or

Communication Patterns

We have already considered communication patterns, or networks, in Component Two of this Study Unit

and Component Two of Study Unit One. So all we need to do here is a little revision.

Having looked through the Components mentioned above, draw diagrams for the patterns of communication between groups with 3, 4, 5 and 8 persons.

Our diagrams are shown in the next Figure.

SOME PATTERNS OF COMMUNICATION AND INTERACTION

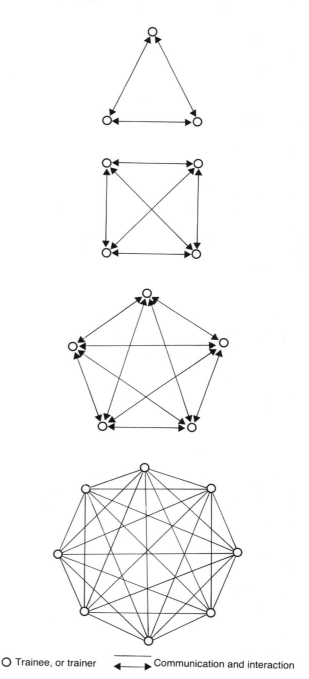

○ Trainee, or trainer ◄──────► Communication and interaction

FIGURE 205

The diagrams in Figure 206 make it clear how complexity increases dramatically as you enlarge the group.

Now try drawing diagrams which show how the patterns would look where you have a hierarchy developing and where a group has sub-divided in to cliques.

HIERARCHIES AND CLIQUES

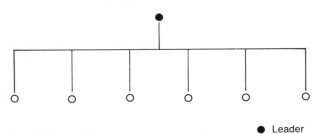

Simplified hierarchy

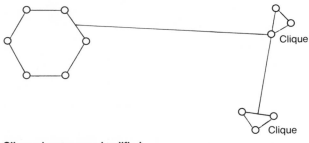

Cliques in a group, simplified

FIGURE 206

You can see from Figure 206 how cliques and hierarchies can disrupt group communication and interaction patterns. Where possible, you should always try to prevent sub-groups forming on a strong or permanent basis as they lead to restricted interaction and to conflict.

We now need to get down to examining in detail how the group discussion is carried on and we shall structure the rest of this Component as follows:
The Trainer's Role in Group Discussion.
Member's role in the Group Discussion.
Advantages and Disadvantages of Group Discussion.
Checklist for a Group Discussion.

If you glance back at Figure 163, you'll see that we are examining the last of the first level units of analysis, "Operating in Groups".

So, let's begin with

* The Trainer's Role in Group Discussion
We have already looked at the general functions of the leader in group discussion and you should refer to Figure 191 in Component Three where you can see the job of the group leader explained in broad terms.

Remember that whilst the group discussion is a trainee-centred strategy for delivering the learning in that the trainee can participate actively, it is also trainer-centred because the trainer often acts as official, or unofficial, group leader. In group discussion, this trainer-centred aspect is much weaker than in the lecture method and in some lessons. This is why we have previously called it a mixed strategy.

So let's examine the trainer's role under the four stages which he will follow in discussion work.
1. Preparing and planning the group discussion.
2. Beginning the discussion.
3. During the discussion.
4. Ending the discussion.

* Stage 1. Preparing and planning the group discussion.
Here are the important aspects of the trainer's role during this stage:
Physical Environment: The trainer must ensure that the physical environment of the learning space in which the discussion is to take place is suitable for the work in hand. Especially, he must ensure appropriate seating which allows face-to-face interaction of the persons in the group.

ENSURING FACE-TO-FACE-INTERACTION

FIGURE 207

As you know, the arrangement shown in Figure 207 is not the best for group discussion, but we think it makes the point about the "face-to-face" nature of group interaction!
Pre-requisites. The trainer must have ensured in previous training sessions that the trainees have the information and knowledge necessary for them to be able to benefit from and contribute to the discussion.

Knowledge of groupwork. Similarly, the trainees must have some understanding of how groups work, the nature and demands of discussion and what can be achieved by this method. The members must accept the value of doing the preparatory groundwork necessary and the trainer must have ensured that this work has been done.

How is this done?

The trainer must give a preparatory lecture, supported by a handout incorporating the main points on groupwork explained in this Study Unit. Preparation for groupwork, especially in the initial stages, should be phased, with the trainer monitoring each phase.

Type of leadership. The trainer must be aware of the varieties of leadership and which style he uses naturally, or which style he tends to adopt. The trainer must also know the effects which leadership styles have on the effectiveness of the group.

The three types. A decision has to be made as to which of the three types of group discussion are to be used whether planned, partly planned, or unplanned.

Stages in group formation. If the group has met before, the trainer should have identified at which stage of group formation the group finds itself in. He can then handle the topics to be discussed most profitably.

People in the group. Similarly, for a group which has held discussions previously, the trainer will need to know the dynamics of this particular group including group characteristics (personality, cohesiveness, laws, commitment), the group structure (individual variables, type of group), and the group interaction patterns (communication, behavioural and barrier).

Objectives. The trainer must have the objectives of the forthcoming discussion established clearly.

Content. He must also be aware of the topic, issue, problem or decision which the group are to discuss.

Pre-planned questions. The trainer must preplan the major questions which the group are to be asked, together with an outline of what is expected in a suitable answer.

Review. If the trainer has previously handed out information about the topic for discussion and proposes to review it at the beginning of the session, then he must make appropriate notes before hand.

* Stage 2. Beginning the discussion.
What the trainer does at the beginning of the discussion itself rather depends upon the type of group, the task and the characteristics of the group. So all, or some of the following parts may be observed in the trainer's role:

Gain the attention and interest which are necessary to engender motivation and the consequent participation of the group members.

Brief the group on the objectives of the discussion, which are explained fully and perhaps shown on an OHP or on the board.

Recall the pre-requisite learning.

Guide the group in **selecting** a topic, problem or task for discussion, or inform them fully of what it is to be. Sometimes this topic will be part of a previous learning experience like a field trip which they have made, or video seen, or an article read, or a lecture. If this is so, the trainees will already be motivated to discuss what they have experienced.

Allow participation of the trainees in selecting the topic, or aspects of the topic they want to concentrate on, where feasible. If the members feel involved at this point, subsequent discussion is usually improved. Part of this participation is developed by showing how the proposed topic is relevant to the trainees with questions like: How does this problem or topic affect you? Is discussion likely to help the group? Do the trainees feel competent enough to deal with the topic?

Present some pre-planned questions to warm-up the persons in the group and get the discussion going.

Check the suitability of the learning space and arrange, or re-arrange the seating.

Introduce everybody, or have them introduce themselves, or use "ice-breaker" games at the very first session.

Agree "ground rules" for groupwork at the beginning of the first session.

What do you think these "ground rules" might be?

We suggest:
Don't interrupt others.
Everyone should have a chance to speak.
No smoking (or smoking is allowed).
Members may ask you or someone else for help.
The ground rules can be changed at any time if a majority agrees.
Individual contributions should not go on overlong.

Timing should be made clear, e.g.
"We will talk for 35 minutes, then ten minutes for summing up, so we end at two minutes to eleven."

Break the main group down into temporary sub-groups if the topic is large and complex, giving each sub-group a component to discuss and then report back. In this case, you'll need time for reporting back at the end of the session.

An amusing method to decide on sub-groups is called **"on-parade"**, where the trainees line up, with the most experienced or skilled in a particular topic nearest to the door along the line, to those with least experience at the other end. The sub-groups are then formed from nearest neighbours or mixed, e.g. every third person joins one group.

Otherwise, you may pre-select groups yourself on a basis of say, all stronger or weaker together or randomly, e.g. every other person where they sit at the beginning, or neighbour groups of three or four, or first four in the alphabet and so on.

SELECTING SUB-GROUPS RANDOMLY

FIGURE 208

If you intend to use the pyramiding technique, pair the trainees off immediately before discussion starts.

Should you decide to use a debating technique, then divide the group into (opposing) halves.

HALVING THE GROUP

FIGURE 209

Well, perhaps the technique of Figure 209 is not recommended, but at least you'd get opposing viewpoints!

Whilst you can place all those who agree with a topic statement on one side and those against on another, in the traditional fashion, you can also ask trainees to speak for a view with which they disagree, changing sides halfway through the debate.

Present the topic or issue for discussion in a short lecturette if necessary. This enables you to set the scene, inform the trainees of the basic elements of the discussion subject and give some guidance on the order in which the topic will be considered. It is also useful to identify any major sources for further reading or research.

You are now ready to undertake your role in Stage 3.

* Stage 3. During the discussion.
Obviously, during the discussion itself your participation varies according to how things are going, but the following are important. Have a try at identifying your own part in recent discussions before you read our suggestions.

Define problems and issues rather than solutions.

Don't talk too much yourself; keep a low profile.

Don't pit your wits against the trainees; mostly you are bound to win, anyway.

Be neutral, trying to show both sides of an issue.

Be prepared to have your own preferences knocked down.

Act as a consultant, guiding and helping when needed, but only when really needed. Try to make yourself a sort of "information centre".

Don't use overt authority; that will kill discussion.

Be responsible for keeping to a discussion timetable.

Ensure face-to-face interaction.

Give access to boards and OHP's.

Provide any materials necessary and distribute.

Keep the group working fruitfully.

Judge on disputes between persons in the group but only when you have to.

Offer advice and comment, when asked.

Ensure that the objectives of the group are being attained and that the discussion is pertinent and following profitable lines.

Establish an atmosphere of freedom and friendliness.

Encourage the weaker members especially and

Ensure maximal trainee interaction, communication and participation.

Give everyone an equal opportunity to participate.

Consider all contributions, or make certain they are considered.

Respect well-supported and honest viewpoints which differ from your own.

Avoid confrontations as this restricts learning, especially as most trainees find aggression daunting.

Be aware of non-verbal cues, such as facial expressions and gestures, so that you can have a feel for the group reaction.

Clarify difficulties, correct misinterpretations and errors, define new concepts and terms.

Assist the trainees to express and clarify their ideas.

Encourage trainees to think through problems.

Stimulate lines of approach which may result in trainee follow-up after discussion.

Summarise progress periodically, if necessary.

Act as "devil's advocate" by deliberately being controversial, presenting an opposing viewpoint.

TAKING THE OTHER SIDE

FIGURE 210

Organise contributions by nodding at the next contributor or holding up your hand to restrain too many people trying to talk at once.

Ask provocative questions, if no-one wants to talk, or start talking, but don't be rude.

Control trainees who want to monopolise the discussion, or do not recognise them if they have made numerous contributions already.

Quieten angry members by joking, redirecting the discussion or, if you have to, ask for hush.

Don't allow the trainees to wear out a theme.

Allow occasional silences; the trainees might well need to pause for thought.

Remember, remember, the Golden Rule that learning is achieved in a group by participation of the members through successful interaction and communication.

How do you do this?

Engender learning by: encouraging the trainees to talk; asking each other to speak; regarding you merely as a member of the group; sub-grouping; making a "round" where everyone makes an uninterrupted statement on some aspect of the topic; encouraging the trainees to ask questions rather than you asking; addressing their remarks to each other and not to you; using buzz groups; by asking open-ended questions which the trainees develop themselves.

And, of course, by using the techniques which we have described already in this section on what the trainer does during the discussion.

This leaves a consideration of what the trainer does when

* Stage 4. Ending the discussion
Here you want to

Help the group to a conclusion, a decision or find a solution to the problem.

Assist the group to select one or two conclusions if several are available, by agreeing a consensus or majority decision.

Decide if any further action need be taken on the topic or issue in hand.

Sum-up finally, by yourself, or ask the trainees to do so.

Note significant areas of agreement or disagreement which still remain.

Link the current with previous learning.

Suggest or **outline** the topics for the next discussion.

Give sub-groups the opportunity of reporting back.

Feedback information on progress accomplished.

Evaluate the discussion and its findings.

Clearly, the role of the trainer is important and there are many aspects to it, as we have tried to show. You will probably derive best value by reading and rereading the last few pages on the trainer's role in group discussion and considering how far you have implemented our suggestions in discussions which you have held.

You should then find that our recommendations spring to mind naturally for you to use in future discussions. Our next major topic in this Component is

* The Members' Role in Group Discussion
You may wish to incorporate these suggestions as to what a group member should be doing in a discussion into your **ground rules**.

What do you believe your trainees should be doing in group discussion?

Our brief suggestions follow.

In a group discussion each person in the group should:

- **Make** an effort to **prepare** for the discussion by reading literature, manuals and handbooks before hand.
- **State** views, ideas, opinions, interpretations and possible solutions.
- **Give** support.
- **Disagree** where appropriate, but support disagreement with justification and evidence.
- **Suppress** personal objectives for group objectives.
- **Follow** agreed group norms.
- **Make contributions** audibly.
- **Listen** with care, attention and respect.
- **Give information**, proofs, evidence and explanation.
- **Seek information,** proofs, evidence and explanation.
- **Comment** or group procedures and progress.
- **Build on** the ideas of other group members.

- **Redirect discussion** which has become erratic.
- **Try to link** contributions to objectives.
- **Be prepared** to use OHP and board when necessary.
- **Summarise** evidence, re-phrase, re-organise and clarify contributions.
- **Show** positive behaviour.
- **Try** to **counteract and counterbalance** the negative behaviours of others.
- **Make any report** required by sub-groups, if asked.
- **Attempt** to participate at all times.
- **Communicate** clearly.
- **Interact** maximally.

It is frequently useful to train the trainees in what is expected of them before embarking on a series of group discussions. Using our list which shows a member's role as a basis, it is sensible to work through it so that the trainees know what to do when they become group members. Reassure the trainees that most people feel nervous about contributing to a discussion, especially in a newly formed group. Tell them that this anxiety should pass as they become more experienced in group procedures and in making contributions.

Another useful idea is to discuss with them

* The Advantages and Disadvantages of Group Discussion
We'll begin with a survey of
The Advantages of Group Discussion.
These are:—

- All the trainees are involved.
- The expertise of the trainer is available and can be used to direct discussion.
- Critical thinking can be stimulated.
- Group concensus can be achieved.
- Group discussion provides an interesting change of method in delivering the learning and fits in well with other methods.
- The higher levels of Bloom's taxonomy can be achieved as the trainees can demonstrate application, synthesis and evaluation in discussion. This cannot always be attained with other methods.
- Trainees can express opinions and ideas freely.
- Decision-making skills, independent of trainer's support, are fostered.
- Independent problem-solving skills are improved.
- Creative thinking skills are encouraged, e.g. perceiving new relationships, or providing imaginative solutions.
- Oral, non-verbal and written communication skills are improved. The skills of presenting and defending arguments and making sensible, meaningful contributions are practised more in this method of learning than in any other.
- Social skills are exercised and improved: the members have to get on with each other if the group is to be effective. Trainees learn about co-operation, leadership and delegation.
- Members develop an appreciation of the importance of non-verbal skills and non-verbal cues, such as reading body language.

NON-VERBAL CUE

FIGURE 211

— Discussion teaches trainees to expound and defend their values and attitudes and helps them to modify those which are unsuitable. Trainee interaction is one of the most important keys to attitude change. Freedom of discussion breaks down prejudices and wrong conceptions.

— Trainees become aware of the multiplicity of factors involved in any solution, issue or topic.

— Groupwork promotes an intellectual development and rational thinking is best fostered in groupwork.

— Relationships with the trainer improve, as he is seen as less authoritarian, more approachable and having fallibilities like everyone else.

IMPROVED RELATIONS WITH TRAINER

FIGURE 212

— Personality develops through social and group interaction, especially the need for co-operative stances.

— Positive behaviour is enhanced and trainees learn that it is more rewarding.

— Negative behaviour is suppressed and seen as a handicap.

— Self-discipline is necessary to subscribe to group norms.

— Group learning can be cost-effective.

However, there are some
Disadvantages of Group Discussion.
These may be:—

— Discussion can move more slowly and little may seem to be achieved through what seems to be snail's-pace progress.

A SLOW-MOVING DISCUSSION

FIGURE 213

— Negative behaviour may predominate, especially over-domination by a few talkers.

— The group may become hopelessly side-tracked.

— Heterogeneous groups may have to move at a "compromise" speed, too slow for the ablest and too quick for the slowest. Worse still, a "convoy" pace may prevail, i.e. that of the slowest member.

— Some members finish as they start, still having difficulties in making a contribution.

— Trainees often do not prepare themselves adequately.

— The trainer fails to provide adequate preparatory material, or time in which to prepare.

— Leading a discussion requires a change of role on the part of the trainer and he may not relish this, or have an aptitude for it.

— A change of role is also required of the trainee, who has to become active, rather than a passive recipient of knowledge and skills. Trainees may not like this, nor appreciate the different relationship with the trainer, on whom they must depend less.

— Debriefing may not take place through lack of time at the end of the discussion. Much of the effectiveness of groupwork thus becomes lost.

— Assessment of trainees, if required, is difficult.

— Co-operation may be hard to obtain between trainer and trainees and between trainees themselves. Consequently, group cohesion is poor and progress slow.

— Trainees may not be happy at accepting the group's "ground rules" or norms and are afraid to show themselves up in front of their peers. Discussion is then inhibited.

What conclusions do you come to when reading and thinking about these advantages and disadvantages?

Whilst the disadvantages appear formidable, most of them can be overcome in effective, cooperative and cohesive groupwork. By contrast, the advantages are permanent, especially in well-run groups.

Finally, let's look at this Checklist for group discussion, which will serve as a **summary** of this Component.

* Checklist for a Group Discussion

CHECKLIST

In preparing and planning the group discussion, did I

1. Prepare the physical environment, or learning space, efficiently?
2. Ensure that I had given the trainees sufficient information to cover the pre-requisites?
3. Adopt an appropriate type of leadership?
4. Make a clear decision on whether the discussion was to be planned, partly planned, or unplanned?
5. Know what stage in group formation my group was at?
6. Understand the group's characteristics and communication?
7. Understand the group's structure and accommodate it?
8. Foresee individual member's likely behaviour and make plans to accommodate it?
9. Have the objectives for the groupwork defined clearly?
10. Prepare suitable pre-planned and leading questions?
11. Know the topic, issue, problem or decision to be discussed thoroughly?

When beginning and during the discussion, did I

12. Introduce the topic, issue, problem or decision?
13. Explain the objectives of the discussion?
14. Ensure the discussion was relevant?
15. Maintain a balance in trainees' contributions?
16. Remain neutral?
17. Avoid monopolising the discussion and keep a low profile?
18. Make periodic summaries?
19. Give adequate guidance?
20. Keep to the timings?
21. Break the main group down into smaller groups if necesssary?
22. Provide appropriate materials and handouts?
23. Establish a friendly, free atmosphere?
24. Encourage positive behaviour?
25. Suppress negative behaviour?
26. Encourage trainees' participation, communication and interaction?

When ending the discussion, did I

27. Assist the group to make a conclusion, a report, give a solution, express a decision?
28. Give feedback on progress?
29. Suggest ways of using insights gained in discussion?
30. Evaluate the discussion and its findings?

FIGURE 214

Obviously this Component has shown many other items which you could add, but those in the Checklist appear to us to be of major concern.

In the next Component we are going to look at different types of group discussion. So select one now, such as a panel, or seminar and identify the main points which you consider we should discuss.

Finally, there is one major advantage of group discussion which we have kept till last. Can you suggest what this is?

Well, this advantage is that group discussion allows you, as trainer, to regard your trainees as individuals Each group member can benefit from personal participation and interaction. Trainees can express themselves and develop individually to a large degree. You can go much of the way to delivering the learning to each person. Remember the old slogan we gave you previously? That's it: **Banish Learnermass.**

Apply the Checklist in Figure 214 to a group discussion which you held recently. Send your evaluation of the effectiveness of the group discussion and of the group operation to your Programme Tutor for comment, should you want to.

Component 5:

The Seminar and the Panel Discussion

Key Words

 Seminar; definition; seating; patterns of communication and interaction; running the seminar, preparation, running the discussion; presenter's role; trainee's role, checklist; advantages and disadvantages of the seminar; the panel discussion; the expert panel; the trainee panel.

Introduction

In this and the next Component, we are examining some other forms of groupwork which are based upon the group discussion. If you look at Figure 160, Component One, Study Unit Three, "Methods of delivering the learning to smaller groups", you will see that the relevant Boxes are 2, 4 and 5.

Here we are examining two of the major developments of the group discussion; these are the

Seminar and the

Panel Discussion

When we look at each we will follow this plan:

1. **Definition**
2. **Seating**
3. **Patterns of Communication and interaction**
4. **Running the seminar/panel**
5. **Advantages and Disadvantages**
6. **Checklist**

So let's begin with

* The Seminar

1. * Definition

DEFINITION OF A SEMINAR

> A seminar is a type of group discussion where one trainee, or several, prepares a paper on a given topic, issue or problem, which is then presented to the whole group for discussion and analysis.

FIGURE 215

So we see differences immediately from the group discussion which we have considered already as our basic form.

Checkpoint

What do you believe these differences to be?

They are:

— *The trainees, or the trainee, present the material to be discussed rather than the trainer.*

— *Accordingly, the trainer plays much less of a central role in the discussion, i.e. the seminar is a more trainee-centred method of delivering the learning.*

— *Therefore, the seminar will require a different sort of planning from the group discussion.*

— *The trainees, rather than the trainer, are responsible for the success of the seminar.*

— *The seminar is more formal than the group discussion.*

— *It requires a fairly sophisticated type of trainee whose level of attainment is high enough to present and analyse the seminar paper.*

Commonly, a series of seminars can be presented by the trainees around a major topic, so that they form a linked series of discussions.

We must make an important point here: in the literature which you read about groupwork, you will find that the Americans use the word "seminar" differently from us. An American will define a "seminar" in the way that we define a "conference"; their seminars are our conferences that go on for several days. So take care to avoid any confusion which can arise from this differing terminology.

ANOTHER TYPE OF SEMANTIC DIFFERENTIAL

FIGURE 216

2. * Seating
This is the same as for a group discussion, shown in Figures 201 and 202 of Component Three of this Study Unit.

3. * Patterns of Communication and interaction
There are two stages in the seminar and these patterns vary in each.

Consider what these stages are, from what we have told you about the Seminar already and draw patterns for each.

The stages are: **presenting the paper**
discussing the paper

The interaction and communication patterns vary as follows:

COMMUNICATION AND INTERACTION PATTERNS WHEN PRESENTING A SEMINAR PAPER

One presenter

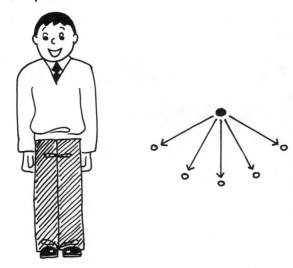

Several presenters

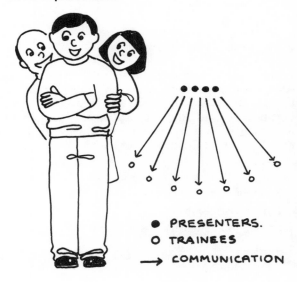

● PRESENTERS.
O TRAINEES
→ COMMUNICATION

FIGURE 217

COMMUNICATION AND INTERACTION
PATTERNS WHEN DISCUSSING THE PAPER

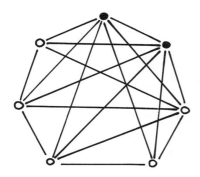

● PRESENTER/S
○ TRAINEES
— COMMUNICATION AND
INTERACTION

FIGURE 218

4. * Running the seminar

There are three main aspects to this:
the trainer's role
the presenter's role
the trainee's role
Let's look at each of these in turn.

The Trainer's Role. There are two parts to this:
Preparing the seminar
Running the Seminar
When **preparing the Seminar,** the **trainer** has these
responsibilities:

— **Select** a trainee, or group of trainees to present the
paper, or ask for volunteers. A group is preferable
when the topic is complex.
— **Select** suitable topics for discussion.
— **Acquaint** the presenters with a Summary of the
paper which is to be presented, about one month in
advance of the seminar.
— **The presenters' summary** must contain this
information:
a) Title of the paper.
b) A short description of the issue, topic or problem
and an abstract of the argument which is to be
presented.
c) The objectives of the topic and of the seminar.
d) The main headings and sub-headings of the
topic.
e) Sources of information, including a reading list,
statistics, descriptive handouts, articles and
periodicals, manuals etc.
— **It is useful to hand a brief version** of this summary
to all the trainees in the group, so that they can read
up the material, as well. This second summary will
usually be shorter than that given to the
presenters.
— **Discuss** the summary with the presenter(s) when
they have had a chance to look at it and sort out any
difficulties.
— **Many presenters are anxious** about giving their
paper, so keep in **close contact** during the period of
preparation. An essential function of the trainer at
this stage is to ensure that presenters have all the
support which they need.

SUPPORTING THE PRESENTER

FIGURE 219

— **Finally,** have a session with the presenter(s) just
before the seminar to **check** that all is well. Make
certain that the objectives of the topics or issue have
been covered adequately. Ensure that timings are
suitable and that the presenter is not talking more
than 20 minutes in an hour-long seminar. Also make
certain that the presenter has a proper sequence to
his or her paper, that this structure is logical and
orderly, that he or she has pre-planned certain vital
questions and answers and that the presenter knows
the norms and ground rules of the group.

when **running the Seminar** the **trainer**

— **Should keep** in the background.
— **Help** the presenter(s) only when essential.
— **Act** as time-keeper.
— **Resolve** any major problems.
— **Help** the group to be self-sufficient and independent.
— **Evaluate** the seminar at the end, both privately and
in public, **judging** the following:
a) The group's understanding of the topic.
b) The quality of the paper presented, including
depth and quality of research and preparation.
c) the quality of the discussion, the views, analyses
and arguments expressed.
d) The quality of the contributions, the perception of
acceptable and unacceptable arguments, sound
and unsound views.
e) The soundness of the group's conclusions.
f) The quality of the actual presentation, including
clarity, pacing, emphasis, voice production and
control, mannerisms, use of visuals, control of
group.
g) The quality of the presenter's handouts.

The **Presenter's Role** is to

- **Prepare** the paper thoroughly.
- **Know** the topic, issue or problem in detail.
- **Consult** the trainer when necessary.
- **Run** the discussion efficiently.
- **Help** everybody to contribute.
- **Assist** the group to reach accurate conclusions and decisions.
- **Avoid** sidetracking.
- **Ensure** the production and issue of high quality handouts.
- **Pre-plan** important questions.
- **Make** interim and final summaries.
- **Keep** to timings agreed with trainer. Suitable timings might be

ACTION	MINUTES
a) Introduction	3
b) Presentation of paper	17
c) Discussion	10
d) Interim summary	2
e) Discussion	5
f) Interim summary	2
g) Discussion	10
h) Final summary	5
j) Conclusions and evaluation by trainer	6
	TOTAL = 1 hour

- **Finally be courteous** and kindly to everybody and refrain from seeking help from the trainer.

The **Trainee's role** is to

- **Provide** an interested audience.
- **Contribute.**
- **Analyse** the arguments, and other contributions.
- **Help** identify the main points and conclusions.
- **Avoid** negative behaviour.
- **Exhibit** positive behaviour.
- **Support** the presenter(s).
- **Apply** the learning to their own situation.

In general, the trainees should show all the positive aspects of group behaviour required in a group discussion.

5. * Advantages and Disadvantages of the Seminar

Advantages
- Allows the group to become more independent.
- A change of group leader (i.e. not the trainer) is refreshing.
- Give trainees, in turns, a chance to prepare a topic or issue very thoroughly.
- Allows trainees, in turns, to practice the techniques of intensive, orderly preparation of a topic.
- Gives them a chance to practice group leadership.
- Allows the trainees to use analytical skills, reach a conclusion, solve a problem, largely independently.
- Allows them an opportunity to practice presentation skills.
- Give an insight and practice in running a group.

Disadvantages
- Can be time-consuming.
- Relies for effectiveness on quality of the paper which is presented and this may be poor.
- Relies on the quality and skills of the presenter, who is usually inexperienced and may be inadequate.
- Relies on an untried group leader.
- Handouts may be poor.
- Needs a group of trainees with fairly high levels of attainment.
- May cause stress.

SUPPORT AND STRESS

FIGURE 220

16. * Trainers Checklist for a Seminar

Did I

Preparation
1. **Give** an adequate Summary to the presenter; emphasising topic objectives; pick a suitable topic?
2. **Issue** a similar, shorter summary to all the trainees?
3. **Offer** the presenter adequate support, including time for discussion?
4. **Allay** any anxiety on the part of the presenter?

During the seminar
5. **Keep** in the background, stay low-profile and neutral?
6. **Timekeep?**
7. **Evaluate** the Seminar adequately?
8. **Evaluate** the paper both privately and (more gently) in public?
9. **Evaluate** the presentation?
10. **Evaluate** the contributions?
11. **Evaluate** the presenter's handouts?
12. **Conclude**, emphasising the main points and objectives?

The Panel Discussion.

1. * Definition

DEFINITION OF A PANEL

A panel is a discussion, held by three to six speakers, which is listened to by an audience, who follow the panel discussion with a general group discussion.

FIGURE 222

So what we have here is a small group discussion between several members of a panel, or panellists, which is overheard by an audience of trainees.

The panellists are selected for their special expertise and experience. Consequently, their views are usually well-informed, open up new insights, are interesting and very up-to-date.

The trainer normally acts as chairman of the panel.

2. * Seating

SEATING FOR A PANEL DISCUSSION

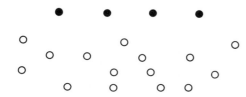

● Panellist
○ Trainees

FIGURE 223

3. * Patterns of communication and interaction
There are two stages in a panel discussion, these are:
Discussion by the panel members.
General Discussion by the whole group.
The patterns are as shown in the next two Figures.

COMMUNICATION AND INTERACTION
PATTERNS DURING THE PANEL DISCUSSION

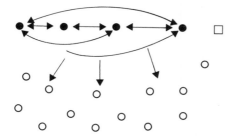

□ Chairperson
● Panellist
○ Trainees

FIGURE 224

It is difficult to show the communication and interaction patterns between the members of the panel, but we have tried to show that the panellists talk and interchange views amongst themselves, freely. The audience of trainees listens passively during this stage.

COMMUNICATION AND INTERACTION
PATTERNS DURING THE GENERAL
DISCUSSION.

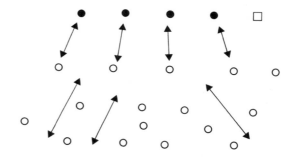

□ Chairperson.
May be located in
centre of panel.

FIGURE 225

Here, the trainee audience asks questions, expresses views, agrees and disagrees with the panel.

The panel discussion is very informal, the panellists talking and arguing freely amongst themselves with little direction from the chairman, who may or may not join in the discussion.

Questions and views from the audience must be directed to the panel. Usually, the trainees do not talk to each other nor question each other.

Generally, the chairperson will signify which member of the audience is to ask the next question.

4. * Running the Panel
The trainer plays an important part in the panel discussion during three phases:
Preparing for the Panel
During the Panel Discussion
During the General Discussion

When **preparing for the panel**, the responsibilities of the trainer are to
— Ensure a selection of high quality, expert and experienced panellists are available.
— Ensure selection of a suitable topic.
— Brief each member of the panel briefly about
  a) the topic, issue or problem to be discussed.
  b) the knowledge which the trainee audience will have about the topic.
  c) the date, time and place of panel discussion.
  d) the size and nature of the trainee audience.
— Ensure that all resources, rooms, seating and lighting are adequate.
— Inform the trainees of the panel membership, topic, time, place and date.
— Provide the trainees with background material so that they are informed about the topic.
— Warn them that they will be expected to ask questions, state views and present arguments, i.e. interact with the panellists.
— Ask the trainees to respect the chairperson's authority and
— Be pleasant, courteous and polite to their visitors.
— Make sure that all of the trainees attend!

WAS IT WORTH IT?

FIGURE 226

Amazingly, as you can see from Figure 226, the trainees (and students in further and higher education) sometimes think a panel is a "talk shop" held by strangers and they think this is one activity that they can skip! This shows inadequate preparation by the trainers. You really have to impress on the trainees the importance of forming a large, worthwhile and appreciative audience. Preparatory reading on the trainees' part and building up their anticipation on your part are fundamentally important in ensuring an audience ready to attend and participate.

Then during the panel discussion, the trainer has the important role of acting as Chairperson, which involves:
— Arranging the seating for the panel.
— Beginning the discussion with a short introduction to the topic problem or issue which is the subject of the discussion, and to the members of the panel.
— Monitoring the discussion by ensuring that
  a) All panel members make contributions of approximately even length.
  b) No-one dominates the discussion.
  c) The panel keeps to the subject of the discussion.
— Ending the panel discussion on time.

Finally, **during the general discussion,** the trainer continues as Chairperson, by
— Inviting contributions from the trainee audience.
— Filling in any gaps in the flow of questions from the trainees by questioning the panel himself, or presenting a personal view, or otherwise generating further discussion.
— Monitoring the discussion by
  a) identifying who is to contribute next.
  b) Indicating that there is time for one more question.
  c) Summing up the discussion and declaring it closed.
  d) Thanking the panel and the audience.
  e) Generally keeping to the schedule of timings.

Concerning the last point, it is very important to keep the various parts of the panel meeting on the time schedule.

For a sixty minute panel discussion, write down what you think is a suitable breakdown in time for various stages.

Our suggested breakdown is shown in the next Figure.

PANEL DISCUSSION: TIMINGS

STAGE	TIMING/MINUTES
Chairperson's Introduction	5
Discussion between panellists	30 (or 35)
General discussion, panel and audience	20 (or 15)
Summing up by Chairperson	3
Closure	2
Total	60 minutes

FIGURE 227

Another type of Panel Discussion. Many panels are formed from "outside" experts, who are brought together to talk about some issue or topic. By "outside" we mean other employees in your organisation who are not part of the training department, but who have special knowledge of the subject under discussion. Another type of "outsider" is the expert brought in from outside your organisation, who might well be a nationally recognised figure. Unfortunately, such persons are frequently difficult to contact, have little time, sometimes call off at the last minute and can demand a fee. As they can reasonably ask for travelling expenses additionally, your hour's panel is going to be a costly business.

So what can you do about this?

The answer is to create your own panel from your group of trainees. The procedure is similar to that of preparing for a seminar, except that you select not one, but several trainees to act as a panel. You prepare them exactly as you do for the seminar, but when the panel day arrives, they do not present a paper, but talk around their subject.

We said that you prepare them **exactly** *as you do for a seminar, but this is not quite true. Whilst the trainees have to do the preparatory work as diligently as they do for a seminar, they do not write out a paper, but concentrate on preparing a* **series of interesting and perhaps controversial statements.** *These they use as a basis for their contributions, during the discussions.*

If you like, you can "beef" up the panel with a couple of experts from your own organisation who will help the trainees along. Panels of this nature tend to be larger than those we described previously, say four trainees, a couple of "imports" and yourself.

They have the advantage of involving the trainees more closely and sometimes of keeping the discussion at a level which all the trainees understand easily.

However, they do not provide fresh faces and may not give the audience a "state-of-the-art" talk, which acknowledged experts can.

Picking your first panel may be difficult.

SELECTING A PANEL

FIGURE 228

As this **trainee panel**, as distinct from the **expert panel** which we described before, is of a different character and therefore operates differently, here are **some tips which will help things to run smoothly:**

- Remember that as trainer-leader you will have less control of the discussion, so everyone must prepare thoroughly.
- As Chairperson, you must ensure that everyone on the panel reacts to questions and talks freely, but you might have to give more guidance than in the expert panel situation.
- In a group discussion the trainer largely plans, prepares and controls the event, but in a trainee panel it is the trainees themselves who do this.
- Make sure that the subject which you give the trainee panel grows naturally out of the training programme, and should be of immmediate interest to the trainees. They will be able to handle this more familiar material more efficiently.
- Give the trainees a chance to pick their own topic, issue or problem.
- Try to select open issues, which have an element of controversy and which the trainee panel and the audience can really get their "teeth" into.
- Although you may adopt the "short-straw" selection procedure shown in Figure 228, for the first couple of panels you should personally pick the most able trainees, so that you get off to a good start.
- Encourage the trainee panel members to break down complex subjects into sub-topics, which each can manage more easily.
- Give them plenty of time to prepare, say three or four weeks.
- You can give the trainee panellists a series of questions to answer. Either you, or they can then introduce those questions and answers into the panel discussion.
- Give the trainee panellists a Summary of the subject, as you would for a seminar.
- Aid the panellists to be effective by these techniques:
  a) Making short contributions up to one minute in length.
  b) As chairman ask open-ended questions which generate answers and probe the topic.
  c) Try to link the various contributions together and to the theme of the discussion.
  d) As Chairperson be warm, friendly and tactful and ensure each contribution is treated with respect.
  e) Make challenging statements from time to time.
  f) Try to introduce new aspects of the subject to the trainees, linking with what has gone before, by short summaries of the previous discussion running into an introduction to another area.
- Make certain to underline the principles of what has been said in your concluding summary. You can put more of yourself into this, should you have kept particularly quiet during the discussion.

So we have two types of panel discussion, the expert panel and the trainee. Both have a useful place, but which do you think you will use most?

Probably the trainee panel, because it is certainly more economical, can be very cost-effective and is easier to arrange.

You may wish to keep your "BIG-GUNS" for the occasional expert panel, highlighting the end of a course.

5. * Advantages and Disadvantages of Panel Discussion

Advantages
— Trainees are exposed to informed opinion.
— Provides considerable interaction between the panel and the trainees.
— Well-expressed views by experts act as a model for trainees.
— Trainees have experience in analysing the statements of others, defending their own opinions and making contributions.
— Trainee panellists have invaluable experience in presenting their material and in oral interchange.
— An expert panel presents fresh focus and new views and is stimulating.

Disadvantages
— Sometimes much ground is covered; sometimes not.
— Discussion may be unsystematic.
— Control of panellists may be difficult.
— Questions and views can come thick and fast and some areas may be left ill-considered or incomplete.
— Heavy demands in articulateness, quick thinking and ability to marshal facts and formulate answers are placed on the trainee panellists.
— Expert panel members can sometimes go "over the top" in detail and technicality.
— The discussion may be difficult to summarise.

6. * Trainer's Checklist for a Panel Discussion

Much of what we said for the Seminar Checklist applies here.

PANEL CHECKLIST

DID I
1. **Pick** a suitable topic, issue or problem?
2. **Select** a suitable panel?
3. **Give** the panellists adequate briefing?
4. **Ensure** that the objectives of the discussion were clear?
5. **Encourage** thorough preparation of the subject?
6. **Give** the panel adequate preparation time and assistance?
7. **Ensure** a good-sized audience who knew when and where to attend?
8. **Make** sure all of the trainee audience could see and hear?
9. **Make** an effective introduction to the panel and the subject?
10. **Monitor** the discussion efficiently?
11. **Make** an effective Summary?
12. **Evaluate** the panel discussion?
13. **Feedback** the results of evaluation to the trainees?

FIGURE 229

///

One item on the Checklist involves several important activities. Which is this "umbrella" item and what activities are included in it?

The item is number ten, did I "monitor the discussion efficiently?" Look back through this Component to see what that involves.

Summary

In this Component we considered the Seminar and the Panel Discussion and defined each.

Although both are derived from the Group Discussion, the Seminar differs in that it revolves around the presentation of a paper which is then discussed generally. The Panel discussion involves a discussion by experts, succeeded by general discussion.

Consequently, the patterns of interaction in both are different from the group discussion initially and then are similar during the general discussion which involves the trainee audience.

In the seminar, the trainer has to ensure the thorough-going and efficient preparation of a paper by a trainee, or group of trainees; he must give considerable support during this stage.

Subsequently, in this seminar discussion, the trainer should keep a low profile, but has to monitor the discussion and summarise comprehensively if the seminar is to be effective.

In the panel discussion, the trainer usually acts as Chairperson. During the first stage, the panellists who are informed and experienced people in the case of the expert panel, and well-prepared trainees in the case of the trainee panel, hold a discussion which is seen and overheard by the audience.

In the general discussion stage of the panel, the whole trainee audience participates with the panellists and the trainer continues as Chair person. Again he monitors the discussion and summarises.

Both seminar and panel discussion must be evaluated by the trainer and the results fed back to the trainees. This evaluation should be made privately, by the trainer reflecting on the events of the day and deciding how to do it better next time. It should also be made in public, working with the trainees and making sure not to offend anyone.

Send one of your evaluations to your Programme Tutor for further evaluation, if you wish.

Component 6:

The Symposium and Brainstorming

Key Words

Symposium; definition; seating; patterns of communication and interaction; running a symposium; advantages and disadvantages; Checklist; Brainstorming; Stages: Introduction; Icebreaker; Defining; Focusing (Focus Statements); Selecting; Brainstorming (Developments); Incubation; Daftest Suggestion; Evaluation; Four basic rules.

Introduction

In this Component we shall look at two further important types of group discussion, the

Symposium

Brainstorming.

Both are widely used, especially Brainstorming, which is suitable for many sorts of groupwork. We shall use the same structure for examining each as we did in the last Component, viz.

1. **Definition**
2. **Seating**
3. **Patterns of Communication and Interaction**
4. **Running the Symposium/Brainstorm**
5. **Advantages and Disadvantages**
6. **Checklist.**

We shall start with

* The Symposium

1.   *** Definition**

DEFINITION OF A SYMPOSIUM

A symposium consists of several formal speeches, given by an expert panel and followed by a general group discussion.

FIGURE 230

We must emphasise that the symposium is much more of a formal occasion, certainly in the initial stages, than are any of the forms of group work which we have considered so far.

FORMALITY AND THE SYMPOSIUM

FIGURE 231

There are other differences and these are:

— The participants, or panel, in a symposium are picked for their special expertise in the subject. Consequently, they are not trainees, but invited speakers, drawn from your own organisation and from outside. They are similar, therefore, to the expert panel in the panel discussion.

— Each speaker gives a lecturette, or a short speech of about ten minutes duration. No questions are asked during these presentations.

— Each lecturette must be limited strictly by the Chairperson to a previously agreed time limit.

2. * Seating

This is similar to the panel discussion. However, during the panel discussion the speaker often addresses the trainee audience from his seat. In the symposium, the speaker usually stands and talks from behind a lectern.

SEATING FOR A SYMPOSIUM DURING THE SPEECHES

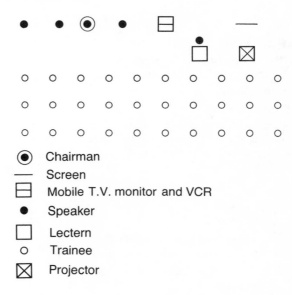

◉	Chairman
—	Screen
⊟	Mobile T.V. monitor and VCR
●	Speaker
☐	Lectern
○	Trainee
⊠	Projector

FIGURE 232A

Often too, the trainees are seated in lines facing the speakers as shown in Figure 232A, although this is not a mandatory arrangement and the seating can be semi-circular. This arrangement changes when the speeches are completed as shown in the next Figure.

Various visual aids are shown for possible use by the speakers.

SEATING IN A SYMPOSIUM DURING THE DISCUSSION

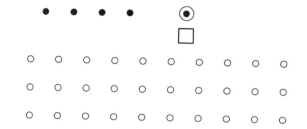

FIGURE 232B.

The Chairperson has taken up a position beside the lectern from which he controls the discussion. Alternatively, the Chairperson may remain seated.

3.   * Patterns of communication and interaction
Once again, there are two stages and these are:
  During the speeches
  Discussing the speeches
These variations are shown diagrammatically as follows:

COMMUNICATION AND INTERACTION PATTERNS DURING THE SPEECHES

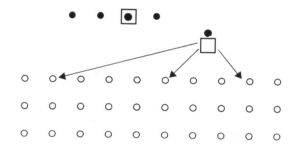

FIGURE 233A

COMMUNICATION AND INTERACTION PATTERNS DURING THE DISCUSSION

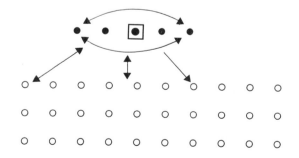

FIGURE 233B

▨▨▨ Checkpoint
The last Figure is not entirely accurate as drawn. Why is this?

The interaction shown between the members of the panel is restricted. **All** *can interact freely with each other. We have drawn it the way we have simply because of the difficulty of showing all of the lines of interaction.*

Incidentally, in both the panel and the symposium, this interaction between the members of the panel, which is such a vital part of these types of group, can be improved by arranging the seating as shown in the next Figure.

IMPROVED PANEL SEATING ARRANGEMENT

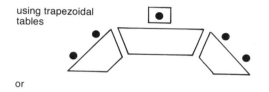

using trapezoidal tables

or

using square and rectangular tables

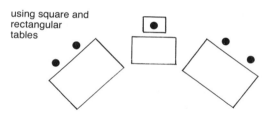

FIGURE 234

4.   * Running the symposium
You will have realised that there are three distinct stages to consider when running a symposium:
  Preparing for the Symposium
  During the Speeches
  During the General Discussion

  Preparing for the Symposium. The situation here is much the same as when preparing for the panel, although there is even greater emphasis on obtaining expert speakers of high calibre. As the Symposium is usually billed to be something special and it may well be costly to bring in experts, you must ensure that it is well publicised.

PUBLICITY AND THE SYMPOSIUM

OYEZ! OYEZ! GRAND SYMPOSIUM

FIGURE 235

Different groups of interested trainees can be brought together for the symposium, to increase audience size.

Usually, the speakers will be of sufficient reputation to attract a wider audience than your trainees, although you then run the risk of the trainees becoming "lost" in large numbers of visitors. Consequently they will become passive. However, there is an advantage in their hearing the views of other practitioners in the subject of the symposium, in addition to the invited speakers.

Naturally, with so many visitors and guest speakers, you will have to be particularly careful to ensure that preparatory administration is smooth and that the physical environment is satisfactory.

A smaller-scale symposium can be formed from speakers invited from within your own organisation, from carefully chosen and specially prepared colleagues.

You certainly can make your own trainees feel that they are involved in the symposium more closely by having them take a part of the work of locating and inviting suitable speakers. All of the mechanics of a symposium like meeting, transporting and acting as guides can be handled by the trainees, under the trainer's guidance.

The trainees can also thank the speakers at the end of the symposium

During the Speeches. Here the trainer acts as Chairperson and his responsibilities are to:
— Announce the subject of symposium briefly and clearly
— Introduce the speakers and note their backgrounds
— Call upon the first speaker

— Make sure that the speaker does not exceed his time. A pre-arranged signal is useful here.
— Make a short transitional statement and then call upon the second speaker.
— Carry on in this fashion until the last speaker is finished. As this is a formal occasion you do not, as chairperson, interject your own views, nor comment upon the speeches.

During the general discussion. You announce that the panel are now prepared to answer questions. Usually, the persons in the audience signify a wish to ask a question by raising a hand and you then indicate who may ask his question. Frequently, you will direct a question from the audience to a specific speaker.

It is better to keep a measure of discipline by insisting on this formal procedure.

After the first responder has answered, you then allow any other person on the panel to add a comment, or disagree. Sometimes, a mini-discussion arises around a controversial statement and the audience enjoys the cut-and-thrust of experts defending their own views and attacking those of the other speakers.

Questioners may also be allowed a second "shot" if the situation warrants it.

Finally, you say, "Can I have a last question". When that has been answered you then make a very brief summary of the discussion, although this is optional.

At this point, upon your signal, a trainee stands up and makes a short vote of thanks.

You then end the session by saying something like, "Thank you, speakers and audience. That ends the symposium."

A difficulty found in this general discussion stage is keeping some speakers to this time limit and you are advised to warn the speakers about this before they start. If you can keep to schedule, your timings for a symposium could look like this:—

SYMPOSIUM TIMINGS FOR FOUR SPEAKERS

STAGE	TIMING/MINUTES
Chairperson's Introduction	6
First Speaker	15
Second Speaker	15
Third Speaker	15
Fourth Speaker	15
General discussion, speakers and audience	18
Summing up by a chairperson	4
Vote of thanks	2
TOTAL	90 minutes

FIGURE 236

SYMPOSIUM TIMINGS FOR SIX SPEAKERS

Chairperson's introduction	6
Six speakers each	10
General discussion	18
Summing up	4
Vote of thanks	2
TOTAL	90 minutes

FIGURE 237

What strikes you about these timings?

Remembering what we said about lectures and the attention span of an audience being 20 to 30 minutes, you can see that we are pushing the audience to remain attentive throughout the speeches.

However, the situation is alleviated by the constant change of speaker, so attention span is lengthened. Try to begin with an interest-catching speaker and end with a "hot-shot" who can pull back the trainees' attention.

In any case, the timings which we have shown are flexible, certainly for the general discussion.

5. * Advantages and Disadvantages of the Symposium

Advantages

1. A symposium is not difficult to run: once the speakers have started off, all the trainer has to do, as chairperson is to conduct the meeting.
2. The speakers give a refreshing change of face, views and attitudes.
3. The trainees benefit from exposure to expert information.
4. By the time the general discussion has arrived, the trainees are usually eager to ask questions about the new material and perspectives which they have heard.
5. It is beneficial for the trainer to keep in touch with colleagues from outside the training department and/or the organisation.
6. It is useful to hear different views on controversial areas, or on emerging areas of research where the speakers often provide a "map", or overview of the current "state of the art".
7. In general, trainees and trainer are stimulated by contact with "new" personalities and are often motivated to find out more about the subject of the symposium.
8. Inviting visitors to attend as part of the audience is similarly beneficial.
9. Using speakers of high reputation enhances the position and reputation of the training department in the organisation.
10. The audience can be fascinated by the cut-and-thrust of argument expressed by experts in the language of the subject.

Disadvantages

1. The symposium can be expensive, sometimes in fees and certainly in travelling expenses.
2. Experts sometimes go off on lines of their own, especially into their areas of special interest and research; they have "bees in their bonnets".

BEE WARE OF SPEAKERS' SPECIAL INTERESTS!

FIGURE 238

3. Consequently, through divergence, the whole of the topic may not be dealt with in the manner which you had in mind.
4. Often, in drawing together experts in a particular field, only that specific area of study is dealt with, which can be restricting and over-specialised.
5. Experts can sometimes become over-technical and have little opportunity to gauge the audience until the discussion stage.
6. The trainee audience is passive for up to an hour and attention may wander, although frequent change of speaker alleviates this.
7. Gathering together four, or half-a-dozen speakers, can be time-consuming and frustrating and the symposium discussion has quite a deal of administration attached to it.
8. Symposia are time consuming: you won't want to bring the speakers and audience together for less than 90 minutes and this may cause time-tabling problems.

6. Trainer's Checklist for a Symposium

Parts of this Checklist are similar to that for a panel discussion. So write out your own Checklist first, consulting Figure 229, Component 5 of this Study Unit.

SYMPOSIUM CHECKLIST

DID I
1. Pick a suitable topic, issue or problem?
2. Select suitable speakers?
3. Give the speakers an adequate briefing?
4. Ensure that the objectives of the symposium were clear?
5. Ensure a good-sized audience?
6. Publicise the symposium comprehensively?
7. Introduce the speakers to the subject efficiently?
8. Keep to the timings?
9. Ease in the next speaker with a suitable transitional statement?
10. Chair and encourage the discussion effectively?
11. Make a summary?
12. Follow-up the symposium by emphasising the main points to the trainees in a later class?
13. Evaluate the symposium?
14. Feedback the results of evaluation to the trainees?
15. Write thank you letters to the speakers?

FIGURE 239

We are now going to look at a method of delivering the learning to smaller groups which is completely different from anything which we have studied before.

This is

* Brainstorming

Although brainstorming has been with us for over 50 years, there is still widespread misconceptions about what it is. The most frequent mistake is to believe that it is a group of people sitting around a table and shouting out any ideas which come into their heads. This is really only a **"bull"** session, which has its uses for generating a few ideas quickly, but does not follow in the "classic" structure of the true brainstorming session.

WHAT BRAINSTORMING IS NOT!

FIGURE 240A

So let's follow our usual pattern of looking at types of groupwork, beginning with a

1 Definition

DEFINITION OF BRAINSTORMING

Brainstorming is creative groupwork in which group members produce a large number of ideas quickly for subsequent evaluation.

FIGURE 240B

Brainstorming is suitable for a wide range of learning situations and it can be used either by itself, or as part of some other method. It can last for a couple of hours, or longer.

It may involve anything from half-a-dozen to about 20 participants and can be quickly organised and run. Optimal size is about a dozen; minimum about five, including the leader.

2. Seating

SEATING FOR A BRAINSTORMING SESSION

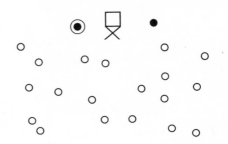

● Trainer
◉ Trainee Writing
○ Trainee
⊻ Flipchart

FIGURE 241

The seating arrangement is best when it is informal, as shown in Figure 241, but any arrangement is O.K. provided that all of the trainees can see the flip chart. Usually the trainer moves around during the session.

3. Patterns of Communication and Interaction

PATTERNS OF COMMUNICATION AND
INTERACTION IN A BRAINSTORMER

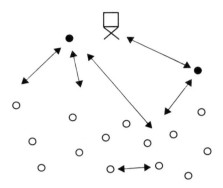

FIGURE 242

Mostly the communication and interaction is directed towards the trainee who is writing on the flip chart and to the trainer. However, anyone can exchange remarks with anyone else, provided these aside conversations are kept short.

4. * Running the Brainstorming Session

There are eight basic stages to a brainstorming session (or "Brainstormer") and they are, in order:—

THE EIGHT STAGES OF A BRAINSTORMING
SESSION

```
1. Introduction.
2. Icebreaker.
3. Define the subject, problem or issue.
4. Focus on the subject (How do you . . . . . ?" Focus
   Statement).
5. Select one Focus Statement (How can you . . . . . ?").
6. Brainstorming (Developments).
7. Daftest Suggestion.
8. Evaluation.
```

FIGURE 243

Let's look at these stages, one at a time, saying what the trainer does and what the trainees do in each.

Stage 1. Introduction. Here the trainer describes the structure of a Brainstorming session telling the trainees that there are eight stages and saying what they are. The stages should be shown on an OHP or written on a board.

During the introduction, the trainer emphasises these points:

— Everybody takes part, calls out his or her ideas when they occur to them.
— The success of the Brainstormer depends entirely on the participation and effort everybody puts into it.

— There are only **four basic rules** and these are:

> **"Nobody judges anybody"**: during the session, no-one must evaluate the ideas of anybody else by saying, for example, "That's a stupid suggestion". As no evaluation of ideas is allowed, judgement is suspended, otherwise the free flow of ideas will be inhibited.
>
> **"Letting go"**: everybody's ideas, sublime or ridiculous, relevant or irrelevant, are accepted. Participants just let their ideas go.
>
> **"Quantity"**: large numbers of ideas are wanted, not a few classy well-thought-out ones. Never mind the quality, feel the width; quantity is what counts.
>
> **"Changing"**: anybody can take anybody else's idea, change and develop it. It is essential that ideas are regarded as common property, free to be taken up by the group, changed and developed.

It's a good idea to have those four basic rules written out on the board and left there during the session. Anybody who transgresses should get a polite "chop" from the trainer.
— Brainstorming is not only work, it is supposed to be fun. We don't know of a session in which we took part in which there wasn't a lot of laughter and wit.

Stage Two. Icebreaker. It's a good idea to have an "icebreaker" next, i.e. a sort of warm-up session. After all, brainstorming is supposed to be a creative method of learning, producing lots of ideas and lateral thinking, so the mental "engines" are unlikely to start well from "cold".

One way of getting the creative juices flowing is to use an icebreaker, where you ask the group to suggest other uses for some everyday object, like a matchbox, drawing pin, paper-clip or bricks. It doesn't matter if the ideas are crazy or unrealistic, that's part of the game.

We illustrate icebreaker ideas in the next Figure.

OTHER USES FOR BRICKS

```
 1. A bed-warmer
 2. A doorstep
 3. A pendulum
 4. Missile for smashing windows
 5. Weapon for clobbering somebody's head
 6. Book ends
 7. Shelving
 8. Maze for mice
 9. A plumb-bob
10. A fulcrum
11. Table legs
12. Loose pavement
13. Keeping a field fire in place (like scouts do)
14. A counterweight
15. Tied to leg of a swimming trainer
16. Other end of a see-saw
17. Base for rocket ship.
```

FIGURE 244

As you can see from the last Figure, the ideas can be useful or ridiculous: that doesn't matter. Making ideas flow, does.

Stage Three. Define the subject, problem or issue.
All that is required is a clear statement of what is to be the subject of the Brainstorming session. Recently, we had an actual session around the following subject.

"The problem of gaining and retaining attention in the classroom."

We shall use that as our example.

Stage Four. Focus on the subject or problem. Here you are focusing more closely on the problem, by simplifying it. You ask yourself and the trainees the **main ways** of gaining and retaining attention. In one sense, this is a parallel activity to making your first level of analysis in Task Analysis, although this is a looser, less tidy and generally less accurate technique.

So you ask the Brainstorming group, in effect, **"How do you** gain attention in the classroom?" This is your, "How do you" question.

Remember, you are looking only for the **major** ways of doing this. So you might actually say to the trainees, "OK. Tell me what you think are the main ways of gaining and retaining attention in the classroom. How do you do this? Let's have some suggestions now."

You and the group now answer the "How do you" questions by making up a series of **Focus statements** on the subject. The best way to do this is to ask yourselves the basic "How do you" questions, as we suggested, each Focus Statement being one of your buzz group's numerous replies to that question. In practice many replies will be minor rather than major points, but press on by accepting them all.

Here are some of the Focus Statements, taken from our Brainstorming session.

1. Be dramatic
2. Provide impact
3. Be novel
4. Shock
5. Be outrageous
6. Attract attention
7. Create interest
8. Motivate
9. Create variation
10. Associate with trainees
11. Take clothes off
12. Be selective
13. Communicate clearly
14. Be offensive
15. Tell jokes
16. Be enthusiastic
17. Use visual materials
18. Create dissonance
19. Develop participation
20. Instil fear
21. Create surprise
22. Use sound
23. Be brief

All of these Focus Statements must be written down on a flip chart and numbered. As you can see, they turned out to be a mixture of important points, which you really wanted and trivia. This doesn't matter; you've made a start.

When you begin Stage Four you are well-advised to use a trainee to write down suggestions on the flip chart rather than doing it yourself. When ideas begin to flow thick and fast in this and in later stages, writing becomes quite a job in itself. You should be free from being tied down in this way. So use trainees as writers, but change them every ten or fifteen minutes because even the writing can become quite tiring.

NEXT PLEASE!

FIGURE 245

Normally, in Brainstorming session of an hour-and-a-half, you should receive between ten and twenty Focus Statements, although this really depends on how far you try to stick to major statements only. In any case, don't be too selective and don't put the participants off by rejecting answers.

Incidentally, you'll find that you need about ninety minutes to complete an average Brainstorming session and you are unlikely to finish in less time than this.

As leader of the Brainstorming, you can contribute Focus Statements of your own. You should have half-a-dozen "up your sleeve" before you begin, to help you start and maintain the flow.

As each flip-chart sheet is filled in, pin it up to the classroom walls, where everyone can see it and the others which have been completed.

You stop focusing when the supply from the audience, the Brainstormers themselves, dries up, or they begin to suggest only minor rather than major ideas.

Stage Five. Select one Focus Statement. As leader, you can either pick one Focus Statement, or ask the trainees to select the four or five statements which appear to be the most fruitful and have the greatest potential for **developing** further suggestions. From those four or five you then select one which you write down at the top of a fresh flip-chart sheet. To this you add these words as a preface: **"How can you . . . . . ?"**

In the actual Brainstorming session which we are describing, the trainees selected Focus Statement 7, "create interest", for development, first.

So you write down, "How can you create interest?" at the top of our sheet. Under it write **"Developments"**.

You are now ready to begin

Stage Six. The Brainstorming. This is it! Your group have now reached the stage of developing each of your Focus Statements. Here are the steps which you take for producing **Developments**.

a) Begin with the Focus Statement which you chose first (Number 7).

b) Have a trainee ready to write suggestions on the flip chart sheet under the heading, **"How can we create interest"**, and **"Developments"**.

c) Call for ideas and suggestions from the trainees saying, "OK. You can see what we are concentrating on. (Point to the heading) I want you to develop ideas on how we can create interest in the classroom. Call out any ideas and suggestions which you have, when you think of them. There's no special order. Joan, here, will write them down under **Developments. Ready? Go!!**"

d) The flow of ideas shouted out should then come quickly. Bounce around the classroom yourself, saying, "Come on then. Who's next? that's a good 'un. Try again. I've got one here. Another, Jack? Well done. Great. Here we go, and so on." Be active, exhorting and energetic.

e) During this time, your writer will be very busily and legibly writing down Developments in the shape of ideas and suggestions, **numbering each.**

BE ACTIVE AND ENERGETIC

FIGURE 246

f) If the pace slows, or the writer gets behind, give a minute's **"incubation"**, saying, "Right. Silence for a minute. Re-read what we've written, then after a minute let's start again!"

g) Another technique is to say, "Now let's look at number six again. Any variation on that?"

h) When the flow of suggestions has dried up finally, say, "I think we've just about exhausted that one. Let's select our next Focus Statement for development, now."

j) Off you go again, repeating the process.

k) Finally, when you have selected as many Focus Statements as you can deal with in the time allotted and have all of the sheets pinned up around the walls, the Brainstorming ends and you move onto the next stage.

Before you do so, a few points about writing down the suggestions which are called out. These are:

— Be sure to have a thick flip chart with plenty of sheets available.

— OHP transparencies are not suitable, because the group cannot read them easily when pinned up.

— Use pins or "blu-tack" to stick up the sheets.

— Pin them up as soon as they're finished.

— Use felt-tipped pen, with a different colour for each development.

— Print, or write legibly, in large letters.

In the actual Brainstorming session which we are using as an example, we had time to develop four Focus Statements. Let's show how the whole session developed in the next Figure.

FOCUS STATEMENTS AND DEVELOPMENTS

Stage 3. DEFINITION: "The problem of gaining and retaining attention in the classroom."
Stage 4. "How do you gain and retain attention in the classroom?"

FOCUS STATEMENTS: How do you . . . . . .
1. Be dramatic
2. Provide impact
3. Be novel
4. Shock
5. Be outrageous
6. Attract attention
7. **Create interest**
8. Motivate
9. Be variable
10. Associate
11. Take clothes off
12. Be selective - what
13. Touch
14. Be offensive
15. Tell a joke
16. **Be enthusiastic**
17. Use visual materials
18. **Create dissonance**
19. **Increase participation**
20. **Instil fear**
21. Create surprise
22. Use sound
23. Be brief

Stage 5. SELECTION of Focus Statement Number Seven: "How can you create interest?"

Stage 6. DEVELOPMENTS
(of Focus Statement Number Seven):—
1. Show enthusiasm
2. Speak in a different accent every day
3. Teach in dark
4. Be unpredictable
5. Be injured
6. Give free gifts
7. Dress up
8. Find out hobbies
9. Promise rewards
10. Put up pictures (visuals)
11. Use audio-visuals
12. Sing a song
13. Ask questions
14. Ask if game for a laugh
15. Use class — speak
16. Have a quiz
17. Walk out
18. Show threatening behaviour
19. **Cause an explosion**
20. Bring in an observer
21. Use humour
22. Bring in an animal
23. Use new technology
24. Make a deliberate mistake
25. Use no chairs
26. Discuss assessment
27. Show exam papers
28. Show relevance to daily life
29. Give out new text books
30. Introduce new teaching style
31. Alter pace
32. Change the teacher
33. Get your act together

Stage 5. SELECTION Of focus Statement Number 19: "How can you increase participation?"

Stage 6. DEVELOPMENTS:—
34. Ask questions
35. Tell story
36. State problem
37. Employ Drama
38. Use Group Work
39. Play a game
40. Debate
41. Ask for written responses
42. Set a concrete problem
43. Provide teaching materials
44. Change environment
45. Show Colour picture
46. Be sympathetic
47. Delegate
48. Cause physical movement
49. Exclude non-participants

Stage 5. SELECTION Of Focus Statement Number 16: "How can you be enthusiastic?"

Stage 6. DEVELOPMENTS:—
50. Show energy
51. Be on time
52. Hands out of pockets
53. Smile
54. Introduce new topic
55. Be smart
56. Be highly involved
57. Be prepared
58. Show thorough knowledge of subject
59. Prepare materials
60. Go on after bell (10 mins)
61. Start early
62. Mark homework
63. Invite suggestions
64. Don't yawn
65. Listen
66. Speak rapidly
67. Inspect fingernails
68. Display outgoing attitude
69. Teach what you want
70. Be the boss
71. Be encouraging
72. Be vital
73. Organise trips
74. Use board
75. Offer to come in Saturday (Hols etc.)
76. Organise Extra-Curricular activities
77. Never say No!
78. Never say Yes!
79. Show emotional involvement

Stage 5. SELECTION Of Focus Statement Numbers 18 and 20: "How can you create dissonance and instil fear?"

Stage 6. DEVELOPMENTS:—
80. Bully
81. Insult
82. Stop play
83. Threat
84. Cause silence
85. Tear up work
86. Mark when you feel like it.
87. Mention short time to exam
88. Police (threat)
89. Whisper
90. Threaten parents visit
91. Challenge norms
92. Offer house points
93. Ask for one pound (money)
94. Use corporal punishment threats
95. Pull hair
96. Cause loss of privilege
97. Discuss future
98. Demean character
99. Remind of past failures
100. Compare with siblings
101. Compare boys with girls
102. Make sexist remarks
103. Make racist remarks
104. Make fascist remarks
105. Make Leftist remarks
106. Make Nationalistic remarks
107. Patronise
108. Use jingoistic remarks
109. Put on spot
110. Stand in corner
111. Ask if up-to-date with reading?

FIGURE 247

What strikes you about Figure 247?

Well, we think that some of the Focus Statements and many of the Developments vary from the useful to the useless and from the sublime to the ridiculous, in some cases.

However, this is part of the character of Brainstorming. You have to take all suggestions, otherwise if you begin selecting some and leaving others out, you will inhibit the free flow of ideas.

Another point worth noting about Figure 247 is that Focus Statement Numbers 18 and 20 were combined into one. This is acceptable if the Focus Statements are of a similar nature. You'll notice that these combined

Statements and their Developments finished off with a lot of laughter even though they are techniques to avoid rather than include in your training.

The material shown in Figure 247 is a little rough and ready, but that's how it came out in the session!

Stage Seven. Daftest Suggestion. As most trainees taking part in the Brainstorming are getting tired by now, you announce selection of the Daftest Suggestion. Here are the steps in this stage:—

a) Write **"Daftest Suggestion"** at the top of a new flip chart sheet. You can pick either a Focus Statement, or a Development. The one which we picked in this session was, "Take clothes off".

b) Now say: "Well, that's certainly a crazy idea. But has it any sense in it? Give me some suggestions about how it may be turned into something useful."

c) Then write down the suggestions. In this case, the Daftest Suggestion resulted in the group highlighting the importance of the trainer being well-dressed, almost to the opposite of the original idea, so some benefit was derived.

In any case, the session ended with a lot of jokes and laughter, which is important.

You are probably saying now, "The session ended? But I thought there were eight stages, not seven!" Well, there is another and that is

Stage Eight. Evaluation. Clearly, when you have finished the brainstorming session you have a lot of ideas and suggestions which are not tidily put together **nor** evaluated. So you evaluate some time **after** the main session using one of the two techniques as follows:—

TECHNIQUE ONE

a) Pick a team of three or four to help you.

b) With your team, pick out the Daftest Suggestions.

c) Have the rest of the work typed up under the headings

Focus Statements ("How do you" statements).
Developments ("How can you" developments).
Exclude Daftest Suggestions.

d) Send the photocopied list around participants and ask them to select and inform you of the best 10% of Focus Statements and the top 10% of the Developments.

e) With your team, award each Statement and each Development one point.

f) Pick the top 25% of the marks and act on those. Notice that we say "act on those". This is because the Brainstorming method is frequently used to solve a problem, or decide on the best ways of doing something. So you need to **categorise the ideas in order of priority for action.** The example we used of gaining and retaining attention doesn't quite fit here, as it requires no immediate action of any sort.

TECHNIQUE TWO

a) This technique uses the resources of your evaluation team only.

b) Prioritise, in rank order, each of the **suggestions** under Developments by **weighing** it against a set of criteria, picked by your team. Your criteria are similar to those used in writing specific objectives. (However, there you were deciding how **far** a trainee had achieved the objective, only).

c) Criteria for weighing the suggestions shown in the Developments of our example concerning attention, could be Cost; Resources Required; Amount of preparation; Constraints Present; Time Needed; Effectiveness.

d) Attach a scale to each criteria related to its comparative importance. For the Criteria we gave, we rate each one on a scale of 0 to 5 (high) except for "effectiveness", rated 0 to 25 (high) because of its importance.

e) Complete the scales for each suggestion, or idea, by the team entering an agreed, or averaged, mark against each suggestion in each column.

f) Here is an example, using a few ideas from Figure 247:

SUGGESTION	EFFECTIVENESS	COST	RESOURCES REQUIRED	AMOUNT OF PREPARATION	CONSTRAINTS PRESENT	TIME NEEDED	TOTAL
1. Show Enthusiasm	25	5	5	5	5	5	50
13. Ask questions	20	5	5	4	4	5	43
20. Bring in an observer	20	2	2	3	2	5	34
23. Use new technology	20	1	1	2	2	2	28
38. Use group work	22	5	5	3	4	4	43
69. Organise trips	20	0	1	1	2	2	26
98. Demean character	0	—	—	—	—	—	0

g) Note that a criterion which you **always include** and always **place first** is that of **"effectiveness"**.

Any suggestion or idea not scoring more than half-marks (i.e. 13 out of 25 in this case) is not considered further. This knocks out the daft suggestions.

Finally, for both techniques, circulate the results of the Brainstorming session to the participants.

What strikes you as being the underlying theme of Brainstorming?

We consider it to be a sort of "instant Task Analysis", using a group to think up the units of analysis. Putting a number of minds together to consider one problem or subject gives a chance for a creative outcome.

5. *Advantages and Disadvantages of Brainstorming

Advantages

1. Encourages creativity.
2. Can be a lot of fun and creates laughter and warmth.
3. Great participation by most of the trainees.
4. Cheap to run.
5. Doesn't require much preparation.
6. Helps trainees think around a subject.
7. Refreshing change of method.
8. Produce types of suggestions and ideas which other methods cannot.
9. Can be used in many other situations, in addition to training.
10. May be used effectively to fit in with many other methods of training, including lectures, group discussions and individualised instruction, especially where plenary sessions are organised to "round off" personalised and performance based training programmes.

Disadvantages

1. Not a very systematic way of studying a subject and the results are unpredictable.
2. Sessions may be difficult to control.
3. Sometimes trainees become silly and make too many daft suggestions.
4. Evaluation is difficult and time-consuming and the trainer has to keep the team engaged, otherwise the work is not done.
5. May only be used as an alternative method to others, otherwise the training could become formless.
6. Some trainees are reluctant to participate. Usually this is a small minority, but non-participants are always there.
7. Sometimes difficult to persuade management that this is actually a genuine training method until they become familiar with it and see the results.

FIGURE 247A

6. *Trainer's Checklist for a Brainstorming Session

We could write quite a long list, but let's pick out the main points only. This will also serve as our Summary.

BRAINSTORMING CHECKLIST

DID WE
1. Follow the four basic rules?
   a) "Nobody judged anybody"
   b) "Letting go"
   c) "Quantity"
   d) "Changing"
2. Follow through each of the eight stages?
3. Develop maximal participation?
4. Create a warm, friendly atmosphere?
5. Keep to reasonable timings?
6. Enjoy the session?
7. Circulate the results of evaluation to the participants?

FIGURE 248

We mention timing in the Checklist; in a Brainstorming session of 90 minutes, typically your timings could be

STAGE	ACTIVITY	TIMING/MINUTES
1.	Introduction	3
2.	Icebreaker	5
3.	Defining	3
4.	Focusing	15
5.	Selecting	6
6.	**Brainstorming**	**50**
7.	Daftest Suggestion	8
8.	Evaluation	Later
		TOTAL FOR SESSION = 90 minutes

We shall complete our examination of groupwork methods directly based upon the group discussion in our next Component.

Component 7:

Using different forms of Groupwork

Key Words

 Brief Brainstorming; Characteristics, Doubles and Spray Brainstorming; Leaderless Groups; Walk-out, Seminar and Syndicate; Workshops; chimes; Wilson Quadro; Colloquys; T-Groups.

Introduction

In this Component we are going to complete our coverage of the methods of delivering the learning to smaller groups which are directly based on group discussion. These methods are shown in the following diagram and are named on the next page.

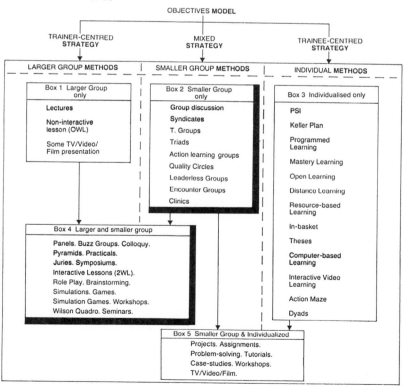

Brief Brainstorming and related methods.
Leaderless Groups.
Workshops and Clinics.
Wilson Quadro.
Colloquy.
T. Groups.

As you will see there are several methods of group delivery, not based so directly on group **discussion**, shown in boxes Two and Four of Figure 160, which remain to be studied after this Component.

We shall consider those from Box Four, that is Games, Simulations and Role Play, in this Study Unit. As the methods shown in Box Five tend more to the subject of our next Package, delivering the learning to individuals, we shall look at them then, remembering that they also play an important part in smaller groupwork.

Let's begin with

* Brief Brainstorming and Related Methods

As we saw from the last Component, Brainstorming can be a quite complicated procedure and lasts usually for an hour-and-a-half.

On occasions, you will find that a **Brief Brainstorming** session will suffice, lasting for only thirty minutes. There are only five stages:

ACTION	TIMING/MINUTES
1. Introduction and Defining	2
2. Focusing	4
3. Selecting	2
4. Brainstorming	15
5. Evaluation then Summary	7

Several stages are omitted in Brief Brainstorming. You do not use an Icebreaker (Stage 2 of full Brainstorming); you amalgamate Introduction (Stage 1) with Defining (Stage 3) into one stage; you omit Daftest Selection. The stages of Focusing, Selecting and Brainstorming are carried out as you would in full Brainstorming, but you allow less time for each.

The major change is in the last Stage, Five. Here the trainer quickly evaluates the ideas and suggestions which have come up in the session, finally making an immediate summary of the major findings.

This summary may be written briefly on the board and copied down by the trainees. There is no follow-up evaluation.

In order to keep the session on a time-restricted basis, the Brainstormers will usually only have time to identify half-a-dozen Focus Statements, select a couple for development and offer perhaps a dozen Developments under each.

Brief Brainstorming acts as a fillip to training and, if used often, quickly becomes a procedure at which both trainer and trainees become adept.

A lot depends on the trainer's ability to evaluate and summarise efficiently.

There are some other techniques related to Brief Brainstorming, all requiring less time than a full session; these are

Characteristics Brainstorming.
Doubles Brainstorming.
Spray Brainstorming.

Let's look at these briefly:

Characteristics Brainstorming.

Here, the original or initial Characteristics of an object, or idea, or techniques are identified and listed. Each characteristic is then examined individually to see whether it can be used some other way, or improved.

The use of a penknife is one example. Initially, the characteristics of a penknife were that it had one or two cutting blades.

Improved characteristics retain the original blades, but also incorporate devices for opening bottles, scissors, nail files, screwdriver heads, tin openers, saw-toothed blades and so on. Even more specialist knives are available with devices for the use of anglers and electricians, etc., rather on the lines of the famous Swiss Army knives.

CHARACTERISTICS COMBINED

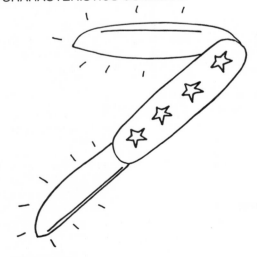

FIGURE 249

The characteristics of an idea or procedure can also be developed and applied in another field. For example, the attributes of the engineer's systems approach have now been widely applied to education, as have those of communication systems.

Alternatively, each characteristic, or the object, or idea, or procedure can be considered against a list of headings suggesting other uses. Such headings could be:

Can it (the object, procedure, or plan, etc) **be**
Adapted for other uses?
Enlarged?
Decreased?
Embellished?
Modified?
Substituted?
Rearranged?
Reversed?
Combined?
Speeded-up?

This technique is very stimulating to Brainstormers and produces unusual ideas, suggestions and uses.

CHARACTERISTICS COMBINED

FIGURE 250

Doubles Brainstorming

Here two separate objects or procedures are combined into one product. Although unrelated initially, the two objects, when combined, result in a dual or multi-purpose item, e.g. chairs with turn-over flaps for writing; multi-purpose a-v trolleys; calculators incorporating date and time displays; multi-purpose combs, etc.

When used with an **idea**, rather than an object, the variables of, say, a problem are written on postcards and the cards then juggled around to provide new combinations of factors and possibly different solutions.

Spray Brainstorming

This is based upon spray diagramming and content mapping, which we considered in Component Six, Study Unit Two, Package One.

In this technique, the Brainstorming group works together to develop a spray diagram, or a content map, on the board. Every branch, or spray, of the diagram is continued until the possibilities are exhausted.

What do you think the differences are between Spray Brainstorming and "ordinary" Spray diagramming or content mapping?

Well, Spray Brainstorming is a public rather than a private effort; the "sprays" are continued further to include every possible relationship and development, logical or not; daftest suggestions are also written down and pursued; the four basic rules of brainstorming are applied; priorities are established by underlining the most significant developments.

Don't forget yet another related form of groupwork, Buzz Groups, which we considered in Component Seven, Study Unit Two, Package Two.

Buzz Groups, like Brief Brainstorming and its variations, can always be used to brighten up other forms of delivery, like the lecture and the lesson. These methods are both versatile and stimulating to the trainees.

* Leaderless Groups

So far, we have considered groupwork in which the trainer usually plays the part of group leader. It can be beneficial for him to step down, allowing the groups to carry on by themselves. Such are known as leaderless groups.

Have we considered a type of leaderless group already?

Yes. The buzz group is an example. However, these are of short duration, say five minutes. What we are looking at here is longer.

There are three types:
  The Walk-Out.
  The Seminar Leaderless group.
  The Syndicate.

The Walk-Out

This is the simplest form. Having started off a group discussion, the trainer says, "You're well underway now. I'm leaving it to you to complete the discussion, I'll be back in half-an-hour. Donna, will you take over as group leader?". And off you go.

On your return, you'll need to check on progress and this can be done by asking the trainee group leader to summarise the discussion. You can add to this, filling in gaps and giving a touch of re-direction if necessary.

Usually, we also explain that we left to give them the chance to air their views even more freely, but especially so that the trainees can experience working independently.

The Seminar Leaderless Group

Here the trainer asks the presenter of the paper also to act as chairperson and group leader. In this case, as for the Walk-Out and the Syndicate, we are interpreting "leaderless" to be "trainerless". Perhaps the latter would be a more accurate description.

Usually, we check with the presenter/chairperson after the meeting as to how things went.

The Syndicate

This is the most elaborate of the leaderless group techniques and has several stages:—

Stage 1. Introduction. The purposes and techniques of the Syndicate method are explained to the trainees. Emphasis should be placed by the trainer on the aim of fostering independent trainee study and research;

organising their own time and work; co-operating as a group; establishing effective social relationships and personal behaviour. If the syndicate product is to be assessed, then details must be made known of how this will be done.

The role of the trainer needs absolute clarification, especially the part he plays in acting as a resource and advice base, closely interested and supporting their efforts.

Stage Two. Describing the Assignments. Each syndicate has an assignment to fulfil. The details of each assignment must be at least as full as the Summary which is given to a trainee preparing for a seminar. The **Assignment Summary** must contain:

> a) Title of Assignment.
> b) A moderately detailed description of the issue, topic or problem and brief abstract of the field of study relevant to the assignment.
> c) The objectives of the assignment.
> d) The main headings of the assignment.
> e) Time available for the presentation of their report in plenary session.
> f) Sources of information, including a reading list, statistics, descriptive handouts, articles and periodical references, manuals, etc.
> g) An indication of the timetable for the completion and consideration of the assignment.
> h) Composition of the Syndicate membership.

The trainer is in somewhat of a dilemma when describing the assignment: too much detail given out circumscribes the work of the syndicate; too little, may let them go astray, drift or even give up. A rough rule of thumb is that the more able and sophisticated the syndicate members, then the less help they'll need; the lower their level of experience and attainment, the more assistance they will require.

SOPHISTICATED TRAINEES NEED LESS HELP

FIGURE 251

Stage Three. Composition of the Syndicate.
Breaking trainees down into sub-groups can always be a problem. We use two main techniques for syndicate work:
a) Place lists on wall; each list shows items a), b), c) and d) from several Assignment Summaries. Trainees then fill in their names in numbered spaces beneath the appropriate Summary, if they want to do that particular Assignment.

b) Split the main group down yourself, giving each Syndicate an appropriate mixture of stronger and weaker trainees.

If you adopt technique a) the trainees have only themselves to blame if things go wrong, but you might finish up with a weak syndicate group.

You must also decide on the number of trainees and how many syndicates there are to be. These numbers are decided by a balance between the number of Assignment topics you want covered and the total number of trainees in your main group.

Generally, each syndicate strength should be about six trainees, range from three to eight.

Stage Four. Meeting the Syndicates. After composition has been decided and each sub-group has received its Assignment Summary, you will wish to have an initial meeting with each group a week or so after they have had a chance to think things over. Sort out problems at this meeting and timetable further set meetings, stressing that you are always available, however, should they need you.

Stage Five. Syndicate Working. This is the important and time-consuming stage. You should give your trainees **at least** one clear month to prepare their Assignments. Don't give longer than that, otherwise they'll lack urgency and delay the start of their work. Each syndicate will need to
a) Divide up the work.
b) Establish links between their individual contributions.
c) Meet to confirm progress.
d) Hold a final meeting to put together the actual presentation of their report.

Stage Six. Reporting. Each syndicate reports its findings to the whole group in full plenary session. Timings will have been agreed previously.

Reports are best made orally, but should not be the reading out of a written report, which can be boring. Each syndicate report should also be written out and presented to the whole group as a handout. Each oral report should be made by several, rather than one trainee, to increase involvement.

After the oral report, time is given for discussion.

Stage Seven. Evaluation. Trainer gives his evaluation of each syndicate report. The main purpose of this evaluation, given after the plenary session when syndicate written handouts have been considered, is to fill in any gaps and emphasise major points.

Some evaluation of the syndicate exercise may be called for from the trainees.

As you can see, syndicate group-work is very trainee-centred. It has several disadvantages and advantages.

Write down what you believe these to be.

Here are our views on the advantages and disadvantages of the syndicate method.

a) **Advantages**

1. After the initial briefing of the trainees, the trainer plays a low-profile role. Consequently, the trainees have an opportunity to practice the organisation of their own learning.
2. Trainee dependence on the trainer is weakened; the trainees become more independent, self-assured learners.
3. Trainees develop the social skills of working in a co-operative group and of having to show positive group behaviours.
4. Trainees become more skilled in the **process** of learning, rather than continuing to be passive acceptors of the **product** of learning.
5. Syndicate work reflects real life, where reports have to be produced in a limited time under a certain degree of stress.
6. Trainees are allowed freedom in the two major aspects of syndicate work: **exploration** in their syndicate discussions, which are leaderless groups; **consolidation**, in plenary session when the reports are presented and discussed.
7. All trainees tend to participate more in trainer-less group discussion, sometimes by 50%

b) **Disadvantages**

1. Syndicate work requires the trainer to adopt a new role as an unobtrusive yet supportive presence. He clarifies and expands, diagnoses problems without giving solutions, gives confidence to the trainees in their own capacities, helps trainees refocus, try different approaches, offers advice. The trainer does not lead, hustle, take responsibility for progress, validate arguments. Disadvantageously, many trainers have great difficulty in accepting or fulfilling this role. The less they are able to do so, the less successful is the syndicate method.
2. Similarly, trainees have to accept a role change. They must not regard the trainer as a manager nor the authority and repository of knowledge. For a time, they must take charge of their own learning, establish their own frames of reference. Many trainees find this difficult, if not impossible to accept.

ROLE REVERSAL

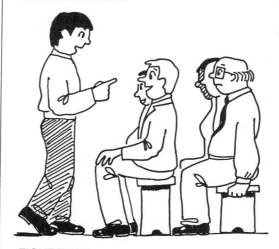

FIGURE 252

3. Trainees make mistakes and assumptions which go uncorrected. They may not know if they are on the correct lines of enquiry and may worry about assessment. Sometimes, they produce boring, amateurish reports.
4. Weaker, or idle trainees can become non-contributing passengers. The trainer may not detect this and it may be difficult to remedy.

THERE IS USUALLY A PASSENGER

FIGURE 253

5. Trainees, other staff and management may think that the trainer using the syndicate method is getting off without doing much work. Based on ignorance, this can be a difficult attitude to dispel.
6. The method is most suited to abler trainees, but it can be modified, by introducing more trainer support, for the weaker.

On balance, the syndicate method is a powerful and effective method of delivering learning to smaller groups and should be used more widely.

Let's move on to some other methods of groupwork, not concerned with leaderless, or trainer-less groups.

* Workshop

A workshop involves a range of group discussion and practical techniques from the comparatively short session of an hour or two, to a few days. It is particularly concerned with mental skills such as problem-solving and decision making, although motor, procedural, social and life skills are practised. Whilst this is basically groupwork, participants can work individually for some of the time.

There are several **stages** and these are

1. Demonstration of the skill(s) by the trainer and/or explanation of the theoretical background, practical context, work situation, problem, etc.
2. Series of tasks set for trainees which involve use of the skill, consideration of the problem, etc. Usually, trainees select tasks most appropriate to them, from a range of options related to the theme of the workshop.
3. Trainees then work in groups, or individually. The groupings may be designated by the trainer, or come together voluntarily. Some workshop members may choose to work individually.
   Trainees consider and practice the skill and/or exercise a procedure, discuss a problem, work through the set instructions. They come up with completed pieces of work, conclusions on a topic, products (mental or physical) from having worked through the task.

4. Practice in one aspect of the skill, task, topic or procedure, etc., may be succeeded by practice in other aspects, depending on the length of the workshop.
5. Groups meet to exchange results.
6. Final plenary session in which workshop training staff may act as a panel. Basic principles and concepts are identified. Groups may also submit reports which are put together into a full workshop report. Workshop is evaluated, sometimes by use of a questionnaire to trainee members.

* Clinic

This is a special type of workshop, usually used for smaller numbers, where a particular real-life problem or series of problems associated with a difficulty, or special aspect of training, is examined in detail.

Sometimes the group meets in one continuous session until the situation is resolved, or gathers together at regular intervals until the problem is solved.

There is no one groupwork method advocated for a clinic: usually a combination of methods is used, depending on the problem and the available time.

Obviously, this method can be used for a variety of managerial as well as training purposes. In training, the clinic members are usually presented with one major problem, or issue, to which they have to hammer out a solution. Examples are the design or redesign of a piece of equipment; reconsideration of the functions of an organisational structure or of a building; re-assessment of a technique or procedure.

The topic, problem or issue must be a real-life one. Usually, trainees involved in clinics are high-level, attending an advanced course, although simpler material may be considered if carefully tailored to the trainees' needs and abilities.

Clinics offer excellent vocational training, dealing with practical matters in a practical way. They are effective in the degree to which a solution is found.

* Wilson Quadro

This is an amusing method of groupwork which generates a lot of work by the trainees. It has two stages:
Preparation
The Competition

Preparation.
1. Explain how the Wilson Quadro works to the trainees.
2. Identify a suitably "meaty" subject, either a topic or a skill, for this activity. Either you, or the trainees can choose.
3. Provide a detailed breakdown of the subject for the trainees, showing:
   Title of subject.
   Synopsis of subject.
   References.

4. Give the trainees three or four weeks to prepare. Each must equip himself with a thoroughgoing knowledge of the topic.

5. Simultaneously, trainees prepare a list of thirty or more questions on the subject. Each question must have a prepared answer.

6. Lists are presented to the trainer for checking on clarity of questions, accuracy of answers and elimination of way-out questions. Questions eliminated are replaced and the agreed list is duplicated. Trainees keep their personal lists secret.

The Competition.
ROUND ONE

7. Trainees are paired off. Names can be drawn out of a hat.

8. Each pair is then matched with one other pair. Thus foursomes are formed. Each foursome is called a **quadro**. As an example a quadro consists of

    Pair One — Trainees A and B.
    Pair Two — Trainees C and D.

9. Pair One then compete against each other, i.e. A v B, by asking five questions of each other. A and B use their list of prepared questions. Spin a coin for who **answers** first (this has an advantage, see below at 11).

10. C and D, the other members of the quadro, have the duplicated copy of A and B's questions. C and D act as umpires, giving one point to either competitor when a correct answer is scored. It is up to C and D to decide if an answer is correct. There are no half marks. Disputes are referred to the trainer for a final judgement.

11. A or B is then declared winner by virtue of who answers most of the five questions correctly. In the event of a draw, A and B continue until one gains a two-point lead, having answered the same number of questions.

    Thus A, or B, could win outright, two-nil, three-two, or four-three, or whatever. If the scores are level at, say two-two, or four-four, then the competitors continue until one of them wins at, say, six-four or eight-six. Remember, A and B must answer the same number of questions.

    However, the first competitor to reach ten correct answers, after an initial draw on the first five questions, wins. He wins, even if he has had the chance of answering one more question (the one which scores the tenth point) than the opponent. This is the advantage of answering first.

FIRST TO TEN!

FIGURE 254

12. When a winner is declared between A and B, roles are reversed with C and D. Thus A and B become umpires; C and D are competitors.

13. Round One ends when either C or D wins.

ROUND TWO

14. The two winners, say A and C, then form a competing pair and compete against each other. B and D, the losers, act as umpires and are now eliminated from the competition.

LATER ROUNDS

15. Winners from Round Two then compete against other winners until a final is reached. Losers from previous rounds volunteer to be umpires, two for each competing pair. The number of rounds depends on the original number of trainee competitors.

16. Finally, one trainee emerges as overall winner.

Marking up.

Throughout the competition, the trainer marks up the results on a **Results Sheet.** The form of results sheets are shown below, completed as examples.

RESULTS SHEET FOR AN EVEN NUMBER OF COMPETITORS

ROUND ONE	ROUND TWO	ROUND THREE	FINAL	WINNER
A v B	A 3-1			
C v D	C 8-6	A 7-5		
E v F	F 3-0		H 5-4	
G v H	H 10-9	H 4-3		H 8-6
I v J	J 4-3			
K v L	K 4-2	K 9-7 bye	K	

QUADRO 1 - ABCD.   QUADRO 2 - EFGH   QUADRO 3 - IJKL

RESULTS SHEET FOR AN ODD NUMBER OF COMPETITORS

ROUND ONE	ROUND TWO	ROUND THREE	FINAL	WINNER
A v B	B 5-2			
C v D	C 2-1	B 10-9		
E v F	E 7-5		E 9-7	
G v H	G 1-0	E 6-4		E 5-4
I v J	J 8-6	J 3-2 bye	J	
K bye	K			

QUADRO 1 - ABCD. QUADRO 2 - EFGH. PART QUADRO - IJK.

The Wilson Quadro arouses tremendous enthusiasm and excitement. It has been known for trainees to agree amongst themselves to pay an entry fee of fifty pence, winner takes all! Using the Wilson Quadro occasionally gives quite a fillip to a course. The trainees certainly put a great deal of work and effort into learning the subject of the Quadro, so that they have a chance of winning.

We try to add a little humour after the event by referring to the winner as "Champ", a few times. Once we provided a cup for the winner to hold until deposed.

QUADRO PHONICS

FIGURE 254

Finally, two last forms of groupwork for our consideration.

* Colloquy

This has the same form as a panel, except that the panellists consist of one or two experts mixed with knowledgeable trainees.

A panel discussion is followed by general discussion with audience participation.

The form is useful when experts are in short supply, but the trainees have to be prepared well beforehand.

This mixed panel form makes it more of a "family" affair.

* T. Group

This is really a training form of groupwork, but is often used in human relations training.

Trainees gather together and identify askward life or job situations, personal problems and weaknesses. They may concentrate on the training and difficulties they are experiencing. After identifying the problem, the trainees talk with complete freedom around it, extending the discussion into any area they wish.

T-Groups help trainees to consider poorly defined areas, or ambiguous human problems and to develop self-awareness in doing so. The group has no specific objectives, but generally consider how they behave individually, how groups behave and how organisations behave.

Usually, the trainer, as group leader, is specially trained for the job of acting as a catalyst. T-Groups are of very restricted use in normal training.

Summary

This Component considered a variety of methods of delivering the learning to smaller groups. Brief Brainstorming is a derivative of normal Brainstorming, of which it is a shorter version. Yet other types of Brainstorming can be developed from it, such as Characteristics, Doubles and Spray Brainstorming.

All offer differing approaches, but are based on the fundamental nature of Brainstorming, which is that of making an oral Task Analysis.

Leaderless groups operate without a trainer acting as group leader and give the trainees greater freedom and responsibility for the success and effectiveness of their group, independent of the trainer. The syndicate represents the most important variation of this type.

Of the remaining forms of groupwork considered, the Wilson Quadro is the most unusual for occasional use; it is based on competition, but as there is only one winner, the edge is taken off this competitive nature.

Our next Components will consider very specialised forms of groupwork, that is games, simulations and role-play.

Before you begin the next Component, try to write down definitions of these types, distinguishing between them.

Finally, hold either a Wilson Quadro or a Brainstorming Session with one of your groups. Send the results of the session to your Programme Tutor, together with your suggestions for improvement, next time around.

Component 8:

Games and Simulations (1)

Key Words

 Definition of a "game", a "simulation"; role-play; simulation-games; history; war, business and social, educational and training games; unique communications and interactions; advantages and disadvantages.

Introduction

We asked you at the end of the last Component to define the word "games" and "simulations". So we had better start by suggesting our own definitions.

DEFINITION OF A GAME

> A game is a competition, or exercise, played by adversaries, with the objective of winning within the rules.

FIGURE 255

▧▧▧ Checkpoint

This definition is not comprehensive. Why is this?

There is a small group of games which are not competitive and which do not involve a contest between the players. Examples of these are "ice-breaker" games, which we described in Component Six of this Study Unit. We should also point out that whilst many games are played for entertainment, those with which we are concerned here are particularly used to enhance learning.

However, our definition holds good, generally.

DEFINITION OF A SIMULATION

> A simulation is an imitation of reality

FIGURE 256

So a simulation is a smaller-scale imitation of the "real-thing" where participants carry through an operation, or exercise, which represents a real system, or a process, or a procedure, or parts of them. The simulation may involve either physical or mental skills, or both.

An example of a simulation which teaches physical skills is a flight-deck simulator used to train pilots. For mental skills, examples include trainees taking over various roles of management and operatives in their department at work, or that of an external body, such as a part of the public service, like a tribunal or interviewing board.

Training simulations and games often involve the participants taking over a role. However, in some simulations the trainee does not interact with other people, e.g. he or she may take the part of a manager, who deals with the contents of the "in-tray", or of a storekeeper completing his returns.

Where the simulation involves and focuses on interaction with others, it can be called a **role-play**.

Let's try to illustrate what we said so far.

A GAME

FIGURE 257

A SIMULATION

FIGURE 258

A ROLE-PLAY SIMULATION

FIGURE 259

Recapitulate this Component.

*We say, **playing a role** is a basic tactic used in many games and simulations.*

*Where the role-playing involves **competition and rules**, the activity is called a **game**.*

*Where the role-playing does **not involve competition** (and often not any rules, either) the activity is a **simulation**.*

*Where the simulation concentrates and **focuses on interaction** between the players, it can be called a **role-play**.*

We can show this information in a diagram.

THE RELATIONSHIP BETWEEN GAMES AND SIMULATION

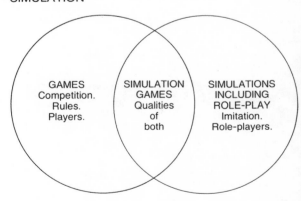

FIGURE 260

You can see from the last Figure, called a Venn diagram, that the area of overlap between games and simulations produces yet another category; **simulation games**. These have the properties of both games simulations and are especially what we are concerned with here.

There are other group and individual methods, based on role-play and simulation, e.g. the case study (group) and the "in-basket" (individual). Place these and the methods we've named so far in this Component into a diagram which shows their relationships and how far they are "real" or more abstract.

Here is our diagram.

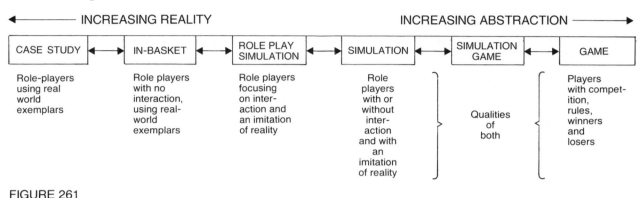

FIGURE 261

We really ought to attempt a definition of "simulation game" now. Try making your own before you read ours.

DEFINITION OF A SIMULATION GAME

> A simulation game is an activity which combines the qualities of a game (players, rules, competition) with those of a simulation (an imitation of reality).

FIGURE 262

In concentrating on simulation games we are going to examine, in this Component:

The History of Simulation Games.
A Rationale for Simulation Gaming.
The Advantages of Simulation Games.
The Disadvantages of Simulation Games.
Conclusion.

In the next two Components we consider Designing a Simulation Game and in the last Component of this Study Unit, Role-play.

You may be surprised at the structure of this Component, as it differs from others we have written, where we usually begin with an explanation of how a method is carried out, leaving a consideration of the advantages and disadvantages until later.

We can't do this with simulation games. There are thousands of games in existence and all have different rules of play. So we cannot inform you **how** to operate the game; the rules in the game box tell you that. However, by looking at Rationale, Advantages and Disadvantages we hope to give you a clear perspective

on the **use** of games and how you can adopt the method to your training.

Let's gain a further perspective by beginning with

* **The History of Simulation Games**

War Games

Gaming and simulation procedures have a venerable history and can be traced to 3000 BC when the Chinese encirclement War Game "Wei-hai" originated. "Go", a Japanese-developed game, still played widely today, and chess are probably derived from encirclement games.

By the turn of the eighteenth century, war games had become popular with armies throughout the world and especially with the German General staff, who developed "kriegspeil" as both an art and a science. The Schlieffen Plan of 1914 was the development of a war game and was followed in the Second World War by a burgeoning of the game approach used for these purposes:

— finding quick and effective solutions to urgent and complex problems.
— providing a novel approach to military training.
— offering an instructional medium which is versatile in keeping pace with changing needs.

Current American budgets for running and developing war games run into millions of dollars.

Business and Social Games.

These developed from war games after 1945 and provided an opportunity of playing for high stakes and making important decisions for comparatively little cost in time and money.

Games vary in length from simple, decision-making exercises which last only a few minutes to elaborate simulations taking several days for a single round of decision-making.

Computer simulations are used widely now, especially where a large number of variables have to be handled.

Educational and Training Games.
Simulation games do not have such a long history of use in education. Their introduction followed a phase of initial enthusiasm, during the late 1950's and early 60's; a sort of "post-honeymoon" regression during the late 60's; a tempered enthusiasm during the 1970's onwards.

Games are now a stable feature of the educational and training landscape and have received a fillip from the increasing application of learning theory to Games and the move away from the early twentieth century image of didactic (trainer-centred) teaching to problem, trainee and discovery-centred methods.

* A Rationale for Simulation Gaming
We shall identify a rationale for gaming partly through our examination of the advantages of the method, but here we must try to answer the question, "Why use games?"

One way of answering this question is to determine whether or not simulation games offer something different to the processes of training and learning which other methods do not.

Research has shown that simulation games have a wide range of disparate natures, but that they do have one important and unifying feature: they are **a form of communication which is unique**. This unique communication leads to **unique interaction**.

In the first two Components of this Package, we spent a considerable time in establishing the importance of communication in the training-learning process. We showed, during our examination of delivering the learning to larger groups and of smaller group work, how communication networks form and facilitate the interaction upon which learning activities are based.

During our consideration of the advantages of simulation games we shall see how it is that they offer a **unique** form of communication. In offering something different, games must also offer something extra to training.

Let's find out what this is:

* The Advantages of Simulation Games
By looking at the advantages and disadvantages of simulation gaming as a method of delivery of the learning, we are evaluating that method.

Learning is about changing behaviour. We can begin our evaluation by considering how far research and experience has shown how the strengths, or the advantages of gaming, are effective in causing positive changes in behaviour in the desired areas of improvement, as follows:
— Motivation and interest.
— Learning knowledge, skills and procedures.
— Attitudes.
— The processes of training.

Note: in this text we are using the terms "games", "simulation games" and "gaming" etc. interchangeably. This is a common practice. We shall examine each of these areas of improvement in turn.

* Improving Motivation and Interest
Although many of the claims of simulation gaming are contested, this is one which seems proved. For participants, games appear to
— Be interesting and involving in themselves. This is irrefutable to those who have played training games.
— Cause greater interest in the topics and skills being learned, although only to a limited extent.
— Can create greater interest in the training and the course in general, provided that the trainer tries to integrate the game with the rest of the course. Only about one in five trainers do this, however.
— Increase interest in and committment to learning, although it is probable that the motivational qualities of gaming merely predispose trainees towards learning.

* Improving the learning of Knowledge, Skills and Procedures
Evidence offers some conflicting conclusions here, but it seems that
— Whilst trainees may not learn a great deal more through gaming than by conventional training techniques, they **retain** what they learn, better, provided they are de-briefed efficiently when the game is over.
— There is some evidence to suggest slow learners show an improvement in learning, greater than expected.
— Games offer trainees a chance to put themselves in "someone else's shoes". Obviously, this is an important strength of gaming and one not conferred by many other methods of training.

The advantages in improving understanding of how to negotiate, use power and organise others, are obvious.

SOMEONE ELSE'S SHOES

FIGURE 263

— It is difficult to reproduce elements of the real world in a tiny package like a game, because of constraints of size, complexity and reproducibility. Effective games, by largely overcoming this difficulty, provide trainees with a learning experience which helps them to relate what goes on in the classrooom to what goes on in the world

In doing so, trainees must concentrate on the principles, rather than learn a plethora of facts by rote.

Games players are "actors" who must learn the rules, understand the alternatives open to them and develop game strategies. So they learn not only principles, but procedures as well and, as "gamespeople", are ready to identify both in the real world.

— The gaming environment encourages the trainee players to explore the situation, recognise and utilise the data inputs appropriately and adapt feedback loops from the outcomes of previous decisions, to provide a foundation for subsequent decisions.

So the game-learning process has a systematic structure and trainees learn how to think systematically.

The trainees learn how to learn, as opposed to becoming learned.

— Games provide an excellent vehicle for trainees to develop their problem solving and decision making abilities.

▰▰▰

Think about this. Write down a list of advantages which simulation games have in providing practice in decision making.

We think these advantages are:
a) The decision making takes place in a risk-free environment where expensive real-life resources and equipment are not lost.

GAMING CAN'T DAMAGE YOUR WEALTH

FIGURE 264

As you see from the last Figure, action and feedback are related closely and the players can learn from their mistakes by amending performance immediately in accordance with results.
b) Gamers must develop the capacity to have a feel for and an insight into evolving situations.
c) The gamer is exposed to irrational intuitive facets of decision making. Trainees have to make decisions at "gut-level" with incomplete data.

d) A large amount of decision-making experience is provided for trainees in a compressed form, priorities have to be established quickly, commitments harnessed to information flows, stress and uncertainty accommodated.

e) Games give flexible frameworks in which to practice decision making. Significant factors must be identified, appraised and planned for.

These are very important advantages of gaming.

— If a trainee games player is to be successful, he must develop winning ways. The game framework provides a "safety-net" within which the trainee can operate. Risky and experimental problem solving strategies can be implemented without fear of permanent damage resulting from the use of wrong methods.

Therefore, games offer scope not only for "traditional" problem solving strategies, but also for intuitive approaches, developed to complement systematic approaches.

Trainees have little chance to develop intuition in formal training, yet intuition needs to be stimulated, given expression and evaluated, as in life itself.

Few other forms of training teach anything about the development of winning strategies by the learner. Simulation gaming covers this aspect of real life uniquely.

* Improving Attitudes

Attitudinal change is notoriously difficult to measure, but there is sufficient evidence to show that simulation gaming helps attain the objective of changing attitudes.

This is particularly so, in these areas:

— Reducing reliance on stereotypes. Everyone possesses stereotypes of many human groups. We talk of "egghead" academics; film "superstars", "innocent" virgins, of "awkward-minded" shop stewards. See if you can identify the stereotypes in the next illustration, giving each a name.

OUR STEREOTYPES — AND YOURS?

KEY

① WIZARD-PRANG PILOT.

② THE LITTLE HOUSEWIFE.

③ SCHOOL MARM.

④ INSCRUTABLE ORIENTAL.

⑤ ALL-AMERICAN BOY.

⑥ HEN-PECKED HUSBAND.

⑦ HORSEY LANDOWNER.

⑧ GREAT LATIN LOVER.

⑨ ABSENT-MINDED PROFFESSOR.

FIGURE 265

Many of our stereotypes are uncomplimentary. They create divisiveness because the stereotypes lack sympathy and understanding. Consequently, their view of the world lacks insight.

However, if the trainee has a role in a game which is that of one of his stereotypes, then views can change. Even if the role is not of a stereotype, experiencing the point of view and likely feelings of somebody else can be emancipating for the trainee. Perceptions are altered.

— Part of this change derives from the improved sensitivity to others and from increased self-awareness on the part of the trainee. This self-awareness also leads trainees to become more perceptive of the attitudes of others and thus to more understanding.

* Improving the Processes of training

— Simulation gaming can offer activity for the trainee both as a member of a group and working alone. Essentially, the gamer has to make his own decisions and stand or fall by them.

In this situation, the trainer becomes a fund of knowledge, a suggestor to the trainee of sources of information which will illuminate the problem, a subtle hinter at appropriate strategies, an agent in assisting progress.

Requests for information by the trainee are informal: he or she decides what to ask for, and when to ask for it; generally, in a well-conducted gaming operation, he or she receives.

So, the learner develops a positive relationship with the trainer, beneficial interactions are promoted, trainers are seen positively and exchanges become more natural.

Authoritarian, trainer-trainee, or teacher-taught relationships are replaced by co-operation.

— Gaming structure provides an opportunity for bold experimentation by the trainee, latitude to manoeuvre knowledge and to explore ideas.

The only penalty possible for this free-thinking and exploration is the adoption of a losing game strategy. Both penalty and rewards are contained within the classroom walls. Experimentation and learning by experience and discovery are enhanced.

— Social skills are improved. Through bargaining, persuading, competing, co-operating, leading and being led, the trainee player practises responsive and manipulative skills. He sees and learns about the capacities and characteristics of colleagues. With knowing comes acceptance.

— Games are self-judging. The outcome decides the winner, indicating satisfactory and unsatisfactory performances. The trainer escapes the role of being judge and disciplinarian. He can analyse learner performance and respond to it, rather than spending time and energy in controlling it. Trainees and trainers see each other in a co-operative light.

— Games emphasise the process of doing something properly, as well as achieving a satisfactory product, or outcome.

— Finally, in this section on the advantages of simulation games, we must remember the point, made previously, about gaming being a unique form of communication. This is a vital consideration in view of the current explosion of knowledge in the world and the heavy requirement of the processes of training to communicate it and of learning to cope with it.

* The Disadvantages of Simulation Games

On the other side of the coin, there are several criticisms which can be made of simulation gaming as a training method.

Consider what these might be, write down a general list, rather than sub-dividing it as we did when viewing the advantages.

We believe the disadvantages of gaming to be fairly substantial. The list which follows is not in any particular order.

— Games sometimes ask players to take roles which they will never fill in real life, e.g. manager, chief executive. This might really be a criticism of the trainer for picking the wrong game. But we must remember that even if the trainee won't ever do the job, at least he will have sympathy for and some understanding of those who do.

ROLE REVERSAL

FIGURE 266

— Simulation games probably train in lower level cognitive objectives (knowledge, comprehension) less well than some conventional methods, although they are sound at higher levels, such as evaluation, synthesis and analysis.

— Poorly organised and inefficient simulations can over-simplify complex reality to such an extent that the trainee develops the dangerous illusion of perfect understanding.

— Competitiveness in games certainly arouses the flow of adrenalin, but over-competitiveness has obvious disadvantages in disrupting classroom harmony.

— Trainers can feel lost in their non-directive role in games. However, this is a characteristic of games which has to be accommodated by the trainer, because taking a "back-seat" fosters trainees' independence.

— Apart from new management tactics which create uncertainty, gaming may require statistical techniques with which the trainee is not familiar.

— As gaming usually models human processes, many of which are ill-defined, any gain in learning is difficult to assess.

— Games are unsuited to short class periods and may be difficult to timetable, consequently.

— Games directly suitable for training are difficult to find as they are not supplied through library channels, nor are many to be seen in bookshops. Advertising is often done in esoteric periodicals, not in normal training use.

— Buying games can be a very costly business, a game often costing £25 to £100 at current rates. American suppliers take months to deliver and may require pre-payment in dollars.

— Absence of key players on "the" day, or one day, can disrupt play.

Methods of Training: Groupwork

> — Apart from resistance to innovation and gaming, trainers may suffer from a lack of guidance and help when gaming for the first time; he is experimenting with the unknown.
> — Some trainers question whether or not games are a part of "serious" learning. They tend to use them as "time-fillers", failing to link the learning and gaming elements together closely.
> — Sometimes a game session does not work. The game fails and nobody benefits. There are many reasons for failure.

Suggest some of these reasons.

Here are a few:
Trainees not prepared adequately.
Time limits and timings gone adrift.
Trainees not organised and briefed on game play.
Game not suited to target audience.
Game not integral to rest of course.
Inadequate debriefing at end of game.

— On the other hand, if the game is successful, then what does the trainer do for an encore?

"NOW FOR AN ENCORE?"

FIGURE 267

— Games do take time to play. Although effective, better use may be made of the time, by delivering the learning by some other method.
— Picking up the point made previously about the game not being matched to the trainee players, it may be necessary for the trainer to design a game to suit the trainees' needs more closely.

This can take a great deal of time and requires considerable expertise. You need less time to prepare a short course of lectures or lessons, say a score, than you do to design one game of modest aspirations.

So, having viewed the strengths and drawbacks of simulation games, what is our conclusion about the part which they may play in training?

* Conclusion

Few training methods have elicited both the promise and the contradiction of simulation gaming.

Simulation gaming certainly appears to increase learner motivation and involvement, improves classroom relationships, offers a unique vehicle for studying, understanding and developing sympathy and empathy for real-life processes, problems and roles.

The disadvantages of the employment of the gaming method argue for a judicious, controlled use of games of part of the total training strategy. None of the handicaps of this method seems to be a terminal limitation, most can be overcome or alleviated, except that the direct betterment of lower-level learning of knowledge and facts is dubious when compared with more traditional methods.

Maybe simulation games are undoubtedly the answer, but some trainers aren't sure what the question is, yet!

Nevertheless, simulation games can provide an interesting and stimulating alternative to other types of training.

The more complex simulation games give a flavour of the human dilemmas of decision making and problem solving; of using opportunistic strategies; of winning and losing; of frustrations and rewards; of the interweaving of people and situations; of finding out how to develop social relationships and encourage positive patterns of behaviour.

Gaming provides learning experiences which cannot be gleaned from text books and traditional sources of information.

Even simpler types of role-play games, like case histories, which have many of the pluses and fewer of the minuses of more sophisticated gaming, help the trainees to find out more about themselves.

Summary

The conclusion which we have just made serves as a Summary. Perhaps we can emphasise a few points by the following checkpoint.

▨▨▨

Answer "TRUE" or "UNTRUE" to the following statements.

1. Games contain rules, competition, winning and losing.
2. Role-play underlies many simulations and games.
3. Case studies are sometimes more realistic than games.
4. Simulation-games are a unique form of communication and therefore of interaction.
5. Games are usually good trainee motivators.
6. Organising a game requires a change of role for the trainer.
7. Playing a game requires a change of role for the trainee.
8. Gaming provides more latitude for independent action by the trainees.
9. Games improve attitudes by weakening stereotypes.
10. Simulation gaming is best used in collaboration with other methods of delivering the learning.

You should have answered TRUE to all of the statements.
Each statement underlines an important aspect of games.

By examining the advantages and disadvantages of simulation games, we have tried to show you the unique character of the gaming method. You can now decide what part they may play in your training.

If we ask you the question, "Who's game?" we hope you'll say, "I am!"

If you are, there'll certainly come a time when you want to use and play your own games, so that they fit the needs of your training more exactly than those which you buy. This means you'll wish to design your own simulation game. So that's what the next Component is going to be about.

Component 9:

Games and Simulations (2)

Key Words

 Elements of communication; general characteristics of games; thirteen steps in designing a simulation game.

Introduction

In this Component we are explaining how you may design a simulation game for use in your own training.

 Checkpoint

What do you consider to be the advantages of designing your own game?

We believe these to be:
1. *The game you produce should* **fit your needs exactly** *and closer than games which might be available for buying or borrowing.*
2. *The process of designing a game leads you to a* **thorough understanding** *of how games operate.*
3. *You will actually* **learn a great deal yourself** *about the* **concepts and interrelationships** *of the subject of the game. However much of an expert you are, designing a game is very effective at* **resolving issues in your own mind**, *rather like teaching a topic actually helps your own understanding of it.*
4. *Once you have designed a game and are efficient in the practice of the necessary procedures, you can set the trainees the task of designing a simple game themselves.*
   They *then benefit in the way which we have just described. Such an experience proves to be very worthwhile and it is stimulating.*

Simulation games have to be **competent communicators** and **generators of fruitful interaction** between the trainees. They have to establish a **learning environment** in which the main **elements of communication** are included.

What are these elements?

Information and messages.
People.
Networks of communication and interaction.
The game materials.

Simulation games should provide opportunities for the players to observe and analyse the effects of the interrelationships between materials, people, information and messages.

We must always bear this in mind when designing games.

In this Component we shall examine:
Some of the general characteristics of games.
Steps in designing a simulation game.

It will help to explain what we are describing if we use an example game. For this purpose, we have chosen a game which we have designed recently and which is sufficiently generalist in nature for it to have a wide appeal and understanding amongst trainers from a wide variety of backgrounds.

This simulation game, which is unpublished, but has been used in our training, is called "CITY".

* Some General Characteristics of Games

The simulation games which we are considering here are the more advanced, or complex ones. Simple games show fewer of these characteristics, but they work in the same way.

So what are these characteristics?

SIMULATION GAME CHARACTERISTICS

— Games are **simplified versions, or models,** of reality.
— This simplicity is achieved by **reducing complex systems** and operations into a series of simpler actions carried on in the game.
— These actions are controlled by the **specific rules** of the game.
— Games are mainly used for showing how **systems** (communication, interaction, information flow, historical, economic, management, decision making, etc.) **operate and react** to changing conditions.
— The trainee participants play in a **controlled environment** which is free from risk.
— Players adopt **certain roles**, parallel to those found in real life.
— **Interaction** between the players **involves conflict and competition** between the players, as well as various degrees of co-operation.
— This **co-operation** is best shown where the trainee players form teams, which **bargain and negotiate** with other teams.
— **Players and teams make decisions.** The success of these decisions is based on the players understanding and effective use of the **key features** of the game model.
— Decisions result in **"pay-offs"** where the players are rewarded or deprived in some way.
— "Pay-offs" are determined by the **success of the decisions** which in turn depend upon **players' performances** and sometimes **chance**.

THE PAY-OFF

FIGURE 268

— Players have the chance to **control events** over a **pre-determined length of time.**
— As **games "compress" time,** the patterns and trends of events are seen clearly. In a similar fashion the relationships between cause and effect can be identified.
— Consequently, **feedback on the correctness and consequences** of **decisions is rapid**.

RAPID FEEDBACK

FIGURE 269

— Often simulation games are divided up into **stages**, each stage representing a period of **real time**.

FIGURE 270

AN OLD REAL-TIMER

FIGURE 271

So simulation games as a **unique form of communication, interaction and learning experience,** try to provide **insights** into the **dynamics of real-life systems,** how they **evolve and change** and the **forces** which act upon them.

Now let's look at the sequence of steps which you should follow when you are designing a game.

* Steps in Designing a Simulation Game

Step One: Specify the Training Aims and Objectives

Before you begin specifying the training objectives of the game, there is one important question which you must ask yourself. What do you think it is?

We'd say that you must make the query: "Is there a real need to construct this game at all?"

If you don't ask this question, you could be wasting an awful lot of your own time and resources. After establishing the need, you must still assess whether or not some other method of instruction would be more effective than a game.

Naturally, when making your assessment you must bear in mind the advantages, disadvantages and particularly the characteristics of simulation games. If your appraisal shows a game to be the most effective method of delivery, then design it!

Whilst your training objectives, with the different backgrounds of trainers in mind, can vary across a wide range, let's try to establish a common ground by looking at the Aims and Objectives of CITY. As the name implies, this is a simulation game about urban systems.

CITY: Training aims
The game, CITY, is played to

1. Show the dynamics of urban development across a prescribed time-span, mid-nineteenth century to the present.
2. Test various models of urban growth.
3. Allow players to observe and experience the interactions and evolution of the processes which shape a built environment.

CITY: General Training Objectives

1. To clarify the relationships and interaction between land uses and economic forces within a framework of planning principles.
2. To highlight decision-making processes where a polychotomy of interests is involved.
3. To familiarise game players with the causes and effects of selected decisions made through time.
4. To provide a framework for the testing and examination of past or proposed actions which cannot be tried in reality.

CITY: Game-Specific Training Objectives
After playing CITY, the trainees will be able to:

1. Illustrate the evolution of spatial patterns of land-use in an industrial urban area since 1860.
2. Compare this evolutionary process with the "concentric zone", the "sector" and the "multiple-nuclei" models of city structure.
3. Evaluate these models.
4. Analyse the extent to which urban rent, rate and land-value gradients determine the deployment of commercial, residential, industrial, public utility and public institution land uses.
5. Comprehend the roles of the major town builders: entrepreneur; politician; banker; local government officer and planner; people's pressure groups.
6. Analyse the interpersonal relationships and interactions involved in negotiation and working co-operatively as a member of a team.
7. Demonstrate an improvement in the social skills necessary for working in a group and accepting victory or defeat.
8. Practice the skills involved in the making of decisions on the development of an urban environment.
9. Plan the use of the game resources in the built environment.
10. Discern opportunities and marshal resources to exploit them.
11. Value the first-hand experience of the simulation of the processes, geographic, human, economic and historic, which together make up the grand process and dynamic of building a city.

Even if you do not have a background in geography, history, town planning or economics, we are sure you'll derive benefit from our explanation of those aims and objectives. They show the general "shape" of training objectives and, if modified, have a general validity for other types of simulation.

We emphasise we are talking about **training objectives** here, involving the attainment of knowledge, skills or attitudes. There are other types of objective, which are called **game goals.** These are what the game players are trying to achieve in playing the game itself, e.g. winning. These are shown in Step Four.

Step Two: Devise a Scenario
Here you are determining the scope of the game in terms of the issues to be examined, its setting in time and, in the case of the CITY, the geographic area. You are "setting the stage".

What sort of questions do you believe you should ask yourself when developing a scenario? It will be useful for you to have in mind an actual game which you wish to design. If you do have a game in mind, you'll need to have sorted out your objectives before you tackle this stage.

The types of questions which you could ask yourself are as follows:

1. Who are my target audience? (Remember to use information from Entering Behaviour Analysis).
2. At what level do I wish to pitch the game?
3. How many players are to be involved? What is the largest and the smallest number who can play?
4. Will the game calculations be manual or computed?
5. What sort of accommodation, in which the game is to be played, do I require?
6. What is the length of the game-playing period?
7. Can I timetable this?
8. Have I prepared the trainees with the necessary facts, information and skills so that they can benefit from playing the game?
9. What game-time span does the game cover?
10. How long does each round of the game represent in real time?
11. Are material resources available and adequate?
12. Is the preparation of materials completed?
13. How many members of staff are to be involved?
14. Who is responsible for running the game on the day?

These questions are only examples; you can add your own to fit your game. Use information from your design system to help you answer these questions.

Incidentally, CITY is an American or European industrial city and the game begins about 1860. Each round of the game represents five or six years of real time. Topographic features are reduced to representations of higher ground, rivers and river bank sites.

Urban functions, land use and topographic features are represented by cards, each of which equals an area of one hectare.

Step Three: Identify Key Roles

Here you identify and describe briefly the key roles in the process which your game is illustrating, whether they are individuals, groups, organisations or institutions.

Some examples from CITY, where key roles are those of:

a) **The Entrepreneur**, who buys and sells land, builds and negotiates, carrying out the entrepreneurial functions of western society. Each team represents a group of entrepreneurs.
b) **The Banker.**
c) **The Official.**
d) **The People.**
e) **The Politicians.**

CITY TYPES: KEY ROLES

KEY
① OFFICIALS
② THE 'PEOPLE'
③ POLITICIANS
④ BANKERS
⑤ ENTREPRENEURS

FIGURE 272

What they do in the game is shown under Step Four. Figure 272 might help you to build up an image. Try to keep them young looking – these are trainees acting these parts.

We have described the key role of one type of player only, the Entrepreneur, in order to save space.

You begin to think of the way in which players are to be deployed at this stage, e.g. the size of groups into which your typical target audience will be subdivided.

Step Four: Define the Game Goals

Here you define the **game goals**. We use the word **goals** to draw a distinction between the **training objectives**, which are the specific **learning** objectives, which the trainees are trying to attain (see game-specific objectives under Step One) and what the players are trying to achieve **in the game itself**, i.e. the game goals.

Broadly speaking, in CITY, the game goals are for the players to achieve greater **wealth and influence**. If you glance back at Step One, you will see that game goals are nothing like game-specific objectives.

To emphasise this distinction, here are the game goals of the players in CITY:—

> **Entrepreneur**: to increase wealth by making personal profit by competition and negotiation with other entrepreneurs who are not in their team.
> **Banker**: to loan money and make a profit.
> **Official**: to plan a suitable urban environment and keep local government financially viable; act as Clerk to Council; build Council House estates.
> **People**: to express the need for a suitable environment and facilities.
> **Politician**: to carry influence; further team goals; respond to the needs of the people and of local government.
> **Recorder**: to record the activities of each team.

All players compete for Game Points, either as a member of an entrepreneurial team, or in the cases of the Banker and of the Official, individually.

Step Five: Determine the Players' Resources

Each player begins the game with certain resources, which increase or decrease according to the player's success in the game and his employment of an effective game-winning strategy, or of a game-losing strategy.

Here you have to decide, **in outline**, what these resources are to be. In CITY, they are:—

> Entrepreneur: game money, land and buildings.
> Banker: game money.
> Official: money, taxes, land, authority and buildings.
> People: capacity to influence politicians and local government.
> Politician: influence and voting power.

You can see that participants' resources may range from tangible assets such as money, land and buildings to intangible advantages such as influence and authority.

Subsequently, when you write the **Game Manual**, or the **Player's Manual** as it may be called, you will have to define precisely what these tangible assets are, e.g. how much money each player has at the beginning of the game.

Step Six: Determine the Decision Criteria

Here you are determining the decision criteria, or "rules", which the players use in deciding what actions to take.

These basic criteria are the framework within which the player's make their decisions in the game.

Suggest what some of these criteria might be for CITY.

Our suggestions are that a game player must make his decisions bearing in mind these **criteria**:—

> a) **The game goals** described in Step Four. Each decision must be made so that it helps the player to fulfil the goals laid down for his role. Thus each goal becomes a criterion, or standard, against which decisions are measured.
> b) **The player's resources** described in Step Five. Decisions must be made in the game bearing in mind the resources available to the player at the time of making the decision.
> c) **The character of the role** which the participant is playing. It's a bit unfair to expect you to identify this criterion, because we haven't really covered it yet in this discussion. However, one of the last design steps which you make is to write a Player's Manual which fills out the detail of your design steps and tells the trainees how to actually play the game.
>
> In this Manual you will describe, in detail, the characteristics of the role which each participant is playing.

CITY TYPES

FIGURE 273

Obviously, each player must make decisions bearing in mind the characteristics of the role they are playing by saying to themselves, for example:
"Now, what is the Banker likely to do in this situation?"
d) Finally, **decisions** are made according to the **state of the game** at the time when the decision-making is going on. Decisions must be made in the context of the state of play, using such criteria as the financial condition and resources of the player, for example.

So you must bear in mind that a player requires a constant flow of information. In CITY this information would be about capital available, interest rates, cost of building, rates, current negotiations, etc.

Consequently, during this Step of the game design, you are ensuring that the players have all the information which they need to make a decision and they are aware of the criteria which shape the decisions.

Step Seven: Determine the Interaction Between Players

Here you are making certain that the game design which you are forming is going to produce effective interaction between the players. You have to sit down and think how the **resources, roles and goals** of the players will build up patterns of interaction and basically what these patterns are likely to be.

The best way to do this is to draw a diagram of the interactions. Our diagram for CITY is shown next.

CITY: PATTERNS OF INTERACTION BETWEEN PLAYERS

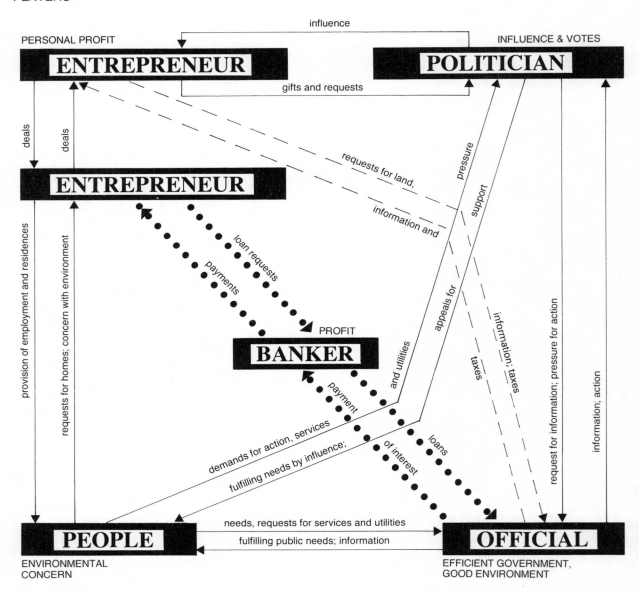

FIGURE 274

When you have completed your diagram showing the patterns of interaction, you will be able to see if the patterns look realistic and balanced, or if there are any gaps, or if a key role appears to be under or overworked.

This is obviously an important diagram because if gaming is best understood as a form of communication, then these inter-player relationships represent that communication as a sort of conceptual map.

Step Eight: Identify Constraints

In this step, you are deciding what constraints are to be introduced into the game. These restraints appear in the form of game rules which the players must observe.

In CITY, there are three main types of **game rules**:
Natural rules
Man-made rules.
Game rules.

Natural rules.

These take note of natural phenomena and make the simulation game more realistic. In CITY, natural rules are embodied in the presence of a river, suitable only for riverside industrial sites; higher ground, suitable only for higher quality residences. You also have to remember simple natural rules, like the fact that rivers flow downstream! Obviously, this affects building.

Additionally, you have to decide which natural phenomena to ignore. In CITY, for example, we did not include presence of woods, or grade "A" agricultural land, or steep slopes, all of which prohibit building. To have included them would have made the game more complex, but also more realistic. You have to decide on the balance which you want.

Man-made rules

In CITY, these are concerned with items like the zoning of land. Someone in the game has to make decisions about when the rules are to be applied and one player's role will include a designation for this purpose.

Game rules

These facilitate the proper functioning of the game, e.g. who opens play; order of play; length of a round, etc. You will not wish to determine the rules in detail at this stage; that is for the Player's Manual, but you will want to be thinking them over.

This is a very significant aspect of designing a game. Designing is a creative process and when you are focusing on one part of the game, other ideas keep popping up in your mind. Document these ideas carefully until you can slot them into a suitable place in the design. Creation can be untidy, unless you take great care.

You should decide, at this stage, who is to be arbiter in the case of disputes about the rules, but you should keep the rules to a minimum, allowing players as much freedom of action as possible.

Step Nine: Decide on Scoring

You now have to decide on the rules for and methods of scoring, i.e. the "win" criteria. Scoring must be related to the degree of achievement of the players game-goals (Step Four).

In CITY, because there is a diversity of game-goals, e.g. wealth, viability of the local authority and success by the People in exerting pressure, these goals must be translated into a common "coinage", i.e. a **game Points System**.

Details of your scoring system will appear in your Player's Manual.

Step Ten: Determine the Form of Presentation

You are now in a position to decide on the physical presentation of the game itself. Many games are board games, e.g. Monopoly. Others require quite complicated pieces for the players to manoeuvre, e.g. chess. The materials of which the game is made vary according to the purpose of the game, but there is one common rule which should be observed: keep the presentation as simple as possible.

CITY, being a game which reflects land-use patterns through time, must have flexible artefacts, the main one of which is a land use card. This is a converted Waddington's playing card, which can be bought in a blank-faced form. Each card bears a symbol showing a particular land use.

Other items of presentation include game money; Finance and Game Point sheets (A4 account sheets); People Problem sheets, defining a need of the people to be resolved by negotiation (A4 sheet typed); Success Cards (Waddington cards showing Game Points gained for successful negotiation).

As you can see, these are simple cheap materials, consisting only of

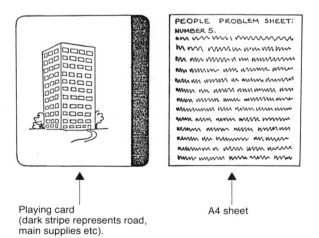

Playing card
(dark stripe represents road, main supplies etc).

A4 sheet

The form of presentation must ensure that those aspects of real life reproduced in the game are abstracted properly and are represented accurately in a simplified form which is easily playable.

So make sure that the physical presentation allows the purpose of the game to be fulfilled and keep the presentation simple.

Step Eleven: Determine the Sequence of Play

You now decide on the order of play, i.e. who does what, when. The decision you make here is an outline one, to be expanded later in your Player's Manual.

In CITY, the sequence of operations is simple; each team places land-use cards on the table, in turn. When all teams have placed, one round is ended. Players may negotiate freely throughout the rounds and there are no time constraints in placing or negotiation.

Step Twelve: Debrief

The final stage in the sequence of play is always the debriefing. This is one of the most important stages and must be organised carefully. As we are looking at Role-play in the next Component and that includes a debriefing stage as well, we shall examine it in detail then.

However, we must emphasise now that the **essential point of debriefing is to examine just what has been learned** in the simulation game which has just been played.

This is not a stage to be skipped, or hurried.

FIGURE 275

As you can see from the last Figure, the trainees are not always keen on debriefing, coming as it does after the excitement of the game. But it has to be done, the sooner the better.

You have now concluded the stages which form the basic structure of the game and made many of the major decisions which face you.

Finally, you must now use the design principles which have been established, in the construction of the actual game. This you do by

Writing the Player's Manual

Making the game artefacts (game pieces, board etc.)

Step Thirteen: Write the Player's Manual

Offering advice on how to write the Player's Manual is not easy.

Why is this?

It is difficult because of the multifarious types of game which different trainers will be designing: there will be as many varieties of game as there are of trainer, subjects and trainees.

Consequently, we are going to offer you a series of headings covering the main points which ought to appear in your manual, with some illustrations from CITY where appropriate.

Do remember that your manual is based upon the twelve Steps of game design which we have just described. The Steps describe the **process**; in writing the Manual you're using this process to make your final **product**: the Manual itself and the game artefacts.

So what do you need in the Manual? Let's have a close look. Here we go!

* Introduction
You begin with an introduction which puts the game into its setting.

In CITY we said:

"CITY is a game which stimulates the circulation of a European or American industrial city (or town) during the period 1860 to the present. Each round of play represents 4 to 6 years in the development of the town, but major human events, like wars and major natural catastrophes, like floods, are omitted.

There is no set period of play, but the number of rounds ranges between 20 or 30; each round should take 10 or 15 minutes of play."

Keep your introduction short. The players want to play!

* Game Goals
State clearly what are the game goals of players who are participating.

For CITY, this is, "To score Game Points".

* The Players
Describe the parts which the players play, e.g. in CITY, there are Entrepreneurs: 2 to 5 in each of 4 or 5 teams.

Banker: 1 Banker
Official: 1 Official
People: 3 or more People Representatives at any one time, each being one of the Entrepreneurs in each team. Politicians: 5 politicians, each being one of the Entrepreneurs in each team.
Organiser: 1 non-playing Organiser, who administers the game session (probably the trainer).
Recorder: 1 in each team; records team's activities.

* What the Players do
Describe the activities which **each** player is involved in during the game, by writing out a **Role Sheet**, e.g.

Entrepreneur: who tries to score Game Points for his team by making a profit on the buying and selling of buildings and land. The Entrepreneur pays for buildings to be erected, collects rents, pays taxes (rates etc.) and acts as agent for the collection of mortgages. He may negotiate freely with any other player at any time during the game.

Entrepreneur's Game Points are scored according to a set scale shown in Schedule Six, "Final Account Sheet" (see end of Component).
Carry on in this fashion for all the players' roles in the

game. Your players must be able to turn to their role sheets and find information there which describes the scope of their activities, their functions, powers and resources (if relevant) to the full.

Some Role Sheets may also contain personality portraits of character.

*Composition of Teams
If your game includes team play, you must describe the composition of each team, as follows:

Number in team.
Selection of team leader (if necessary).
Roles of each member of the team.
Variations in composition according to number of players.

*Playing Materials
Describe the playing materials which you use to present the game and what each artefact is for.

In CITY, we explained the use and appearance of:—

Land-Use Cards: of which there are twelve types, giving the numbers of each which are available. Examples of land-use cards are Commercial, Industrial, Residential etc.
Game-organiser's Cards: e.g. Cathedral, Town Hall, Central Square, River, Higher ground.
Money: denominations described.
Playing Surface, e.g. a board, or a flat surface of certain size.

* Resources
Describe the initial Resources with which each team, or player, begins the game. If money, show denominations issued, central stock etc.

* Schedules
If players have to complete schedules showing their transactions, describe the nature of these schedules, how they operate and how the players complete them.

In CITY there are schedules for; Buying, End Value, Returns, Redevelopment, Payments and Final Account Sheets for each type of player.
As an example we include Schedule Six, which we mentioned before. You won't understand all of the detail of this, but it does show the form of a typical schedule.

* Play of the Game.
This is the big one. This part of your Manual shows how the game is played. In order to ensure players know what to do when actually playing the simulation, the Manual should be issued a week, or so, before play begins so that players have a chance to familiarise themselves with it and query any problems.

The CITY Player's Manual includes this information in the section on Play of the Game:

Before Play begins: organisation of board, or playing surface; distribution of resources; selection of teams; issue of roles, i.e. any information to help the game run smoothly.
Play: number of rounds likely; what each player and each team may actually do during play; rules of

play; operation of each round, buying and selling; other transactions possible; responsibilities of each role.

Order of Play: who begins; how play is carried on; how a round is completed; what may be done in each round.

End of Play: what and who signals the end of play; calculations of Game Points; concluding work of game organiser; declaration of the result; announcement when de-briefing will take place, collection of materials.

Examples: Most Player's manuals contain a few examples of how play is conducted.

Organiser's Manual. Depending on the complexity of the game it may be accompanied by an Organiser's Manual. This is a more detailed Player's Manual which helps the organiser to answer questions, solve problems, gives exemplars and generally have enough background information to ensure that the Game runs smoothly.

Usually the Organiser's Manual is not seen by the players, who probably have sufficient detail to deal with already.

YOU MUST KNOW HOW TO PLAY THE GAME

FIGURE 276

In educational and training games, the Organiser's Manual often contains a useful section on the designer's views of lessons which may be learned by playing the game, plus some subject background.

It may also include follow-up exercises, references and suggestions for further study.

Summary

As a summary we shall list the Steps of designing a simulation game. These are shown in the next table.

STEP	DESIGN ACTIVITY
1.	Specify the training Aims and Objectives.
2.	Devise a scenario.
3.	Identify Key Roles.
4.	Define Game Goals.
5.	Determine the Players' Resources.
6.	Determine the Decision Criteria.
7.	Determine the interaction between players.
8.	Identify Constraints.
9.	Decide on Scoring.
10.	Determine the form of Presentation.
11.	Determine the Sequence of Play.
12.	De-brief.
13.	Write the Player's Manual.
	Introduction.
	Game goals.
	The Players.
	What the Players Do.
	Composition of teams.
	Playing Materials.
	Resources.
	Schedules.
	Play of the Game.
	Examples.
	Organiser's Manual.

We have described the steps in designing a fairly complicated game and used CITY as an example.

Obviously, you must familiarise yourself with the full sequence of design steps and modify that sequence to suit the simulation game which you are designing. Less complex games require less detail in each step of the design sequence, but it is unlikely that you can miss out a single step. This would disrupt the sequence and leave a gap in the organisation of your game.

Game designers do make mistakes. Consider what these might be. We begin the next Component by suggesting the commonest mistakes which designers make.

Schedule Six: "Final Account Sheet" — Entrepreneurial Team

This Schedule is issued by the Banker to each Entrepreneurial team at the end of the game and is used by the team Recorder to calculate the Game Points which his team has gained. The basis of the calculations is shown below.

Entrepreneurial Team

Holding		Game Points value	Game Points scored
For each **Residential** land-use card placed on playing board (i.e. built property)			
Lower Grade	score	4	
Medium Grade	score	8	
Higher Grade	score	12	
High Rise	score	14	
For each **Commercial** land-use card placed on playing board (i.e. built)	score	24	
For each **Industrial** land-use card placed on playing board (i.e. built)	score	20	
For each Success Card gained (People Problem agreed by City Council)	score	20	
For every £1 Million held in Cash (less 20 points for original £20 Million holding)	score	1	
Total of Points Scored			

Deduct game points

For every land-use card held but not played on playing board (i.e. property not built); irrespective of type of land use	deduct	5	
For every £1 Million still owed in loans to other players	deduct	4	
Total of Points Deducted			
Total Points Won or Lost		+	−
GRAND TOTAL			

Lastly, design a simulation game, either partly, or completely. Send your game to your Programme Tutor for evaluation, if you wish.

Component 10:

Role-Play

Key Words

 Common design mistakes; steps in designing a role-play, objectives, setting-up, scenario, roles; definition of role-play; type of role-play; key-role brief; running a role-play; "fishbowl" and "parallel" tactics; debriefing, reactions, reality, transfer of learning; advantages and disadvantages of role play; characteristics compared; conclusion.

Introduction

We have seen how playing a role is a fundamental part of many simulation games. Consequently, we propose to take a closer look at role-playing in this Component.

However, you will recollect that we said in Component 8 that some types of simulation consist of role-playing and nothing else. They do not have the structure of rules, nor the competitive element necessarily, of games or simulation games. These simulations are called **role-play situations**.

Here, we shall describe how to design and run a role-play simulation. By examining this method in detail, you will understand better the part which playing a role has in gaming in general.

Before we do this, we intend to make a link with the last Component by telling you what are those mistakes which game designers made commonly. You'll recollect we asked you to think about this at the end of Component 9.

COMMON MISTAKES GAME DESIGNERS MAKE.

1. **"Straightjacketing"**. Don't be overwhelmed by trying for too great a realism in your games. After all, they are models, or abstractions of reality. Make 'em too realistic and you'll be lost in a plethora of detail.

"STRAIGHTJACKETED"

FIGURE 277

As the last illustration shows, symbolically, "over-realism" reduces interaction. "Straightjacketing" can reduce imaginative solutions and exploring new avenues in a game.

2. **Too much Luck.** Try to avoid introducing excessive chance and luck into the game. The famous game Monopoly, excellent though it is, suffers slightly from this, as those who have played will know. If you are unlucky enough to receive a poor holding of property during the early stages, where what you get depends on the throw of the dice, you are handicapped for the rest of the game.

3. **Too little Time.** Give the simulation game enough time to be played out. There is nothing so annoying as closing the game prematurely, just when everyone is really swinging.

4. **Assuming Objectives will be fulfilled.** Don't assume all of your objectives will be attained. Games are unpredictable; some areas you'd hope to cover may be missed completely and others over-emphasised.

5. **Inadequate Preparation.** Make sure your trainee players are adequately prepared for the game, both in knowledge, skills and attitude.

6. **Irrelevant Scoring.** Make certain that your scoring system is relevant to the game-goals. Don't reward irrelevant conduct or poor game strategies.

7. **"Tat" Presentation.** Don't present your game with game (money, cards etc.) pieces and artefacts which are "tatty". It is a fact that "tat" presentation always downgrades the game in the eyes of the players.

"TATTY" PRESENTATION DOWNGRADES.

FIGURE 278

8. **Lack of Multi-level variety.** Try to ensure that your game has a multi-level approach and varies in degrees of sophistication so that all levels in a group of heterogeneous ability and experience will be fully extended when playing. Try a "something for everbody" approach.

9. **Too much Speed.** If your game teaches facts or skills, don't design it so that the players can rattle through it without learning the facts or skills properly.

10. **Believing in the immaculate conception.** You may think that you have conceived a game immaculately. It's almost certain that you haven't. So be prepared to evaluate, review, revise and improve, as you would for any other training method. You'll only lose "face" if you stick to a simulation game which doesn't work efficiently.

FIGURE 279

So much for those mistakes which are easy to make when designing games.

Now, what about **role-play**? Here is the structure of this Component:

Steps in designing a role-play.

Running the Role-Play.

Debriefing in role-play and simulation games.

Advantages and Disadvantages of the role-play method.

Conclusion on delivering the learning to smaller groups.

Now, let's look at the Sequence of steps you may follow when designing a role-play.

* Steps in Designing a Role-Play

Role-plays are less structured than simulation games.

Why is this?

The reasons are as follows:
— *They have no rules.*
— *They involve little or no competition.*
— *An award system does not have to be constructed, e.g. there are no game points.*
— *Playing a role is virtually the* **sole** *activity of the event; in simulation gaming there's a lot more going on.*
— *There are no game pieces, few artefacts; consequently, presentation is easier.*

Thus, we have fewer design steps. Some of the design steps do parallel those of the simulation game, so we shall "skate" over those.

As always, let's begin with

Step One: Specify the Training Aims and Objectives

This step is carried out in much the same way as that of writing aims and specifying training objectives which are to be fulfilled by playing a simulation game.

Do remember that role-play is even less predictable than is the game method and that's not very reliable in assuming outcomes itself!

There are two major types of training objectives which role-play may achieve. These are:—

— Role-play which **practises skills** and techniques, or subject principles and problems.

— Role-play which deals with **attitude change**, feelings, emotions and change in understanding.

Examples of practising skills could be training interviewers, acting as a receptionist, assisting someone to complete a form.

Examples of role-play dealing with attitude change involve a huge range of activities which aim to develop the trainee's capacity to handle complex situations spontaneously, e.g. dealing with delicate issues, counselling, negotiating and communicating. Trainees are placed very much in a discovery-learning, trainee-centred, learning situation here. This is the commonest form of role-play.

Now, there is one important difference here between writing specific training objectives for a game and for a role-play. Whilst the mechanics of writing the training objectives are similar in each case, **the training objectives of the role-play also act as the role-play goals.**

You'll recollect that we wrote both training objectives **and** game-goals when designing a simulation game. However, in a role-play the players do not have to achieve any goals just for the role-play alone. Thus, there are no equivalents to the game-goals of gaining money or power which can be translated into game-points, for example.

So, the training objectives are also the role-play objectives.

Let's look at an example. Suppose our role-play was about the controversial issue of. **"The inadequate promotion of women in the organisation".** What could our training objectives be for that topic?

We suggest the following:

"After the role-play the trainees **should** be able to:

1. Analyse the reasons why few women are promoted.

2. Identify the nature of possible prejudice against women.

3. Explain the current management attitudes towards the promotion of women.

4. Analyse the attitudes of women towards accepting responsibility.

5. Evaluate the job performance of women in the organisation.

6. Appraise the effects of women's previous experience and background on their promotion prospects.

7. Analyse the work relationships of male and female employees.

You can see that these training objectives are what the whole role-play is about. Thus, the equivalents of game-goals are not needed.

Mind you, role-plays are unpredictable. After the role play the players might have decided that there is no prejudice against women at all. That's half the fun of role-plays! If that is the decision, you can see that the training objectives are not invalidated, however.

Also, you can see why we stated that "the trainees **should** be able to . . . . . ." instead of our usual **"will** be able to". Now you know why!

Clearly, your training objectives should decide the type of role-play which you mount.

Step Two: Setting-up a Role-Play.

Once you have your training objectives specified, you can start setting-up the role-play.

Why do you have to set up a role-play? How does this differ from setting-up a lecture, or a discussion?

It's quite a lot different. Lectures and group discussions are a routine part of training, but a role-play is unusual. So the trainees have to be prepared for it. If you said, "We're having a role-play now", without previous warning, there might be some panic!

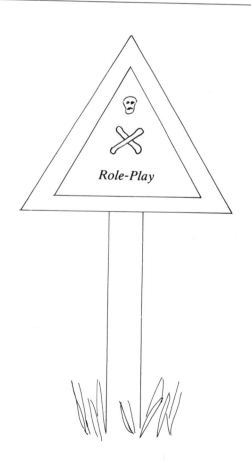

Role-Play

Thus, you set-up by telling the trainees reassuring facts like: a role-play is merely a form of simulation where the focus is an interaction between the players; it's called a "role-play" because the word "role" comes from the description of the roll of parchment on which the actor's part was written; they really don't need to act, they just have to be themselves playing a part; they don't have to learn lines; nobody is going to criticise their performance.

You might try some **warming up** games. Examples are:

"Following phrase": one trainee says a phrase, or a sentence from a story, the next follows and so on around the group.

"Non-Stop": pairs of trainees talk at each other about a selected topic until one dries up or hesitates.

"Colours": pairs of trainees pick a colour each and try to persuade each other that their colour is the better. All pairs talk together without listening to other pairs.

Warm-up games are usually played immediately prior to the actual role-play.

So talk to the trainees, especially those who have not enjoyed a role-play previously, or have not taken part before. Help them to get the "hang" of it before they start. Try defining role-play to them.

▰▰▰

Incidentally, can you remember where we explained the term "role-play", previously? What did we say?

We explained the meaning of role-play in Component 8. Slightly modified, our full definition is shown in the next Figure.

A DEFINITION OF ROLE-PLAY

> A role-play is a simulation which involves and focuses on interaction between the players, without a structure of rules or competition.

FIGURE 280

Sometimes, role-plays become a little competitive, but competition is not **in-built,** although players must argue their cases, or point of view.

OK. So you have set-up the role-play by preparing the trainees for it, psychologically as much as anything else.

By now, the next Step should be forming in your mind; this is to

Step Three: Devise a Scenario.

As for simulation games, this is an exceedingly important step. Perhaps even more so, because when the role-play is taking place you can't rely on a structure of game rules to keep it going in the right direction, nor on competition to push it along. So your role-play scenario has to be comprehensive and written well.

What do you do when devising a scenario?

1. **Refer to your training aims and objectives.**
They will indicate to you which of the two major types of role-play you are into.

▰▰▰

What are these two types?

Have a look at Step One again where it tells you that they are a
— *Role-play which practises skills and techniques or principles and problems of the subject in hand.*
— *Role-play which deals with attitudes, feelings and emotions.*

You write your scenario to fit the type of role-play. So, either

(a) use scenario material which embodies each part of the skilled or technical procedure, or identifies the principles or outlines the problem.

or,

(b) use scenario material which gives full expression to and explanation of the trainees' attitudes, feelings and emotions.

In (a) for example, you might be role-playing the techniques of successfully closing a sale, or negotiating a deal. Your material must set a realistic scene and give the trainees a chance to show their efficiency in implementing the principles of sale-closure or negotiating. In completing a complex form, one trainee would ask another all of the difficult questions which can arise in form-filling, or present some awkward problem for the advising trainee to deal with, when the form doesn't seem composed to handle the problem.

Examples of (b) would be for you to write your scenario around a controversial issue which is associated with strongly held attitudes and feelings. Such issues could be included in role-plays as the length of working hours and conditions of work, where you'd have one group of role-players **for** certain changes and one group **against**; on making a decision whether to sack somebody, or not; on potential colour discrimination in the firm; on a public enquiry into a proposed site for a new retail outlet.

Remember that your specific training objectives give a framework around which you can build your scenario.

Look back to Step One at the training objectives for the topic of "The inadequate promotion of women in the organisation". You can see the ground which you have to cover and how you can write your scenario around the issues identified by the objectives. Make sure your material allows each objective to have an "airing".

Remember, too, that it is possible to combine the two types of role-play described in the last checkpoint, into one exercise. Such a dual role-play would embody a skill, or a technique, where trainee attitudes and feelings are also involved.

Incidentally, which type of role-play would you be writing, i.e. a) or b) when considering the women and promotion topic?

Certainly, this is b), i.e. "a controversial issue which is associated with strongly held attitudes and feelings".

---

2. Refer to your design system (see Package One) for information on:—

— What the trainees have in the way of previous experience and background (Entering Behaviour Analysis). You don't want to write a scenario that's over the heads of the trainees.

OVER THEIR HEADS?

FIGURE 281

— Your resources: can you do this role-play with the resources which you have e.g. is there a suitable room? Try looking at your Resource Analysis.
— The constraints: well, do the constraints hamper you? For example, what are the views of management and colleagues on role-play? Is it not really serious stuff to them?
— Is there a need for this role-play? And how does it fulfil the needs brought out by Needs Analysis?
— Did your Task Analysis identify the knowledge, skills or attitudes you're dealing with? Or are you having a shot in the dark?

DON'T BE BLINDFOLDED: USE TASK ANALYSIS!

FIGURE 282

— We've talked already about identifying your aims and training objectives and you know where they come from!

— Your Synthesis of Content ought to have given you a clear idea of your role-play topic, issue or skill. It's often a good idea to prepare a handout to show what training content has gone into your scenario. If the trainees are shaky or content let them have the handout before the role-play; otherwise issue it afterwards, for revisionary purposes.

3. Write a brief introduction, setting the scene.

This will help you do what you must always do: brief the players at the beginning of the role-play. The introductory brief will help clear your mind, too.

An introductory brief should have two parts:
— a short, background history, i.e. where you were;
— the "now" situation, where you are now.

Examples: "The Workshop was built by George Spriggs in 1910. Since then . . . . . .". And, "We have arranged a meeting today to talk about . . . . . .".

4. Place your role-play action in a definite simulated location.

E.g. "We're meeting in the boss's office".

5. Decide on what supportive documents you need and reproduce them.

E.g. newspaper cuttings; "official" memos; pseudo-instructions from management; various statistical data, e.g. a downturn in sales, wastage rates, overseas product briefs (should we introduce our new iced-orange drink into Antarctica?) letters outlining previous action, etc.

It is preferable to issue supporting documents before the role-play, so that the trainees are prepared for the situation. You don't want them reading up during the role-play, as that slows down the pace, but they can quote from documents to establish their case, of course.

Step Four: Identify the Roles.

This is the most important stage in role-play design. Whereas in simulation games you can use "cardboard" characters of no great depth, in role-play the structure of the action depends upon four types of role.

What do you think these types are?

We suggest the following:
1. Key Roles
2. Supporting Roles
3. Standby Roles
4. Observer Roles

Let's examine each of these in turn.

1. Key Roles.

These are "key" in the sense that they are the most significant roles and they are those which keep the action moving.

These roles have certain **characteristics**; these are:

---

a) The key roles are those between whom the bulk of the significant action takes place.

b) They deal with the central issues of the role-play.

c) They offer the role-players the best chance of influencing the role-play itself and affecting its directions.

d) The key roles themselves are capable of being developed by the players along lines which they think are significant.

e) Key roles have **role goals,** i.e. what the key character is trying to achieve in the role-play, e.g. prevent the building of a new factory; buy a building site; make a sale; sack somebody; negotiate with the union; influence votes in a committee; introduce a change; push a new product. Role Goals are **not** training objectives and they are **not** the same as game-goals. They are specific to one role-player only.

Write the key roles in two stages. These are:
a) The Personality and Background of the key-role character.
b) The Action undertaken by the key-role character.
Let's look at each of these stages, in turn.

a) Considering the **"personality and background"**, write a **Key-Role Brief** giving information on:

The personality of the key role character: don't overdo this. The trainees are not taking on someone else's personality. They are using their own personalities to put a role across. So they are not acting in a real sense; give them plenty of room for manoeuvre by making only a few suggestions about experiences they've had which could cause them to react in certain ways. Let the role-players work out for themselves whether they are angry, prejudiced, emotional, authoritarian or democratic, receptive and responsive, dogmatic, aggressive, or whatever.

The background is important and you have a balancing act to do. You want to give enough information to equip the player to fulfil the role, but you don't want to make the brief overlong.

HE MUST BE WRITING A KEY-ROLE BRIEF

FIGURE 283

So, write your background to the key Role Brief so that it contains adequate information, but just enough information, on what the key role character has in the way of:

> ✱ Resources, i.e. knowledge and skills, wealth, power and authority, social and organisational position.
> ✱ Goals, i.e. what the key role character is trying to achieve in the role-play situation. If there are options open to the character, describe them.
> ✱ Attitudes, i.e. motivations, beliefs, concerns and what pressures he is under.
> ✱ Handicaps, i.e. those constraints which limit action, e.g. ability, health.
> ✱ General Background, i.e. family, education, experiences, etc. This background section very much depends on the type of role-play you are writing, of course.

b) Now, viewing **the action undertaken by the key-role character,** write your Key-Role Brief to cover:—

> ✱ The other characters whom this key-role player will interact with.
> ✱ How, when, where he will meet them?
> ✱ The length of time during which the interaction takes place.

Now, give this key-role character a name. Not a daft name like Miss Bright, Mr. Shifty or Mr. Sexy, but something which won't saddle them with an embarrassment.

Finally, remember the Golden Rule: **don't tell them they're "angry", or "happy"; let the players work it out for themselves.** And emphasise that they are playing themselves, not putting on an Oscar-winning acting performance portraying somebody else.

2. Supporting Roles.

These "beef up" the action and support the key roles. Supporting roles are used especially to provide information for the key characters and to give a background for them, e.g. family members, secretaries, minor professionals, clerks, advisors, counsellors, officials, minor managers, etc.

Your briefs for supporting roles will be very short: show what support they offer, in outline, and how they can fill in the action.

3. Standby Roles.

These are used where you may need flexibility in the number of roles available to deal with different sizes of group.

Usually, your role-play will involve 10 to 15 trainees; 20 is about your maximum. So cover your range from 10 to 20 with stand-by characters.

4. Observer Roles.

Include the remainder of the trainees. Do make them feel part of this role-play by asking them to evaluate what has gone on. Give a structure for this, such as

How far were the training objectives achieved?

Did the role-play proceed smoothly without "hiccups"?

Did the role-play appear to be reasonably realistic"?

Did the key characters fulfil their role goals"?

Have a look at the next Figure, which should help impress these roles on your memory.

KEY-ROLES

SUPPORTING ROLES

OBSERVER-ROLES

STANDBY-ROLES

FIGURE 284

You may wish to devise observer roles which have a definite function such as reporters (assess interaction and the order of play) recorders (note major points only) time-keeper, etc.

The Role Briefs can be typed on a sheet of A4 paper, or on a card, for permanence. Don't forget to remind the players, by typing on the card, "only to be used before the role-play begins".

Add a note saying, "This Role Brief gives you essential information only. You should invent any other information which is required as the role-play proceeds. Keep it realistic!"

You are now ready to start the role-play itself. We shall deal with this next, but don't forget that there is another Step in designing a role-play and this is "Debriefing". As this follows naturally after the role-play itself, we shall deal with this last.

* Running the Role-Play

As you can see, role-plays do require a lot of work to prepare. However, they are easy to run. Part of the reason for this is that a well-prepared role-play should largely run itself. Also, as the organising trainer you will wish to keep out of the "limelight" in the role-play, so that the trainees can develop the action themselves. Their taking the lead, instead of you, is one of the things it's all about.

There are two main ways of running a role play. Basically, you can use either the
  Fishbowl tactic, or the
  Parallel tactic

Fishbowl Tactic.

Here the players meet in the centre of a rough circle of observers.

THE "FISHBOWL"

FIGURE 285

This is the commonest way of holding a role-play.

When running a Fishbowl role-play, the following phases can be observed:

> **The Lead-in.** You should give a **starting signal.** If the players have had some experience of role play, all you need to do is to say, "OK. Off you go".
>
> Otherwise you can signal the start by saying something like "Right. We're having a meeting to discuss . . . . . . Jack, would you take over as chairman now, please", or, "You were working in the machine shop, when . . . . . .".
>
> **The Play.** The play has now started and all you'll have to do is
> — keep your intervention to a minimum.
> — intervene only when players are drying up, by making a helpful suggestion for an aspect of the topic to be pursued.
> — feed in new information which changes the situation. This is a common practice which develops the role-play by presenting new approaches, or problems to the players.
> — prevent the "Apocalypse" situation, where players over-invent and call upon unrealistic resources to solve their problems, e.g. debar trainee statements like, "Well, I've just been left two million pounds by my auntie and that solves our financial problems".
>
> **The End.** Again you must signal the end of play, sometimes offering a, "Five minutes to go" warning.

The Parallel Tactic.

This is used where the action is small-scale. You pair off the players, add an observer to each pair and then let them play out the action in small groups. So you have several role-plays being carried out simultaneously, in parallel.

This tactic is suitable for role-plays such as interviews, dealing with a customer, negotiating a sale, filling in a form.

The whole group meets together at the end, to exchange views on what has happened.

This meeting together leads us to the final step in the role-play, which is

* Debriefing in Role-Play (Step Five) and Simulation Games (Step Twelve).

We said in the last Component that we would "kill two birds with one stone" by considering debriefing of role-play and simulation games together. This is a matter of convenience, but do remember that "Debriefing" is Step Five in the role-play design sequence, as you'll recollect from our previous comments to this effect in the previous Step Four.

One important point needs emphasising: don't skimp the debriefing. Much of the benefit of the role-play or game is derived from the debriefing.

Is there any other major consideration of a general nature which you should bear in mind about debriefing?

Yes, there is: hold the debriefing as soon as possible after the event, when memories are fresh and enthusiasm still runs high.

Debriefing, Step Five in designing a role-play and Step Twelve in a simulation game, should have three stages:
  Reactions
  Reality
  Transfer and evaluation of learning
Let's look at these individually.

Reactions.

Players usually have strong feelings about the actions which took place in the event, whether role-play or game.

Help them to express these reactions by asking them questions like:

"What was your most frustrating experience in the event?"

"What did you like about your role?"

"What did you dislike about your role?"

"How did your part help you to actually feel something about the situation?"

"Why did you find it beneficial to stand in someone else's shoes?"

Remember to:
— Keep your questions open-ended.
— Deal with the reactions of each key-role first: then supporting roles; then observer roles; then general comment on the roles and reactions.

— Make sure each role-player has a chance to speak.
— Try to keep the questions to descriptive answers about feelings and reactions and not about appraising or assessing the situation.
— Help the player to unwind by coming out of role.

Reality

Here you find out how real the players thought the roleplay or game was. Ask questions like,

"What similarities did you observe between the event and the real world?"

"How real did you think the role of . . . . . . was?"

"Was the game organised like a real-life situation?"

"If it was, how was this effect obtained?"

"How real do you think your decisions were?"

Transfer and evaluation of Learning

This is a very important part of debriefing where you try to draw out the lessons of the game. Here you are establishing and reinforcing what has been learned.

You are trying to make the shift from the role-play or game to the real world situation and real problems. The trainees have had the common experience of the event; you and they are transferring learning from the event to real life.

Have a look at the next Figure which shows what you do.

TRANSFER AND EVALUATION OF LEARNING

What you do:

— Draw conclusions about what happened.

— Decide why these happenings occurred.

— Analyse what interactions took place between the players.

— Assess the way the players behaved, and why.

— Identify the decisions which were made and how and why they were made.

— Identify any new or unexpected points or actions which arose and why and how they were caused.

— Establish whether different behaviours would have brought different or better results.

— Make connections with previous and future learning.

— Establish how the event could be made to provide a more effective learning situation.

— Itemise the main learning which took place in improving skills, or increasing knowledge, solving problems, making decisions or changing attitudes. The items identified should be recorded permanently.

— Show how the learning can be connected with and extrapolated to real life.

— Assess how far the training objectives were fulfilled. If they were not all achieved, use part of the debriefing session as an ordinary lesson to cover those objectives which were missed or not achieved adequately.

— Appraise the extent to which the role-goals were achieved.

— Evaluate the event as an effective training method and a learning experience and how it may be followed up.

You do not:

— Criticise players' performances.

— Withhold advice, assistance or resources.

— Cram the debriefing into an inadequate time. Effective Debriefing often takes as long as the actual role play or game; that's a good balance for you to timetable.

FIGURE 286

FIGURE 287

Certainly, for a complex game or role-play, there's no way you can compress the de-briefing into a spare 20 minutes. If you **"cram-debrief"** you may as well not have held the event.

* Advantages and Disadvantages of the Role-Play Method

By now, you'll have a pretty good idea of what these are. So write down your own lists before you look at ours.

ADVANTAGES AND DISADVANTAGES OF ROLE-PLAY.

Advantages

1. Role-playing is trainee-centred; consequently, it is motivational and stimulating.

2. It involves massive trainee communication and interaction.

3. Everybody takes part in the learning activity.

4. Allows trainees to practise social skills and the skills of articulating, decision making, problem solving, negotiating and manipulating.

5. Creates opportunities for trainees to empathise with others. Empathy is a way of putting yourself in someone else's place.

6. Shows the rewards for co-operative and positive behaviour; gives penalties for negative behaviour.

7. Like gaming, gives immediate feedback to the trainee on effective strategies and conduct, and to the trainer, on trainee progress.

8. Brings elements of real-life into the classroom.

9. Can effect attitude changes for the better.

10. One of the few areas of training where feelings and emotions are given free rein.

11. Is a refreshingly different method of training and offers unique learning experiences to the trainees. Like gaming, role-play is a uniquely different form of communication and interaction.

Disadvantages.

1. Role-play results can be unpredictable. Many of your training objectives may not be achieved whilst others receive too much consideration.

2. May give the trainees an impression of perfect understanding, when the real-life situation is more complex.

3. Can be wasteful of time: role-plays do not deliver the learning in certain areas as well as other, more direct methods.

4. Role-play may not be regarded as a serious form of training by other trainers, by management and even by the trainees, who wax frivolous.

IT MUST BE A ROLE-PLAY!

5. An effective role play requires considerable resources of time for preparation and play and sometimes of space.

6. If the trainer is skilled in preparation and the trainees are capable of role-playing, then the experience will be worthwhile. Sometimes, neither trainer nor trainees are adequate and the role-play is a "zero-experience".

7. Faulty preparation of the trainees means they haven't the knowledge or skills to benefit; you may not find this out until the role play is underway.

8. Some types of learning, like the acquisition of knowledge, don't lend themselves to the role-play method.

FIGURE 289

Summary

Now, let's have a different form of summary. We have picked out some of the main characteristics of role-play and of simulation gaming and we are going to compare them. Cover the two right-hand columns of the next Figure and say whether role-play and simulation games have the characteristics shown in the left-hand column. If they have, write YES, or if not write NO, or perhaps, MAYBE.

COMPARISON OF CHARACTERISTICS

CHARACTERISTICS ROLE-PLAY AND SIMULATION GAMES	ROLE-PLAY	SIMULATION GAME
1. Are realistic	YES	MAYBE
2. Have game rules	NO	YES
3. Include competition	NO	YES
4. Need substantial preparation time	YES	YES
5. Include a scenario	YES	YES
6. Have training objectives	YES	YES
7. Have game goals	NO	YES
8. Have role goals	YES	NO
9. Have key roles	YES	YES
10. Have subsidiary roles	YES	MAYBE
11. Have observer roles	YES	NO
12. Have much trainee interaction	YES	YES
13. Require a scoring method	NO	YES
14. Require presentation materials	NO	YES
15. Have strict sequencing	NO	YES
16. Require debriefing	YES	YES
17. Have player's manuals	NO	YES
18. Have organiser's manuals	NO	YES
19. Have a complex design process	MAYBE	YES
20. Are a unique form of communication	YES	YES

FIGURE 290

Finally, we shall list the Steps in **designing a role-play.** These are shown in the next Figure.

DESIGN STEPS

STEP	DESIGN ACTIVITY
1.	Specify the training aims and objectives.
2.	Set-up a role-play.
3.	Devise a scenario.
4.	Identify the roles.
5.	Debrief.

FIGURE 291

* **Conclusion on Delivering the Learning to Smaller Groups**

In this Study Unit we have been concerned to describe to you methods which are suitable for delivering the learning to smaller groups. This meant that we considered the delivery methods shown in Figure 53, Component 4, Study Unit 1 of this Package and in Boxes 2 and 4 in that Figure. We redrew that diagram in Figure 160, Component 1, Study Unit 3.

So, our study has focused on learning in smaller groups. We looked first at definitions of groups and groupwork, then at group dynamics and people in the group.

Using the group discussion as our basic method, we went on to view variations of the group discussion method such as seminars, panels, symposiums (symposia) Brainstorming, syndicates, Wilson Quadro and colloquys, etc.

We finished by looking at games and simulations and at role-play which represent "extreme" forms of groupwork and have unique qualities of communications and interaction.

We have seen how the continuum of delivery

strategies moves from a trainer-centred strategy at one end, to a trainee-centred strategy at the other. The trainer-centred strategy includes methods of delivering the learning to larger groups. The trainee-centred method mainly involves presenting learning opportunities and experience to individuals.

The central part of this continuum is occupied by a mixed-strategy involving methods of delivering the learning to smaller groups. (Check with Figure 257, Component 8, Study Unit 2, Package 1 and Figure 161, Component 1, Study Unit 3 of this Package).

However, the boundaries between the strategies are not clearly defined, because many larger or smaller groupwork methods can be varied to suit different sizes of group. Larger groups can be broken down and smaller group methods then used. A thorough understanding of how the delivery methods operate will allow you to use them flexibly in your training. You will be able to select the methods which are most beneficial to your trainees in any training situation.

In the next Package we move on to methods of delivering the learning to individual trainees.

However, whatever method you choose, you must always try to reach the individual trainee with your training activities, as far as that is feasible. We are still trying to

"Banish Learnermass."

Study Unit 3: Objectives

On completion of this Study Unit, trainers will be able, for training in their own place of work, to effectively:
1. Define a "group".
2. Define a "group discussion".
3. Define "group structure".
4. Define "group dynamics".
5. Identify the objectives of learning groups.
6. Implement groupwork satisfactorily.
7. Analyse group characteristics.
8. Analyse group structure.
9. Analyse group interaction and communication patterns.
10. Explain the trainer's role in group discussion.
11. Explain the trainee's role in group discussion.
12. Compare the advantages with the disadvantages of group discussion as a way of learning.
13. Compile a Checklist of points necessary for effective group discussion.
14. Identify leadership roles in a group discussion.
15. Identify varieties of leadership style and how leadership style affects groupwork.
16. Arrange appropriate seating patterns for groupwork.
17. Define and implement:
    Seminars.
    Panel Discussions.
    Symposiums.
    Brainstorming Sessions.
    Leaderless groups.
    Workshops.
    Clinics.
    Wilson Quadro.
    Colloquys.
    T. Groups.
18. Define a "game", a "simulation" and a "simulation game".
19. Describe the history of simulation games.
20. Express a rationale for simulation games.
21. Compare the advantages of simulation games with their disadvantages as methods of learning and communicating.
22. Explain the general characteristics of simulation games.
23. Design a simulation game.
24. Avoid the common mistakes made in game designing.
25. Design a role-play.
26. Run a role-play.
27. Debrief a role-play and a simulation game.
28. Compare the advantages with the disadvantages of role-play as a method of delivering the learning.
29. Value the part which groupwork can play in effective learning.
30. Evaluate the part which groupwork can play in training.

Voluntary Package Assignment

Answer **one** of the following questions, sending it to your Programme tutor for comment and evaluation, if you wish. Interpret the term "groupwork" to apply to any of the different forms of group and groupwork described in this Package.
a) Observe a small group discussion and comment on how the various behaviours which you can identify either facilitate or hinder the working of the group.
   or,
b) Drawing examples from the operation of an actual group, show how "group dynamics" work in practice.
   or,
c) Analyse the structure of a group with which you are familiar. Evaluate the extent to which this structure affects the efficiency of the group.
   or,
d) Observe a group in operation. Over a single session, or a series of meetings, gauge the effectiveness of the group by checking group performance against a Checklist(s). You should either compile your own Checklist, or use lists from this Programme.
   or,
e) Design a simulation game, or a role-play.
   or,
f) Observe either a simulation game or a role-play being played. Evaluate the effectiveness of the game or role-play and of this method of training.
   or,
g) Write an essay of about 2000 words on the importance of effective communication in the processes of learning.
   or,
h) Explain a variety of models and strategies of learning. Compare the efficiency of the models and of the strategies in providing effective learning in your place of work.
   or,

j) Make out a series of Lesson Plans for a part of a training course. Justify your selection of Lesson Plan format.
or,

k) Plan a skills lesson. Implement the lesson and evaluate it thoroughly. Show how you would improve the lesson the next time you give it.
or,

l) Plan and implement a 2WL lecture. Evaluate your performance and the quality of the trainees' learning. Suggest improvements if you think they are necessary.
or,

m) Negotiate a suitable piece of coursework, of your own choosing, with your Programme tutor. On completion send it to the tutor for comment and evaluation.

Finally, let's have a look at the Aims and General Objectives of this Package. The Specific Objectives have been stated already, after each Study Unit, although you should remember that those lists are not intended to be comprehensive.

Package Two: Aims

a) To provide sufficient information and training material in the form of a distance-learning Package to enable trainers to produce effective and efficient groupwork, simulation games, role-plays, lessons and lectures.

b) To consider the Objectives and Process Models of learning and training.

c) To examine various strategies and methods for delivering the learning.

d) To consider the part played by communication in training and learning.

Package Two: General Objectives

To

a) Familiarise trainers with the concepts and precepts of many and various forms of groupwork.

b) Assist trainers to design and operate effective groupwork.

c) Demonstrate to trainers how simulation games, role-plays, lessons and lectures are designed, planned and implemented.

d) Evaluate the fundamental part which efficient communication plays in producing effective learning.

e) Improve the calibre of trainers as effective communicators, both in writing and orally.

f) Improve the capacity of trainees to communicate effectively.

g) Evaluate the part which effective groupwork, simulation games, role-plays, lectures and lessons can play in trainers' own training methods.

h) Evaluate the efficiency of various strategies for delivering the learning, especially trainee-centred, trainer-centred and mixed strategies.

j) Compare the advantages and disadvantages of the Objectives and Process Models of learning and training.

k) Assist trainers to implement suitable strategies, methods and models in their own training.

BIBLIOGRAPHY

A consolidated Bibliography is shown at the end of Package Four.

The next Package deals with individualised instruction.

THE TRAINING TECHNOLOGY PROGRAMME

Volume 2

METHODS OF TRAINING: GROUPWORK